The
POLITICS
of
COLOMBIA

POLITICS IN LATIN AMERICA
A HOOVER INSTITUTION SERIES

General Editor, **Robert Wesson**

Copublished with Hoover Institution Press,
Stanford University, Stanford, California

The
POLITICS
of
COLOMBIA

Robert H. Dix

PRAEGER

New York
Westport, Connecticut
London

Library of Congress Cataloging-in-Publication Data

Dix, Robert H. (Robert Heller), 1930–
    The politics of Colombia.

    (Politics in Latin America)
    "Copublished with Hoover Institution Press, Stanford
University, Stanford, California."
    Includes index.
    1. Colombia—Politics and government—1974–
I. Title.   II. Series.
JL2811.D59 1986   320.9861   86–021168
ISBN 0–275–92315–0 (alk. paper)

Library of Congress Catalog Card Number: 86–021168
ISBN: 0–275–92315–0

First published in 1987

Praeger Publishers, 521 Fifth Avenue, New York, NY 10175
A division of Greenwood Press, Inc.

Printed in the United States of America

The paper used in this book complies with the Permanent
Paper Standard issued by the National Information Standards
Organization (Z39.48-1984).

10 9 8 7 6 5 4 3 2 1

To the memory of my parents

CONTENTS

LIST OF TABLES

FOREWORD

Colombia is not easily understood. It is typically Latin American in its mixture of Spanish and indigenous peoples, and in its economy based mostly on tropical agriculture, especially coffee and the coca leaf. Distinctly different from its neighbors—Venezuela, Ecuador, and Peru—which it physically resembles, it is a country of contradictions, like the contrast of its steaming jungles and snowy volcanoes. Of all South American nations, Colombia has seen the most violence, yet it has had the least militaristic government, and it is the only country of South America governed today by the same parties as a century ago. Its society is among the most unequal in Latin America— that is, among the least democratic—but it has the best record of a democratic, or at least constitutional, government in South America. It has an outstanding literary and cultural tradition, despite a national university that is virtually nonfunctional because of political disorder.

Few truly understand this paradoxical country, but Professor Robert Dix certainly comes close. In 1967 he wrote *Colombia: The Political Dimensions of Change*, which was widely regarded as the best treatment of Colombian politics of the 1960s. He has now revised and deepened his analysis.

Because Colombia has been relatively neglected by scholars, this work fills a considerable gap. In his thorough and thoughtful treatment one sees behind the stereotypes of drug dealing and guerrilla terrorism to perceive the complexities of a remarkable nation, important to both the United States and the destiny of Latin America.

Robert Wesson

PREFACE

Some 20 years ago I completed the writing of my first study of Colombia (*Colombia: The Political Dimensions of Change*, Yale University Press, 1967). The formalized Conservative-Liberal coalitional arrangement called the National Front had barely reached the midpoint of its designated 16-year duration. Then, the question was how to prevent a recurrence of the recently past partisan violence and unaccustomed military rule. The success of the National Front in accomplishing those goals, in company with other significant changes in the society and polity, has in some ways created a new Colombia. A country that in 1960, shortly after the inception of the National Front, had less than half its population living in urban settings, by 1982 had some two-thirds of its population living in cities and towns. Industrialization has increased, agricultural diversification and commercialization has proceeded apace, and dependence on coffee exports has diminished. Literacy has also risen sharply.

Politically, genuine and peaceful competition between the two principal parties has by the mid-1980s replaced the party hegemonies and interparty warfare of the past. Considerations of economic policy and development have become more central; the government is both more deeply involved in economic planning, and legally and institutionally more equipped to do so. Political tensions remain high, but they are now not so much between the traditional parties as between the country's governing elites, on the one hand, and those in the system—workers, peasants, students, to some extent even the urban middle class—who feel left behind in the emerging new order of things. Urban and rural violence, and a rampant drug traffic, have provoked the recurrent invocation of a state of siege and contributed to periodic signs of friction between the armed forces and the government.

The concerns and the modes of politics, as well as the economic and social contexts in which Colombian politics unfolds, are therefore rather different in the mid-1980s than they were some two decades earlier. At the same time, the key institutions and political actors remain in many ways remarkably similar. The new Colombia, in some respects almost unrecognizable, is in other regards very familiar. This present excursion into the politics of Colombia is therefore somewhat in the way of an update of the earlier one, albeit in less detail. It is more than a mere factual addendum, however. Its themes and its coverage reflect the new concerns and the new scholarship of the intervening years. The international linkages of politics receive considerably more attention this time, as does the process of policy making. The comparative dimensions of the analysis are perhaps more explicit, and the earlier history of Colombia is more extensively treated by way of background. In the end, this book hopes to introduce the reader new to matters Colombian to an intriguing and relatively little-known variation of the human political enterprise; to those familiar with my previous work on Colombia, the book may serve as a summation of one individual's view of the country's politics based on many years of (off and on) observation and research.

The earlier book was rooted in several years' sojourn in Colombia (1957–60) in the service of the U.S. government, plus subsequent visits of an academic nature. It was published at a time when little of a scholarly kind was available in English about Colombian politics (Vernon Fluharty's *Dance of the Millions* [Pittsburgh: University of Pittsburgh Press, 1958] was the principal exception). Since that earlier book, the distractions of other scholarly interests and, more recently, illness have restricted my visits to Colombia, much to my regret. My last trip to the country was in 1974. To some degree compensatory, however, and in the end making this book possible, has been the vastly expanded literature on Colombian politics—produced by Colombians and non-Colombians alike—upon which, for the reasons suggested, this book relies perhaps to an unusual degree.

Those scholarly debts are abundant, and should be amply clear from the footnotes and bibliography of the present work. Special acknowledgment is due, however, to Fernando Cepeda Ulloa, dean of the Law School of the Universidad de los Andes in Bogotá; Gabriel Murillo Castaño, chairman of the Department of Political Science at Los Andes; and Enrique Ogliastri Uribe, also of the Universidad de los Andes. My thanks to Jonathan Hartlyn, Gary Hoskin, Harvey F. Kline, and Elisabeth Ungar B. for materials kindly supplied; and to Robert Wesson, the editor of this series. As goes without saying in such enterprises, the use and interpretations of all materials and counsel rests with the author.

Both credit and my gratitude go also to Margaret Greenwood and Alice Olson, who handled the typing chores.

Finally, my wife, Mary, graciously contributed her considerable editorial talents to the review of the manuscript and spurred me to its completion.

Colombia

The
POLITICS
of
COLOMBIA

INTRODUCTION

By a variety of standards Colombia is one of the most important and exceptional countries of Latin America. With more than 28 million people it ranks fourth in population in Latin America after Brazil, Mexico, and Argentina. With 444,000 square miles it is fifth in area behind Brazil, Mexico, Argentina, and Peru. Its economy, in these recent years of inflation, recession, and expanding foreign debt throughout the hemisphere, is, though hardly without its problems, flourishing in comparison with most. Under President Belisario Betancur (1982–86), Colombia has taken on new importance in the international politics of Central America and the Caribbean. Not least, like few other countries in the region, Colombia has had a series of civilian, nonauthoritarian governments for over a quarter of a century. Indeed, with the possible exception of Costa Rica, there have been fewer years of military rule in Colombia than in any other country in Latin America.

Yet remarkably, considering both its size and its other attributes, Colombia may be the least attended to, by scholars and media in the United States, of all the countries of Latin America (with the possible exception of the recent negative attention paid to the drug traffic). Two recent texts, one by two historians, the other by a political scientist, make the point.[1] Both seek to compare and contrast Latin American countries with regard to their "routes to development." Each selects half a dozen Latin American countries to elaborate its thesis and make comparisons. In neither book is Colombia included. At least as far as politics is concerned, Colombia has lacked the mystique of a revolution come to power, as has occurred in Mexico, Cuba, or even Bolivia, and now, of course, Nicaragua. Nor has it had the glamor of Argentina's Juan and Eva Perón, or the challenge of understanding why a country like Argentina, with so many presumed assets and an apparently successful early start on the road to democracy and economic development, has failed so miserably at both. No set of military rulers has seized power with the expressed object of carrying out a revolution, as in Peru, or of suppressing or preventing its possibility and setting the country on a new developmental path (often involving gross violations of human rights), as in the recent pasts of Brazil, Argentina, and Uruguay, or currently in Chile.

Perhaps most important, Colombia has been difficult to categorize and, hence, to cite as a model. It is certainly neither revolutionary nor authoritarian in any commonly accepted usage of those terms. Yet to call its politics "democratic" is to stretch the meaning of that word somewhat. For, despite the absence of military rule and Colombia's vaunted two-party system, its politics has been among the most violent in the region, the state of siege more often in force than not since the early 1950s, and both its institutions and its patterns of domination more continuous with its past than perhaps those of any other nation in Latin America. Colombia, in short, is a paradox, difficult to classify and generally lacking in the kinds of political innovations that tend to attract the foreign or comparative scholar, or the foreign press. The principal exception to this latter statement has been Colombia's experiment with a form of "consociational democracy" in the years after 1958.[2] Called the National Front, it mandated a two-party sharing of power (including periodic alternation of the presidency) for a period of 16 years that has helped to assure relative political peace.

COLOMBIA AND LATIN AMERICA: SIMILARITIES AND UNIQUENESS

For all the difficulty in placing it in a scholarly pigeonhole, and for all its uniqueness, Colombia is nonetheless quintessentially Latin American in a number of ways.[3]

First, it is culturally a fragment of the Mediterranean branch of European civilization, and particularly of its Iberian variant, as that civilization had evolved by the 16th century, the time of the conquest and colonization of Nueva Granada (the future Colombia) by the

Spanish conquistadores.[4] Thus Latin America, including Colombia, was colonized by a mother country that had experienced little of the Renaissance and none of the Reformation. Its language was Spanish (or Portuguese, in Brazil), and its religion late-medieval Roman Catholicism. Its Church, having joined in alliance with the Spanish kings to expel the Moors from their last redoubt in Europe, now extended that association to the joint conquest of the New World and the conversion of its native inhabitants. The cultural values and the social structure also, naturally enough, mirrored those of 16th-century Spain and Portugal. An important part of that heritage was the corporatist and patriarchal pattern of governance that pervaded Spanish imperial rule.

Colombia, like most of Latin America, became a fusion of cultural and ethnic strains through encounters with the Indians of the New World and the importation of slaves from Africa. While in Colombia, as in the region as a whole, Iberian culture predominated, the resultant cultural and racial mixtures created a society quite distinct from that of the mother country. Indeed, the Colombian pattern is probably as typical as that of any in the hemisphere in having been founded neither in one of the major centers of Indian civilization, as in Mexico or Peru, nor in one of the least advanced, while at the same time including, but in lesser degree than in, say, Brazil, significant numbers of persons of African heritage.

Colombia has further shared with most other countries of Latin America more than a century and a half of political independence. For Latin America, within a few decades of the independence of 13 of the British colonies to the north, became part of the first wave of "new nations" created out of erstwhile European empires, a very long time before the creation of the new nations of much of Africa and Asia in the wake of World War II.[5] Along with that independence came republican institutions—except for very brief interludes of "empire" in Mexico and the retention (until 1889) of a descendant of the royal house of Portugal on the throne of the new Brazilian state. Formal independence did not necessarily mean fully realized independence (especially in an economic sense); nor did adoption of the institutions of republican government always signify their effective functioning. Yet, together, early independence and republicanism gave Colombia a framework of institutions and a legacy of historical experience in their operation that sets it, as most of Latin America, quite apart from much of the rest of the Third World.

Yet another area of affinity between Colombia and most other parts of Latin America is the fact that it is neither preindustrial nor postindustrial, but industrializing. By comparative world standards Colombia (and Latin America as a whole) is somewhere in the middle range of countries according to such standard indices of development as gross national product (GNP) per capita, urbanization, literacy, and life expectancy. According to the categorizations of the World Bank, every Latin American country fits the designation "middle-income economies," as distinct from "low-income economies" or "industrial market economies."[6] Within Latin America, Colombia tends to rank near the middle range; it is neither among the most developed nor among the least.

The further implication of the fact that at least the major Latin American nations, including Colombia, are well into the process of industrialization is that conflict within the countries tends increasingly to center on the issues and dilemmas it raises. Prominent among these issues are differences over how both the costs and the gains of that process are to be distributed. Since, in contrast with the great majority of other Third World countries, ethnic conflict has seldom played much of a role in the politics of independent Latin America, class, group, and regional conflict incited by the ongoing industrialization of the country has played an increasingly salient role in Colombian politics, essentially undiluted by crosscurrents of ethnic politics. This is not to say that the politics of social class is always the predominant axis of conflict in Latin America—it surely is not in Colombia. The competition for power and status among cliques within the elite may count for as much. It is to say, nonetheless, that the countries of Latin America as a group are confronted by the problems and tensions of a relatively advanced stage of the industrializing process in ways that most countries of the Third World still are not, though Latin America continues to share with the latter such problems as highly skewed income distribution and excessive dependence on a single export crop.

Last, Colombia has in common with the rest of Latin America— as well as with most Third World countries, of whatever political hue—a dependence on (or a vulnerability toward) the external world that has deeply affected its economy, its society, its politics, and even its culture. In what sense, to what degree, and with what implications may be debated (and will be in due course), but the reality is inescapable. In the case of Colombia, and generally of Latin America,

TABLE 1.1. Latin American Comparative Data

	Area (thousand sq. mi.)	Population (millions)	GNP per Capita (dollars)	Life Expectancy (years)	Percent Urban	Percent Literate
Argentina	1,073	28.4	2,520	70	83	94
Bolivia	424	5.9	570	51	45	68
Brazil	3,287	126.8	2,240	64	69	69
Chile	286	11.5	2,210	70	82	96
Colombia	**440**	**27.0**	**1,460**	**64**	**65**	**81**
Costa Rica	20	2.3	1,430	74	43	90
Cuba	44	9.8	n.a.	75	68	n.a.
Dominican Rep.	19	5.7	1,330	62	53	70
Ecuador	105	8.0	1,350	63	46	86
El Salvador	8	5.1	700	63	42	71
Guatemala	42	7.7	1,130	60	40	57
Honduras	43	4.0	660	60	37	60
Mexico	760	73.1	2,270	65	68	88
Nicaragua	57	2.9	920	58	55	88
Panama	29	1.9	2,120	71	53	88
Paraguay	157	3.1	1,610	65	40	85
Peru	496	17.4	1,310	58	66	82
Uruguay	72	2.9	2,650	73	84	96
Venezuela	352	16.7	4,140	68	84	88
Latin America (av.)			1,701	65	59	81

Note: Socioeconomic data are for circa 1982.
Sources: Data compiled from World Bank, *World Development Report 1984* (New York: Oxford University Press, 1984); (for literacy) Inter-American Development Bank, *Economic and Social Progress in Latin America. 1984 Report* (Washington, D.C.: Inter-American Development Bank, 1984); (for area) Robert C. Kingsbury and Ronald M. Schneider, *An Atlas of Latin American Affairs* (New York: Praeger, 1965), p. 4.

this dependence or vulnerability has in the 20th century been especially strong in relationships with the United States. Any realistic citizen of Latin America must come to terms with the fact that he or she exists in a hemisphere for which the United States has assumed a particular responsibility or even suzerainty. This is perhaps even more true for Colombia, which fronts on both the Caribbean and Pacific coasts of South America and is proximate to the Panama Canal.

Colombia therefore has much in common with those other countries called Latin American—in its culture and historical origins, in the time frame of its independent life and its republican constitutional framework, in the level of its economic development and the nature of the resultant conflicts, and in its vulnerability in the face of external forces and political actors, notable among them the United States. Moreover, within the Latin American universe Colombia manages to be fairly "typical" in these respects, insofar as any country can be said to be so.

In spite of these many features in common, Colombian politics has a number of qualities that set it quite apart from the politics of its neighbors, making it difficult to classify or categorize and posing more than a few challenges for comparative analysis. Those differences include the following:

1. While in all but a very few of the other Latin American countries (Uruguay, Paraguay, and perhaps Honduras) the parties or proto-parties of the 19th century have long since faded away or survive only in residual form, Colombia's Liberals and Conservatives remain the political vehicles of choice for most Colombians even as the 21st century approaches.

2. Concomitantly, parties of a Social Democratic, Christian Democratic, Radical, Marxist, or Populist stripe have been perennially weak in Colombia. The only political movements seriously to challenge the traditional parties and their leaderships have come from within the ranks of those parties. Such challenges have invariably failed.

3. The armed forces have played less of a political role than in virtually any other Latin American country, having held the reins of state for only some half a dozen years and otherwise having had little voice in the seating and unseating of presidents. Today Colombia

ranks 17th among the 19 Latin American countries in both military expenditures as a percentage of GNP and military manpower as a percentage of the working-age population.[7]

4. Conversely, the Roman Catholic Church has had a political and social importance beyond that of the Church in virtually any other country of the region, at times helping to make and unmake presidents, influencing elections (as well as more violent forms of political combat), and generally having a profound impact on the political socialization of Colombians.

5. Nationalism, while hardly absent, has proved an unusually weak political reed in Colombia, more so than in most comparable Latin American countries. Despite the role of the United States in excising the province of Panama from Colombia at the turn of the century, anti-imperialist campaigns have had little salience; nationalism has never been the catalyst for a major political party or revolutionary movement, as it has been in a number of instances throughout the hemisphere.

6. Colombia has historically been, and remains today, one of the most violent societies in the world in its internal politics. Perhaps only in Mexico (with its post-1910 revolution) have more deaths resulted from political violence in a Latin American country. Most such violence in Colombia has occurred in the name of one of the country's traditional parties. More recently, guerrilla bands intent on effecting a revolution, and accompanying government repression, have taken the place of the partisan violence of the past. The country's burgeoning drug traffic, though only indirectly political, has recently added its share of violent acts.

7. Paradoxically, in view of violence that sometimes seems endemic, Colombia has had one of the best records of democratic practice in a region where admittedly the standards have not as a rule been high.[8] Elections, while certainly not always fully free or truly competitive, have since early in the country's history generally been regular and often meaningful. While access to the tools of effective political participation (including education) has certainly not been equitably distributed, political and civil rights have usually been respected, at any rate for the politically articulate.

8. As already implied, Colombia's property-owning elites and their representatives have managed to retain control over the political system essentially unchallenged by the representatives of the middle class or labor, let alone the peasantry. New individuals from these latter groups have been added or co-opted by the elites, but the basic structure of power has changed only slightly; even many of the names remain the same. The real structures of power in Colombia may be as little altered as anywhere else in Latin American compared with what they were, say, 50 or 100 years ago. Colombia's elites have been abetted in their efforts at self-preservation by their periodic ability to reach accommodation on sharing power at moments of acute crisis for the system.

9. Finally, Colombia's "route to modernization" has been distinctive, and by comparative standards quite successful. Through a mixture of conservative and progressive approaches to economic development and social reform,[9] control has remained essentially in elite hands while operating within an at least quasi-democratic framework. The whole has constituted a "reform from above" that contrasts with the patterns of revolution, reaction, and more broadly based democracy prevalent in other parts of the hemisphere.

THE STUDY OF COLOMBIA

The following chapters seek to elucidate these and other ways in which Colombia differs from other Latin American countries, given the other, extensive, similarities and Colombia's fairly typical socio-economic profile. We will try, where possible, to account for those differences. In the process it will be necessary to confront several puzzles: How does one reconcile Colombia's high level of violence with its quasi-democratic institutions and practices? How does one account for such a politically weak military on a continent where the obverse has been predominantly the case? Or for the persistence of the two historic parties, whereas they have largely disappeared elsewhere? Or for the weakness of the Colombian Left? And how does one explain the elite's ability to control and manage change under civilian and relatively democratic institutions so successfully?

For Colombia has changed—rather dramatically—since the early 1960s in its rates and degrees of urbanization, industrialization, and the commercialization of agriculture, as well as in its level of literacy. There have been political changes, too, some of them of considerable importance. But what impresses more is the continuity of political institutions and practices even after the intense interparty violence in the years after 1946; a four-year, military-led dictatorship in the years 1953–57, followed by an interim year of rule by a military junta; and a 16-year arrangement to share power between the parties (1958–74). A final paradox is, therefore, how Colombia has been able to maintain such a degree of stability in its political institutions while undergoing significant transformation in other areas of its national life.

Will Colombia's political future continue to mirror its past to the same extent? One school of thought would project that future as most probably bureaucratic-authoritarian (B/A), much along the lines of Brazil (1964–85), Chile after 1973, and Argentina 1966–73 and 1976–83. Such a B/A regime would comprise an alliance of the military with civilian technocrats, foreign capitalists, and some native capitalists. It would seek to roll back the participation of labor and others in the political process, thereby holding down wages and permitting the future "deepening" of the process of capitalist development. There are those who would argue that Colombia already de facto resembles a B/A regime, despite its nominally democratic form.[10]

Others would argue the inevitability of a socialist revolution, later if not sooner, roughly along the lines of Cuba or Nicaragua and presumably founded on the victory of one or more of the guerrilla bands now fighting in the countryside. Failing such a scenario, Colombia's political future would, in this view, hold the prospect for an increasing level of class conflict—arguably already at hand in the forms of enhanced levels of strikes, land invasions, and guerrilla activity—and a reordering of the party system along class lines.

Still others project the gradual democratization of Colombia's current quasi democracy by the more effective and reasonably rapid incorporation of nonelites into the political process.

Failing any of these, more of the same may be in prospect—that is, continued elite rule and "reform from above" within a framework of democratic institutions.

We will begin with two historical chapters, divided essentially by the year 1930, when the modern history of Colombia can rightfully (though somewhat arbitrarily) be said to begin. The subsequent chapter on the economic, social, and cultural contexts of politics will encompass such topics as political culture, the structure of the economy, the class structure, and regionalism. Political actors such as parties and interest groups will be the topics of chapters 5 and 6, respectively, followed by a description and analysis of government institutions in chapter 7. Chapter 8 will describe and analyze both the policy-making process and policy outputs, both domestic and foreign. The conclusion will seek to pull together the main threads of the book, to characterize the nature of Colombia's politics in comparative perspective, and to suggest the lines of the country's future political evolution. Reconciling the relative success of civilian, republican institutions with high levels of violence and a manifestly inequitable social order, and long-term stability with rapid social and economic change, will constitute the central themes of the analysis.

NOTES

1. See Thomas E. Skidmore and Peter H. Smith, *Modern Latin America* (New York: Oxford University Press, 1984); and Gary W. Wynia, *The Politics of Latin American Development*, 2nd ed. (Cambridge: Cambridge University Press, 1984).

2. For the concept of consociational democracy, see Arend Lijphart, *Democracy in Plural Societies* (New Haven: Yale University Press, 1977). The term refers to a variety of democracy whereby "The centrifugal tendencies inherent in a plural society are counteracted by the cooperative . . . behavior of the leaders of the different segments of the population" (p. 1). This is accomplished through various antimajoritarian devices, such as grand coalitions and mutual vetoes. For applications of the concept to Colombia, see Jonathan Hartlyn, "Consociational Politics in Colombia: Confrontation and Accommodation in Comparative Perspective" (Ph.D. diss., Yale University, 1981); and Robert H. Dix, "Consociational Democracy: The Case of Colombia," *Comparative Politics* 12 (April 1980): 303–21. Colombian politics has had marked consociational features at least since 1910; see Alexander W. Wilde, "Conversations Among Gentlemen: Oligarchical Democracy in Colombia," in Juan J. Linz and Alfred Stepan (eds.), *The Breakdown of Democratic Regimes*, vol. 3, *Latin America* (Baltimore: Johns Hopkins University Press, 1978), p. 34; see also chap. 2 below.

3. Latin America is here taken to mean the 19 independent republics of Iberian origin in the western hemisphere. Haiti, Puerto Rico, and the recently independent former British and Dutch colonies in the Caribbean are not included.

4. For the concept of the "fragment" as applied to Latin America, see Richard M. Morse, "The Heritage of Latin America," in Louis Hartz, *The Founding of New Societies* (New York: Harcourt Brace and World, 1964), pp. 123-77.

5. Cf. Seyour Martin Lipset, *The First New Nation* (Garden City, N.Y.: Doubleday, 1963).

6. World Bank, *World Development Report 1984* (New York: Oxford University Press, 1984), pp. 218-19.

7. Charles L. Taylor and David A. Jodice, *World Handbook of Political and Social Indicators*, 3rd ed. (New Haven: Yale University Press, 1983), vol. 1, pp. 24-27, 37-42. In each case only Mexico and Costa Rica rank lower.

8. Colombia is rated third in Latin America in political rights (with a score of 2 on a 1-7 scale), and fourth in civil rights; Ibid., pp. 58-65.

9. For the distinction between conservative (stressing productivity and close ties to the international economy) and progressive (stressing income redistribution and economic autonomy, as well as production) approaches to modernization, see Wynia, *The Politics of Latin American Development*, chap. 5.

10. For the concept of bureaucratic-authoritarianism, see Guillermo A. O'Donnell, *Modernization and Bureaucratic-Authoritarianism* (Berkeley: University of California, Institute of International Studies, 1973).

2

THE HERITAGE OF HISTORY

Colombia shares with its continental neighbors the Spanish colonial heritage, and some of the broad outlines of its subsequent development as well; yet in the 19th and 20th centuries it has also shown some marked divergences from historical patterns elsewhere in the former Spanish empire. In fact, many of the attributes of Colombia's current political system, and many of its contrasts with others in Latin America, were already sharply present in the 19th century and the earlier decades of the 20th. Arguably more so than in almost anywhere else in Latin America, Colombia's present mirrors the patterns of the past.

FROM COLONY TO REPUBLIC

Colombia shares with the rest of Hispanic America a colonial heritage according to which legitimate authority rested in the Spanish king, who was bound only by natural and divine law, and by the extent to which his fiat could feasibly be carried into effect in a distant place. Assisting the king in the administration of his colonial realms were, principally, the Council of the Indies and the Board of Trade. The Council was a combination of bureaucratic legislature and court of appeals for the colonies. The Board sought to enforce the mercantilist policies of the monarchy and to keep its overseas realms in economic thrall. From these two bodies there emerged myriad laws and regulations governing the empire in minute detail, from the organization of municipalities, for example, to the price of salt; not surprisingly, many such regulations proved impossible to enforce. In addition, there was an elaborate hierarchy of officials, headed by viceroys, that extended the royal authority down to the provincial and municipal levels.[1]

The future Colombia was neither a focal point of Spanish rule, as were the early viceroyalties centered at Mexico City and Lima, nor was it an unimportant backwater of empire. The first permanent settlements were established at Cartagena on the Caribbean coast (1533), which soon became a major transshipment center for the export of bullion to Spain and the importation of slaves and other "goods," and at (Santa Fé de) Bogotá (1535). Initially dependent on the viceroyalty of Peru, by 1717 (and again, more enduringly, after 1739) Bogotá had become the center of the newly created viceroyalty of Nueva Granada, encompassing what are today Venezuela, Ecuador, and Panama as well as Colombia.

The edifice of empire ultimately depended on Madrid. Much has been made of the *cabildos*, the municipal councils in which the Creoles (those of Spanish descent born in the New World) took part. Spain had municipal traditions that had taken firm root in response to defensive needs in the warfare against the Moors prior to their final expulsion from the Iberian Peninsula in 1492; and municipalities, and their councils, were at once established in the New World. During the colonial era, especially at the beginning, the *cabildos* often had certain powers in such matters as taxation, licensing, and public works. As virtually the only bodies in which Creoles had representation, they were later to play a leading role in the movement for independence. But as the colonial era wore on, most of the *cabildos* lost whatever degree of autonomy they had had. Membership became principally honorific, and seats on the councils were frequently purchased or went to appointees of the Crown. They accordingly decayed as effective organs of local self-government. With some exceptions in the early years, they seldom became problem-solving bodies for their communities.

Only exceptionally under Spanish imperial rule were there popular uprisings. When they did occur, they did not usually challenge royal authority but were directed against the actions of particular officials or the imposition of particular taxes. Not the king but his administrators were blamed. Such was the case with the most notable instance of violent protest in Nueva Granada prior to the independence struggle, the so-called *comuneros* uprising in northeastern Colombia in 1781.[2]

In short, Spanish rule bequeathed to Colombia, as to the rest of Latin America, a tradition of the ruler from whom all authority flowed and to whom all allegiance was due. It was a heritage of absolute, though not arbitrary, rule. Yet, although seen as ultimately benevolent and paternalistic, it was not a rule that envisaged participation by the monarch's subjects in the decisions of government.

Along with the structure of royal authority in Spanish America there had grown up a society based on exploitative mining and agriculture. The social and national origins of the settlers of Latin America, the values they brought with them, the purposes for which they came to the New World, the nature of the new frontier and the way in which it was conquered, the availability of indigenous labor, and the policies of the Crown contributed to that result.

The conquerors of Spanish America came from a society in which the ethos of medieval Europe still held sway, heightened and accentuated by some five centuries of intermittent crusades against the Moors. Their object in going to America was not to found colonies as a means of reestablishing the life of the mother country on a frontier that promised freedom from religious, economic, or political persecution at home. Rather, the goal was religious conversion or economic exploitation, implying in both cases domination over the native populations. While Colombia was not the site of advanced Indian empires of the dimensions of those of the Aztecs or the Incas, the Chibchas of the Andean highlands were sufficiently civilized, and sufficiently numerous, to provide a labor base for the conquerors. Elsewhere, along the Atlantic coast and in some of the interior valleys of Nueva Granada, African slaves were their substitutes.

Certain policies of the Crown similarly conduced to the formation of quasi-feudal societies in Spanish America. The kings of Spain, eager for both new sources of revenue and additional converts to Holy Mother Church, encouraged the process of conquest and conversion by granting an important measure of authority over the Indians, and at times over large tracts of land, to the conquerors and to the Church and its missionary orders. The Crown attempted, at times with some degree of success, to retain ultimate title and responsibility, and to mitigate abuses. However, the overall effect of royal authority in the American branches of its empire was to forge a society of exploitative economic and social power in which distinctions of race often reinforced those of social class.

Thus in most of Latin America, including substantial parts of the viceroyalty of Nueva Granada, there arose parallel to the machinery of royal rule a structure of social, economic, and potentially political power that lacked the formalized ties of vassalage and certain other qualities of true feudalism, but that in its decentralized foci of power based essentially on ownership or control of land and labor, in its hierarchical relationships of dependency of the many on the few, and in a number of its social attitudes and values, resembled a feudal society.

There was an underlying tension between this quasi-feudal society and the imperial state, evidenced in de facto resistance to royal edicts and by discrimination—economic, social, political, and intellectual—imposed on the Creoles by the agents of the mother country. To be sure, Indians, slaves, and those of mixed blood were in a far worse position than the Creoles, ruled not only by royal officials but more directly, and often more oppressively, in their economic and social lives by the Creoles. Although on occasion there was an Indian or slave uprising, and although some of the lower classes willingly participated in the armies of the wars for independence (on both sides), it was generally the members of the Creole elite who led the struggle for independence. It was certainly they who came into its inheritance. Thus it might be said that independence constituted the victory of the quasi-feudal society over the paternalistic state that had bound that society together for three centuries.

Independence, when it came, nevertheless did not result directly from the slowly festering resentments of the Creoles. Spanish rule might have continued for many years had it not been for the Napoleonic occupation of the Iberian Peninsula in 1808, and the deposition and exile of the legitimate king. These actions of Napoleon set off a train of events, whose details we do not need to consider here, that led several of the *cabildos* in Spanish America to declare their independence. Bogotá in the viceroyalty of Nueva Granada did so on July 20, 1810; the port city of Cartagena, on November 11, 1811. This foreshadowed Colombia's fractured 19th-century unity, and the country still celebrates two independence days. Long and bloody war followed with Spain, and with Spain's adherents in the colonies. The struggle was climaxed by Bolívar's victory over the Spanish at Ayacucho in Peru in 1824, although Colombia's independence was virtually assured by Bolívar's victory at the Battle of Boyacá on August 7, 1819.

In North America independence had been conservative of legitimacy, in the sense that it was fought to preserve those "rights of Englishmen" which both Crown and Parliament were seen as trying to abridge. Independence to the south, on the contrary, wholly destroyed the only legitimate authority and the only source of "rights" there had been. Both revolutions did away with monarchy and ushered in republics. But in the one case legitimate authority in the colonies already emanated to a considerable extent from below; therefore, the end of the monarchy required little more than its rather easy replacement by elected governors or a president. In Spanish America, on the other hand, the king had been the source of all authority, as well as of grants of economic and social power in the form of monopolies, deeds to lands, and encomiendas (trusteeships) of Indians. The wars of independence in South America, instead of preserving legitimate institutions from outside, arbitrary interference, as they largely did in the north, destroyed the fabric of authority. In the political sense, then, the revolutions for independence in South America had a much more radical impact than the (North) American Revolution.

Instead, in most of the Hispanic American countries, including Colombia, the end of imperial rule left a "legitimacy vacuum." Whereas what remained following independence in North America was a wide array of institutions (charters, assemblies, town meetings), as well as a system of values, on the basis of which a republic realistically could be erected, in the fledgling nations of Latin America there remained a series of more or less isolated local societies, a congeries of powerful landowners and regional *caudillos* (strongmen) with their respective clienteles, deprived of the central power that had once provided a common suzerainty. With the monarchy gone, along with its New World agents, the driving force of public life became the attempt by local chieftains to seize the apparatus of government. The caudillo, sometimes a regionally based landowner or strongman, sometimes coming from the ranks of the army, made his appearance on the stage of Latin American politics.

The attempt was made, of course, to erect a new, republican legitimacy. Those who had led the revolution against Spain were imbued with the ideas of the French and American revolutions, of Rousseau and Paine, of the Declaration of the Rights of Man and the

U.S. Constitution. These sources had been the intellectual inspiration for independence; they were accordingly the sources to which the leaders of the new states turned. Elaborate constitutional documents were the result, complete with bills of rights, the separation of powers, provision for periodic elections, and sometimes a federal organization of the state. Such was the case with (Gran) Colombia, beginning with the Constitution of Cúcuta in 1821. These constitutions were not the product of bargaining among interests and regions, nor the expression of an already existing attitudinal and institutional framework of republicanism. They were instead the embodiment of the best imported conceptions of liberty toward the fulfillment of which, presumably, the new nations were to grow. Thus attempts to apply democratic procedures such as a widespread suffrage often led to electoral fraud and intimidation, as those who held the real power exerted it to retain control.

There were yet other consequences of independence and the long struggle on its behalf. They included the ferocity and destructiveness of the wars, which impoverished the new states and gave a heritage of violence to societies already imbued with some of its supporting values. In some countries, though not in Colombia, the wars enhanced the role of the military and led to its emergence as virtually the only focus of national cohesion, and as a channel of social and political advancement for the ambitious and the less privileged. Independence also destroyed the old imperial unity and replaced it with many new centers of sovereignty, most of them at first uncertain of their possibilities of holding together as nations. But the fundamental implication of independence for Latin American political life was without doubt the radical alteration that had taken place in the pattern of authority and in the sentiments that attached to it while leaving relatively undisturbed the pattern of social and economic power as it had emerged during the three centuries of colonial rule. When to the struggles to hold the reins of the new republican authority were added profound divergences over the nature and goals of the state, the stage was set throughout much of Latin America, and notably in Colombia, for a century of civil strife.

THE 19TH CENTURY: ERA OF CONFLICT

A sense of the identity and extent of their new nation was at first quite weak among Colombians. The outlines of the Colombian state that was eventually to emerge were for a time obscured by Bolívar's attempt to hold together as one nation, called Gran Colombia, the former viceroyalty of Nueva Granada. Following the breakup of Gran Colombia in 1830, it was several years before it was certain that a large portion of southwestern Colombia would not join Ecuador. Panama, which had remained a part of Colombia, effected its independence as late as 1903, albeit assisted by the United States. Still, after about 1840 the disputes that led to warfare among Colombians were for the most part not over the extent of the national boundaries (although they often involved the relative autonomy of states or regions in relation to the central government). Nor was the central problem of establishing the legitimacy of Colombia's republican regime the fact that there was any appreciable number of monarchists desiring the return of Spanish rule or the establishment of a new prince, whether foreign or domestic. Once independence had been firmly won, there were few who wished to revoke the deed.

Rather, what divided Colombians politically was, in the first instance, the raw struggle for power among *caudillos*, families, cliques, and regions, in a society from which the guarantor and mediator of a hierarchical social order has been eliminated. However, that struggle was deepened and channeled by disagreements concerning the extent to which, with the monarchy gone, the other fundamentals of colonial society should be retained, or be replaced by the institutions and attributes of 19th-century liberalism. On the "liberal" side were those engaged in the export-import trade who saw their own, and the country's, future in close trading ties to the burgeoning industrial West, with Colombia's role the exporter of agricultural products; on the other were the "conservatives" not so tied and more exclusively involved in agricultural production for domestic consumption.[3] Such conflicts seemed to reach a peak in the late 1840s. Midcentury was also a time of ideological ferment in Nueva Granada (as Colombia was still called), with liberal and utopian socialist ideals, heightened by the example of the European revolutions of 1848, contesting with traditional Hispanic and religious values.

In any case, it is about 1848–49 that one can mark the founding of the two traditional Colombian political parties, the Liberal and the Conservative, insofar as any firm dates can be set. Evidence of their formal organization is admittedly thin in this period. But it is from about 1848 that both the Liberals and the Conservatives carried forward a sense of their own identities, the rudiments of programs, pantheons of heroes, and some minimum degree of understanding among their adherents to attempt to unite on presidential and vice-presidential candidates and for parliamentary purposes in Congress.

It is doubtful, however, whether the crystallization of groups into parties at the time of the 1849 election would have maintained itself even in this somewhat limited sense if the intellectual and social ferment of the period had not been reflected in the acts of the administration of General José Hilario López. For it was during his term of office (1849–53) that liberal, now Liberal, principles which attacked vested interests deriving from the colonial period were vigorously applied. Among the acts of the López government were the expulsion of the Jesuits from the country, the final emancipation of the slaves, a law permitting the free sale of the lands of the previously parceled Indian reservations, and the termination or reduction of such felt burdens on production and trade as the tobacco monopoly. Over the next decade similar actions further divided Liberals from Conservatives in matters of policy and ideology. One was the expropriation of Church lands in 1861 and their subsequent sale at auction by a Liberal government. The constitutions of 1853, 1858, and 1863 embodied the principle of the separation of Church and state, and the (Liberal) constitution of 1863 carried federalism almost to its logical extreme by according the Colombian states many of the attributes of sovereignty.

These steps aroused the bitter opposition of those whose interests, and whose entire conception of society, government, and religion, were threatened; they also generated vehement support on the part of those whose interests and ideas were thereby favored. This period at midcentury, then, constitutes the first real watershed of Colombian history following independence. It saw the origin, or at least the strong reinforcement, of loyalties, hatreds, doctrines, issues, and alignments that have persisted, to some extent, to the present day and have become embodied in two "historic collectivities." From whatever point one dates the precise organization of formal parties, it was clearly at midcentury that the combination of material and ideal interests that was to comprise the stuff of much of subsequent Colombian politics took its shape.

It was also at midcentury that there emerged for a few years, and more clearly than at any other moment in 19th-century Colombia, the outlines of class warfare. The occasion was conflict between artisans organized into the so-called Democratic Societies that had proliferated in the late 1840s, and the intellectuals and free traders, largely members of the upper class, who supported the midcentury policies of the Liberals. Those policies had a considerable adverse impact on nascent Colombian industries and handicrafts. The result was, as one Colombian scholar has put it, that ". . . the urban proletariat attempted to impose its solutions on the nation, [but] the bourgeoisie, supported by the rural masses, defeated the urban workers."[4] There were armed clashes between *los de ruana* (those in ponchos) and *los de casaca* (those in frock coats) in several cities; congressmen were at times intimidated by mobs; and the artisans supported a brief military dictatorship under General José María Melo in 1854. Within a few months, the combined opposition of the civilian elites brought an end both to the dictatorship and, effectively, to the Democratic Societies and the claims of their supporters. Political conflict during the rest of the century was not mainly along class lines.

The seven civil wars and innumerable regional or provincial revolts that erupted between 1850 and the end of the century were in considerable part a function of personal, family, and regional rivalries. And for much of the 19th century both parties stood essentially behind policies of laissez-faire in foreign trade, while issues such as federalism sometimes cut across party lines.[5] Yet to a notable degree the strife between the parties also entailed a clash of two sets of economic interests and two political cultures: one, that of 19th-century liberalism struggling to be born; the other, the traditionalist outlook inherited from Spain. That clash, common to some degree in many Latin American countries during the 19th century, seems to have been unusually bitter in Colombia.

To note the causes of its particular intensity is to enter the realm of speculation. Certainly the dispute over the role of the Church seems to have been more acute than in most Latin American countries and more subject to polarized positions. Colombia was the first country in Latin America to separate Church and state. Yet in 1886 that stand was reversed, placing Colombia ever since among those Latin American countries in which the Church's position has been strongest. It may have been that domestic social and economic forces, such as the artisans, and the tobacco growers and merchants, were stronger in Colombia in the mid-19th century than elsewhere, and therefore regarded the residues of colonial restrictions and institutions more seriously. Or regionalism, more virulent in Colombia than almost anywhere else in Latin America during the last century, may have given the personal rivalries of caudillos and clans a dimension less apparent in other nations. Whatever the reason, and whatever other factors may have been involved, the uncommon frequency and extent of Colombia's 19th-century civil wars was surely fed by the clash between traditionalism and the liberalism of the age.

One consequence of the Liberal policies of midcentury was that Colombia's economy became decidedly more individualistic and laissez-faire, much less encumbered by the restrictions of institutions and practices inherited from Spain. However, free trade helped to ruin the artisan industries that had survived the colonial period with the aid of tariff protection during the years 1830–46. After a boom the tobacco trade also declined, another victim of foreign competion.[6]

In addition, the hacienda system seems to have been reinforced rather than weakened by the measures of the 1850s and 1860s. Some laws, such as the abolition of slavery, did work in a contrary direction, but the expropriation of Church properties and the right of the Indians to sell their lands contributed to the extension of the privately owned large estates during this period. The Indian often became the dupe of the large property owner, of the merchant, or of the shrewd or the daring, in a world of liberal individualism he did not comprehend. The frequent result was the sale for a pittance of the small plot he had obtained in the earlier subdivision of the Indian *resguardos* (reservations), his descent into poverty and the status of submissive sharecropper or peon, and the loss of an Indian identity that had been sustained by life in his own community. The auctioning of Church lands constituted a significant reordering of agrarian property relations. Those in a position to take advantage of such a restructuring were those already wealthy or those with good connections in the government. In any case, the expropriation of Church lands certainly did not create a class of yeoman farmers.

By the early 1880s the conjunction of an economic and fiscal crisis with dissension within the Liberal Party had placed Rafael Núñez in the presidency with a program of "regeneration." Núñez, once a "radical" Liberal, was now a moderate who sought political allies among Conservatives. Under his leadership the federalist period of Colombian history was brought to an end by the centralist constitution of 1886. Designed to create an "elective constitutional monarchy" by greatly enhancing the powers of the presidency, the new constitution embodied the principle of political centralization and administrative decentralization, thus ending the semi-sovereign status of the Colombian states. Furthermore, the relationship between Church and state was settled on terms in the main satisfactory to the Church. While Church lands were not restored and the "freedom of cults" was affirmed by the constitution, the basis was laid for a major Church role in education and other aspects of Colombian life, and for a concordat with the Vatican (signed in 1887). In matters of economic policy, the "regeneration" sought to stimulate domestic production by a modest revision of the Liberals' free-trade policies. Finally, the Núñez administration witnessed the end of the era of Liberal rule that had persisted, with the exception of the years 1855–60, since 1849. The Conservatives were now to dominate Colombia for an even longer period, until 1930.

The Liberals did not accept with grace the demise of their power, or the reversal of the principles that most of them had promoted for four decades. Civil wars ensued in 1885, 1895, and 1899–1902, all of which the Liberals lost. The last of these was the worst, costing a reputed 100,000 lives and contributing to the nation's inability to prevent the secession of Panama.[7] It was not until 1910, when the constitution's "monarchical" features were modified, that the Liberals acquiesced in the constitution of 1886.

Despite the strain of violence in 19th-century Colombian politics, there were other ways in which, as Francisco García Calderón expressed it, "Political life was less imperfect in Colombia than in other Latin democracies."[8] Presidential successions were largely determined by peaceful processes, albeit sometimes through fraud and other less violent means than revolution. And the opposition did on occasion triumph in an electoral contest, both in the period of fractional struggles preceding the formation of parties and after 1848, notably when the dominant party was divided, as in 1855.

Colombian politics during the 19th century was "less imperfect" than that of some of its neighbors in its relative lack of some of the excesses of *caudillismo* and *continuismo*, two persistent features of Latin American political life. The former term refers to government by a series of charismatic chieftains. *Continuismo* is the practice that entails the continuance in authority, or in effective power behind the scenes, of an individual or of a family dynasty, either without regard for legal amenities or, more usually, by molding constitutional forms to the purpose. Of course, neither *caudillismo* nor *con-*

tinuismo was foreign to Colombia in the 19th century (or, for that matter, in the 20th). During the early decades of the republic, for example, heroes of the wars for independence often attained the presidency. Yet on the whole the caudillo was less important, and dictatorship less frequent, than in most other Latin American countries.

A number of facts support such a contention:

1. Military involvement in politics was infrequent, and generally ineffective when it occurred.

2. Colombian caudillos did not create their own parties, as has been common elsewhere in Latin America. While military or civilian caudillos often had personalistic followings, they almost invariably acted in the name of one of the traditional parties. The parties, rather than particular dynasties or individuals, were the inheritors of their work, and most caudillos were canonized by either the Conservatives or the Liberals.

3. Congress functioned throughout most of this period and frequently showed itself to be independent of the desires of the executive (although there were many instances of executive domination of Congress). In fact, it was a dispute between General Tomás Cipriano de Mosquera and Congress that led to the former's overthrow in 1867.

4. An incumbent president was often unable to impose a successor on his party (though there were also some successful attempts). This was the case even with Colombia's greatest military caudillo, General Mosquera, during his first presidency (1845–49).

5. Only four presidents held the office more than once, none but Rafael Núñez in successive terms and all, during at least one of their terms, for relatively brief or otherwise limited periods. Only one president actively held the reins of power for as many as eight total years, and in only one case for as many as six consecutive years. Colombia has had no counterpart to Mexico's Porfirio Díaz or Venezuela's Juan Vicente Gómez.

6. With the exception of the period 1886–1910, all Colombian constitutions have limited the presidential term to either two or four years. Most of them have also prohibited the immediate reelection of

the president. "No reelection" and relatively short terms for the chief executive were during the last century, and have been since, traditions that have in general been embodied in Colombian law as well as followed in practice.

7. Finally, of the three full-fledged dictatorships in 19th-century Colombian history—that of General Rafael Urdaneta (1830–31), that of General Melo (1854), and that of Mosquera (1861–63)—none lasted as long as a year and a half.

It appeared that the Colombian elite and the traditional parties had reached a consensus of sorts opposing strong-man rule. This bespeaks a unity of outlook and common interests that at certain critical junctures was able to transcend other differences. The degree of economic, demographic, and political balance among Colombia's variegated regions may also have played a role in preventing easy domination of the country by a national caudillo.

Colombia therefore emerged from the 19th century with the paradoxical heritage of opposition to dictatorship, including an at times powerful Congress and functioning electoral process, on the one hand, and a propensity to resolve political differences through violence, on the other. The civil war of 1899–1902 (the War of the Thousand Days) ushered in a five-year dictatorship. More significant, the war, although it had ended more or less in Liberal defeat, produced a compromise settlement. At last a kind of political consensus, sundered by the end of the monarchy and further shattered after 1850 by the crystallization of loyalties around two contending political parties, reappeared in Colombian political life. At the same time, given the impact of many of the Liberal reforms (such as the division of Indian and Church lands), the 19th century ended with the economic distance between classes probably even more pronounced than during the period of colonial rule.[9]

THE 45-YEAR PEACE

Following the end of the civil war in 1902 and the loss of Panama, there ensued almost half a century that has been characterized as the 45-year peace, the classic period of Colombian democracy. During this period there were no civil wars and no forcible overturns of the national government. There was not even an attempted revolt worthy of the name, with the exception of an abortive military coup in 1944, when the political system was already entering a period of profound crisis. The parties twice alternated in power peacefully during those 45 years, in 1930 and 1946. From a number of perspectives it appeared that the country's two-party system was finally operating according to the mythical norms of such a system. Some of the features of 19th-century politics were carried into the 20th— electoral fraud, for example—but the rough, violent edges of Colombian political behavior had seemingly been smoothed. Colombians felt they had come of age, politically speaking, and rarely missed the opportunity to point proudly to the contrast with some of their neighbors.

What can account for this change? The particularly long and disastrous civil war at the turn of the century was certainly a key factor in inducing the Conservatives to modify their methods of government, and the Liberals to seek honorable means of accommodation with their adversaries. The fact that the Liberals had been frustrated in 1885, 1895, and the War of the Thousand Days in their attempts to overthrow the government doubtless discouraged further resort to arms. There is likewise some evidence that the war of 1899–1902 had begun to take on faint overtones of class revolution in the countryside. Although the matter bears further investigation, if true, this would be an additional inducement for the elite groups that controlled the two parties to make peace in order to stem the threat to themselves from below.[10] The separation of Panama, resulting from the chaos of civil strife and carrying with it an implied threat of further national disintegration, or absorption by the "Colossus of the North," was a related stimulus to peace.

In addition to these more or less negative causes, the beginnings of economic development and increased international trade, particularly in coffee, were affecting politics. Groups demanding greater centralization of government and more effective administration in order to promote trade and economic growth seem to have been instrumental in bringing about Núñez's "regeneration" in the 1880s. Strengthened now, they emerged from the disorder of civil strife to demand the stability that favored their economic expansion. Values in land that supports a self-sufficient agriculture can survive anarchy; trade and industry cannot.

According to one student of Colombian history, "Although between 1914 and 1930 there was additional economic and political pressure created by a Creole-capitalist textile industry and a foreign-owned oil production, it is the emergence of coffee as the economic basis to Conservative agriculture and landowning which best explains the era of material and orderly progress during the Conservative epoch."[11] In short, during 1890–1930 Colombia moved from an economy based largely on subsistence agriculture to one based substantially on market-oriented agriculture. The production and export of coffee had now in a sense become bipartisan, having expanded from Liberal domains in eastern Colombia to encompass the traditionally Conservative domains of the Antioqueños. Colombian coffee was grown largely on small and medium-size farms, thus providing a wide base of support and legitimacy for the post-1902 political order, as well as affording a channel for enterprise and upward mobility outside the bounds of violence-prone clientelist politics.[12]

Finally, many of Colombia's intellectual lions, members of the "generation of the centenary" (of Colombian independence), sought to move Colombia along new roads, away from the fratricide of the past. They helped to provide the rationale, and to create the climate, for a political truce.

This spirit of conciliation was carried forward by General Rafael Reyes, a Conservative elected to the presidency in 1904. Reyes accorded representation in his cabinet to the Liberals. However, his dictatorial methods, especially the attempt to extend his presidential term from six to ten years, brought about his overthrow, peacefully, in 1909. A constituent assembly was called to amend the constitution. The resulting reform of 1910 was not an attempt to overturn the essential principles of the constitution of 1886. Its main provisions were instead aimed at lessening the possibilities of future dictatorship and of the complete hegemony of one party. Thus it instituted a system of representation that guaranteed the minority a third of the seats at stake in any given electoral jurisdiction, and reduced the presidential term from six to four years.

The constitutional reform of 1910 was the achievement of the Republican Party, an entity composed of members of both traditional parties whose initial purpose had been to overthrow Reyes and reinstitute constitutional government. An erstwhile Conservative, now a Republican, held the presidency in 1910–14. Yet it seems to have been recognized by all but a few diehard Republicans that their party was really only a pause in the period of Conservative rule that had begun in the 1880s; having performed its role, it soon passed out of existence.

During the 16 years between 1914 and the end of Conservative rule in 1930, Liberals occasionally participated in the cabinet or served as ambassadors, and they usually held about a third of the seats in Congress. In presidential elections they were luckless, in part because of fraud. Yet by the election of 1930, the Conservatives were so badly split that they ran two candidates for president. The archbishop of Bogotá, usually a key figure in determining Conservative nominations, wavered between the two. Meanwhile, the morale and effectiveness of the Conservative government were undermined by the onset of the depression; by a strike among banana workers on the Atlantic coast in December 1928, which brought bloody repression and resultant controversy; and by a student-led demonstration in Bogotá in June 1929 that also resulted in bloodshed. The depression, which dried up the foreign loans upon which much of the recent Colombian prosperity had been based, was particularly damaging. The strike of the banana workers, as well as other symptoms of worker and peasant unrest, suggested the need for a new hand at the tiller in order to satisfy or otherwise quell the discontent. Among many Conservatives, as well as among Liberals, *cansancio* had taken hold, a general tiredness and disillusionment with the old faces and a readiness to try new ones.

After some hesitation, the Liberals seized their opportunity. In cooperation with some Conservatives, they called Enrique Olaya Herrera, a Liberal and a former Republican, back from his ambassadorship in Washington to run for president. With the Conservatives divided, Olaya won handily. The really significant thing about the election was that the Conservative president refused to intervene to ensure the election of either Conservative candidate, and that he peacefully turned over power to a Liberal regime, albeit one operating under the guise of a coalition called National Concentration.

Olaya included Conservatives in his administration, and the Conservatives initially retained their control of Congress. However, by the end of Olaya's term the Liberals had gained a congressional majority, and in 1934 the Conservatives offered no opposition to the election as president of Alfonso López, who instituted a full-fledged Liberal regime. This transition—from a Conservative government, to a coalition headed by a Liberal, and then to a Liberal administration—

evidenced the rather special nature of party alternation in Colombia. It is seldom abrupt; a transitional or coalitional regime has usually been necessary to effect the transfer of power at all, let alone peacefully. A like process was to take place in 1946, though in a reverse partisan direction.

Alternation in office between the parties in 1930 was sometimes accompanied by violence. In the Liberal version, some priests and local political chieftains led peasants in armed resistance to the change in the governing party. According to the Conservatives, the violence was launched by the Liberals in an effort to ensure their control of Congress and consolidate their hold on the administration. In any event, virtual civil war raged for a time in the eastern departments of Santander and Boyacá. By the time the army had restored peace, some 6,000 persons were dead.

There was more than one abortive plot against the government during this period, as well as a revolt by army officers in 1944 that was attributed by the Liberals to the agitation against the government by the Conservative press, if not to direct Conservative complicity. Such attempts failed to generate broad support, and the violence that occurred in these years was for the most part localized and sporadic. While the transfer of power in 1930 accordingly did not witness the wholehearted acceptance, on either side, of the role of a loyal opposition, generally speaking the immediate change was acquiesced in by the "outs."

The end of civil war in 1902 marked the beginning of the 45-year peace that the constitutional amendments of 1910 had institutionalized, assisted by the transitional Republican regime of 1910–14. However, there was precious little mass participation in politics or in the material perquisites of the nation's growth. Until 1936, property and literacy qualifications limited the vote; others were simply "voted" by their landlords or by local political chieftains on whom many *campesinos* (peasants) were dependent. Both parties essentially represented elite interests, even though party loyalties extended to the level of the village and the farm. During this period, "Colombia became something like an aristocratic republic, in the style of Rome, Venice, or the Athens of Pericles, with a responsible patriciate, formed by the . . . leading . . . families, whose interests were confounded with the general interest of the state [thus] producing the health of the nation."[13] It was a pattern resembling that of Argentina, Brazil, and Chile during the late 19th and early 20th centuries. The other principal Latin American pattern of this period was that of the "unifying dictatorship" like that of Díaz in Mexico or Gómez in Venezuela. Still other Latin American countries alternated between the two.[14]

At the same time, aside from the fact that this "democracy" afforded little real opportunity for voice or participation to most Colombians, the "out" or minority party often abstained from elections at the national level. Transfer of power occurred only when there was a split in the dominant party that impelled it to present two candidates, while both political violence and electoral fraud and intimidation were at times extensive. Clearly these were a democracy and a political truce that did not fully live up to their names.

Nonetheless, a modus vivendi between the parties lasted roughly 45 years, from 1902 to 1946. Civil liberties were well respected; the opposition did have an opportunity to win at least some seats in national, departmental, and municipal legislative bodies; and even the peaceful transfer of power came to be accepted. Yet the bases of the 19th-century struggle between the parties had by no means been eliminated. The contest for office and employment could still be intense, as indicated by the violence that followed the 1930 election. Even such a highly charged issue as the appropriate role of the Church was more dormant than definitively resolved. Some of the economic foundations of Colombia's Athenian democracy were also being eroded. Thus coffee, while still king, was coming to have to share its place with industry and with other interests in an increasingly complex society. At the same time, the viability of many small farms was diminishing. Most critical of all, perhaps, there were new stirrings among the previously excluded, especially, but not only, in the growing urban centers that would bring to the front new kinds of actors and new kinds of policy considerations. In the process Colombia's vaunted political peace and its version of Athenian democracy would be, for a time at least, rudely shattered.

NOTES

1. A classic study of Spanish colonial institutions is Clarence H. Haring, *The Spanish Empire in America* (New York: Oxford University Press, 1947). A standard history of Colombia is Jesús María Henao and Gerardo Arrubla, *Historia de Colombia*, 8th ed. (Bogotá: Talleres Editoriales de la Librería Voluntad,

1967). Colombia was found by one author to tie for 5th out of 18 Latin American countries in the degree of Spanish colonial "penetration"; David Scott Palmer, *Peru: The Authoritarian Tradition* (New York: Praeger, 1980), pp. 27–28.

2. See John Leddy Phelan, *The People and the King* (Madison: University of Wisconsin Press, 1978).

3. See Charles W. Berquist, *Coffee and Conflict in Colombia, 1886–1910* (Durham, N.C.: Duke University Press, 1978).

4. See Miguel Urrutia, *The Development of the Colombian Labor Movement* (New Haven: Yale University Press, 1979), p. 31; and generally concerning this "class war."

5. For example, Antioquians (Colombians from the department or province of Antioquia), most of them Conservatives, tended to be export-oriented but pro-Church; cf. Charles W. Berquist, "The Political Economy of the Colombian Presidential Election of 1897," *Hispanic American Historical Review* 56, no. 1 (February 1976): 1–30.

6. Urrutia suggests that the economic stagnation of much of the latter half of the 19th century, including the decline of artisan industries, was in part responsible for the endemic conflict of this period; *Development of the Colombian Labor Movement*, pp. 47–48.

7. The total number killed in civil wars between 1830 and 1903 is estimated at 130,000 by William P. McGreevey, *An Economic History of Colombia, 1845–1930* (Cambridge: Cambridge University Press, 1971), p. 176. Some 2.5 percent of the total population may have been killed in the civil war of 1899–1902, compared with losses of less than 2 percent of the 1850 population in the U.S. Civil War.

8. Francisco García Calderón, *Latin America: Its Rise and Progress*, trans. Bernard Miall (New York: Scribner's, 1917), p. 205.

9. Cf. McGreevey, *Economic History of Colombia*, chap. 7.

10. Essentially, though, this "War of the Thousand Days," as Colombians term it, was fought by ". . . two opposing conglomerations of peasants led by lawyers turned generals"; J. León Helguera, "The Changing Role of the Military in Colombia," *Journal of Inter-American Studies* 3, no. 3 (July 1961): 352.

11. Harry Bernstein, *Modern and Contemporary Latin America* (New York: J. S. Lippincott, 1952), p. 636. Between 1905 and 1925, coffee exports almost quadrupled in volume while their value increased some 13-fold; see Berquist, *Coffee and Conflict*, p. 255. See also Marco Palacios, *Coffee in Colombia, 1850–1970* (Cambridge: Cambridge University Press, 1980).

12. Berquist, *Coffee and Conflict*, chap. 10.

13. Rafael Azula Barrera, *De la Revolución al Nuevo Orden: Proceso y Drama de un Pueblo* (Bogotá: Editorial Kelly, 1956), p. 490.

14. For the distinction between these patterns, see Gino Germani, *Política y Sociedad en una Época de Transición de la Sociedad Tradicional a la Sociedad de Masas* (Buenos Aires: Paidós, 1962), chap. 6.

3

MODERN COLOMBIA

The decades since the end of Colombia's 45-year peace have been a period of considerable economic and social change, as well as, at times, intense political turmoil and, briefly, military dictatorship. Yet, overall, the continuity of political institutions and the degree of political stability have been remarkable. Even some of the major individual political actors have been the same (or their immediate descendants) in the 1980s as in 1946.[1]

Of course, modern Colombia does not begin at the arbitrary date of 1946, with the end of the "Liberal Republic" and the inception of a period of violence unparalleled in 20th-century Colombia. Modern Colombia might just as well be said to originate in 1930, with the end of the period of Conservative hegemony, or in 1934, with the reformist regime of Alfonso López, the so-called *revolución en marcha.* That being the case, it seems desirable to begin our look at a changing Colombia in the postwar decades by searching out the roots of change in the preceding era.

THE ONSET OF CHANGE

The roots of change in the years after 1946 can be traced at least as far back as the beginning of the extensive production and export of coffee in the last decade of the 19th century, even before the War of the Thousand Days. With political peace assured after 1902, coffee exports exploded and helped to provide the capital for the beginnings of industrialization.[2] Foreign loans, mainly to government bodies at all levels, to help build public works, and to a lesser degree foreign investors, notably U.S. companies such as Tropical Oil and United Fruit, also helped fuel economic expansion during the 1920s. U.S. loans totaled $4 million in 1913 and reached $250 million by 1929. Payment by the United States of a $25 million indemnity for Panama worked to the same expansive end, as did the general boom in international trade prior to 1930. Meanwhile, the United States, which took 37 percent of Colombian export products in 1913, took 67 percent by 1929.[3] Thus, as the Colombian economy expanded, its ties to the United States grew closer.

The first signs of modern industrialization had appeared in the 1890s; by 1925 the manufacturing sector was producing 7.6 percent of all goods and services. The percentage of economically active persons employed in manufacturing doubled between 1925 and 1953, and those employed in services increased rapidly as well, even though Colombia remained overwhelmingly agricultural.[4] The first modern labor unions appeared among river and transport workers. Urbanization grew at an even faster pace than industrialization. During 1918–53 the proportion of Colombians living in communities of 1,500 or more persons doubled, to 42.8 percent.[5] In some parts of central Colombia, increasing population pressures and the uncertainty of land titles produced land invasions and other evidence of agrarian unrest, while conflict between the banana workers and the United Fruit Company in the Atlantic coast region led in 1928 to the calling in of the army and a bloody "massacre" of workers.

Such transformations, including the repercussions of the latter conflict, undoubtedly contributed to the demise of Conservative rule in 1930. Yet, in contrast with most of Latin America, the world depression that began in 1929 did not inaugurate an era of political instability. The fact that Colombia's economic elites were more unified than conflictual in their goals may partially account for this circumstance; that is, those favoring policies to promote industrial development did not clash fundamentally with landowners, especially those tied to the all-important export trade in coffee. In many cases they were the same people, or closely related.[6] An alliance between the new industrialists and the workers to push aside the landowners therefore did not emerge.

Perhaps most important in accounting for political stability in the face of rapid social and economic change were Colombians' close ties to the traditional political parties and the leadership assumed by one of those parties in addressing the problems of economic and social change, and in co-opting the proponents of change, during the 1930s.

Thus, following the four-year "transitional" term of the coalitional National Concentration regime of President Enrique Olaya Herrera, Alfonso López Pumarejo, the Liberal president elected in 1934, launched his so-called *revolución en marcha.* López and his cadres of Liberal reformers pushed through a series of constitutional amendments in 1936 that laid the basis for an increased role for the state in economic matters. Property was declared to have a social function, and could henceforth be expropriated by judicial decree (normally, however, with prior indemnification). Given this legal basis, the López administration enacted an agrarian reform (Law 200 of 1936) designed to provide greater security and clarification of titles of land ownership, and to redistribute unproductive lands. In other areas the tax burden was somewhat shifted from indirect to direct taxation (including Colombia's first graduated income tax); primary education was both nationalized and made obligatory, the National University reorganized, and federal expenditures on education increased manyfold; new credit institutions were established; national integration was promoted through a program of road construction, the nationalization of the police, and other measures; and a moderate program of "Colombia for Colombians" was promoted in employment and other areas.

The 1936 constitutional reform formalized labor's right to strike (with the exception of public services), a right earlier granted by the Olaya Herrera administration, and the government went out of its way, both in law and in policy, to provide labor a series of guarantees and benefits (including the eight-hour day). Government backing was also afforded the newly founded Confederation of Colombian Workers (CTC). The potential electorate was expanded by abolishing literacy and property qualifications for voting. Finally, in 1936 reforms modified the role of the Church in Colombian society by reducing religious associations to a legal status equivalent to that of other voluntary associations, by loosening the Church's control over public education, and, symbolically, by omitting mention of Roman Catholicism as the religion of the nation.

In some respects such measures remained more impressive in concept and on paper than in their execution. Many workers remained unorganized or outside the law's protection, and in the end Law 200 had only a modest impact on land distribution. Nonetheless, taken together, the López reforms constituted a significant departure in public policy and in government's role in the social order. In a real sense 1934 marks the beginning of the modern Colombian state. Significantly, the "revolution on the march" was carried out under the aegis not of a new party or of a counterelite but under that of intellectuals and politicians, many of them young, from the ranks of one of Colombia's historic parties.[7]

Needless to say, such changes were not without their opponents. In the Conservative view, both property and the Church were under attack, and the Liberals' mobilization of workers and others was a political threat of a new kind. Many Liberal men of property came to resist the reforms, and by the time López returned to the presidency in 1942, both the political climate and the possibilities of further reform had drastically changed. By 1945, López was forced to resign (partly as the result of scandal touching his family), to be succeeded for the remaining year of his term by the Liberal Alberto Lleras Camargo. Lleras proceeded to bring Conservatives into his cabinet and to govern for the remaining year of López's term with a bipartisan coalition of National Union, a forerunner of the later National Front.

CONFLICT, VIOLENCE, AND DICTATORSHIP

It was under such circumstances that the fateful election of 1946 took place. With the Liberals split between the official party candidate, Gabriel Turbay, and the populist Jorge Eliécer Gaitán, the Conservatives, for the first time since 1930, ran their own candidate, Mariano Ospina Pèrez. With only 41 percent of the vote, Ospina won the presidency against the divided opposition. As a minority president and essentially a moderate, Ospina sought to continue the bipartisan coalition, much as Olaya Herrera had embraced bipartisanship when the Liberals had won an election over the divided Conservatives in 1930.

However, political tension remained too high for National Union to succeed, except sporadically. For one thing, the aftermath of the election brought localized violence in some parts of the country, just as it had in 1930, with Conservatives seeking to replace Liberal incumbents and Liberals resisting. Moreover, both the stakes and the rhetoric were higher in 1946, for considerable economic and social change had come to Colombia in the interim, along with López and his *revolución en marcha*. Laureano Gómez, in many ways the real leader of the Conservative Party in these years, was particularly vehement in his denunciations of Liberals—indeed, of all who disagreed with his self-proclaimed mission to save Colombian society from "heresy" and "communism," and to preserve traditional Hispanic and Catholic values. Gaitán had conducted his 1946 presidential campaign not so much against a party as against the "oligarchy" that, in his view, ruled both traditional parties. A dynamic speaker, with both the social background and the physical appearance to make him a plausible tribune of the people, he challenged Colombia's established leaders and institutions in ways they had not been challenged before. In point of fact, Gaitán was more a populist calling for "the moral regeneration of Colombia" than he was a genuine revolutionary, although his program and rhetoric did carry certain socialist overtones.[8]

On April 9, 1948, Gaitán was assassinated, apparently by a mystic and disgruntled job seeker, although there were accusations of involvement (from different quarters) by the Conservative government, the Communist Party, and even the United States. The city of Bogotá, as well as communities elsewhere in the country, erupted in rioting, with most of the police going over to the side of the rioters. Much of the center of the capital was destroyed, clerical and Conservative symbols and institutions taking the brunt of the mob's fury. Although the government survived, and bipartisanship was for a time restored in the wake of this so-called *bogotazo*, the upshot was a new phase of interparty warfare, generally termed *la violencia*, that erupted in various parts of the country with Liberal guerrilla bands explicitly seeking the overthrow of the government and, in a few instances, some kind of social revolution.

This brief period of Colombian history—from Gaitán's antioligarchic presidential campaign to the aftermath of the *bogotazo*—was probably the closest Colombia had come to overt class warfare since the heyday of the Democratic Societies in the mid-19th century. Some Communists and others did attempt to take charge of events. Yet in the end the *bogotazo* was more "the earthquake of a people moved by the assassination of their own voice"[9] than it was an attempted social revolution. It essentially lacked direction and, even if it had toppled the government, it seems likely that either military rule or a government dominated by the leaders of the Liberal Party would have resulted.

The government sought to reassert its authority—often through strong-arm tactics and by intimidating Liberals—not merely in the immediate interests of survival but also in order to be able to impose its will in the next elections. Polarization between the parties and the attendant violence finally led to President Ospina's declaration of a state of siege and the closing of the Liberal-dominated Congress in November 1949, followed by the Liberals' withdrawal from the presidential race scheduled for that same month.

The violence continued following Gómez's virtually uncontested election, as well as under Rafael Urdaneta, who served as acting president much of the time, for Gómez was in ill health. Gómez, long the scourge of both the Liberal Party and of liberalism, convened a constituent assembly with the object of revising the constitution along corporatist lines. Presumably, limiting the suffrage and the role of the "one-half-plus-one" would mitigate the impact of the Liberal majority that had prevailed in the country since the 1930s. However, with the army increasingly called upon to assume a police function in restoring order to rural Colombia, and the more moderate Ospinista Conservatives joining the Liberals in alienation from the regime, General Gustavo Rojas Pinilla, the commander in chief of the armed forces, led a successful coup d'état on June 13, 1953.

Initially supported by most politically vocal Colombians other than Gómez's followers, and including more civilians (mainly Ospinistas) than military men in the cabinet, the new government promptly declared an amnesty and at least temporarily restored a measure of political peace. The regime, however, proved arbitrary and repressive in a number of its actions, including censorship of the press. It also soon became clear that Rojas, instead of acting to restore civilian authority, intended to perpetuate himself in power by forging an "indestructible union" between the armed forces and the people. He sought to create a base for his rule independent of the established parties by creating a Third Force political movement, a captive labor organization, and a social welfare agency run by his daughter along the lines of the Eva Perón Foundation in the late 1940s in Argentina.

Economic problems surfaced in the form of lower coffee prices and accelerating inflation. Rojas further alienated industrialists and others through his tax policies, and the favoritism and corruption that tainted the operations of government. Although on a lesser scale, *la violencia* resumed, now centered substantially in the mountains of central Colombia and with Communist-affiliated guerrillas playing more of a role than formerly. The fatal blow was Rojas's attempt to have himself named president for another four years by the constituent assembly initially convened by Gómez. In the face of student demonstrations, a nationwide "civic strike" that included many banks and businesses, and opposition from the Church and most factions of both major parties, the army forced Rojas out of office and into exile on May 10, 1957.[10] There followed a little more than a year of rule by a five-man military junta and, in August 1958, the restoration of civilian rule. Thus did Colombia complete its only period of military rule in the 20th century and its first period of dictatorial rule since the Reyes regime following the War of the Thousand Days.

LA VIOLENCIA

The violence that had erupted in Colombia in the years after 1946 represented "what is probably the greatest armed mobilization of peasants (as guerrillas, brigands or self-defense groups) in the recent history of the western hemisphere, with the possible exception of some periods during the Mexican Revolution."[11] By the time the original *violencia* had waned in the mid-1960s, it had claimed the lives of an estimated 200,000 Colombians, not to mention many millions of pesos in property damage and crop losses.[12] *La violencia* was also notable for its brutality. Never a civil war with contending armies on recognizable battlefields, the generic term *la violencia* was used to denote a phenomenon that over the years shifted in purpose, as well as in geographic locus and extent (see Table 3.1). Triggered by partisan conflict, and taking place mainly in the countryside between bands of peasants, or between peasants and units of the army or police, it came to encompass motives of banditry, revenge, and economic extortion as well. Generally lacking central direction, the violence was nonetheless at times promoted by government officials or politicians to intimidate the opposition. For the most part the violence fed on itself, with the actions of one side provoking the other, and so on in a vicious cycle. Generally speaking, revolutionary (in the sense of the overthrow of the elites and the whole social system)

TABLE 3.1. The Phases of Violence in Colombia, 1946–84

	Nature	Principal Locations
Phase I (1946–48)	Postelectoral interparty	Northeast (Boyacá, Santander, Notre de Santander)
Phase II (1948–53)	Government (police) vs. Liberals, and interparty, with minor Communist participation	Much of the country, with the exception of Atlantic coast and far southwest
Phase III (1953–58)	Government (army and police) vs. Liberals, with increasing Communist role	Central Andean regions, especially south-west of Bogotá
Phase IV (1958–65)	Government (army) vs. Liberal remnants now primarily reduced to banditry, revenge, and extortion	Central Andean regions
Phase V (1965–75)	Government (army) vs. revolutionary (predominantly Marxist) guerrillas	Scattered, in mountainous and jungle areas
Phase VI (1975–84)	Continuation of previous phase, with the addition of drug traffickers and associated death squads as important factors	Scattered, in mountainous and jungle areas
Phase VII (1984–)	Amnesty for major guerrilla bands; some guerrillas fight on	Scattered, in mountainous and jungle areas; terrorist acts in cities

Source: Adapted in part from Russell W. Ramsey, "Critical Bibliography on La Violencia in Colombia," *Latin American Research Review* 8, no. 1 (Spring 1973): 3–44.

only at the margins and in isolated pockets, *la violencia* eventually gave way to small guerrilla groups of often loosely Marxist orientation pursuing a new set of objectives.

The causes of *la violencia* were complicated and various. They included an array of latent local conflicts and rivalries among families, communities, and political chieftains set aflame by a change in the party in power at the national (and hence the local) level, exacerbated by the events of April 1948 and the attempts of a minority Conservative government to maintain itself in power. Attacks on the clergy in the wake of the *bogotazo*, along with priests' denunciations of Liberals, in some places added fuel to the flames and gave the violence messianic dimensions. Once the violence was under way, those who had seen brothers killed or daughters raped sought revenge on the opposing partisan band, or saw economic advantage in forcing landowners, small or large, from their property in order to preempt it or its crops.

The fact that the state lacked legitimacy in the eyes of many Colombians—that it was regarded as a redoubt of an implacable partisan foe in an era when government had taken on more functions and greater importance than ever before—both intensified sectarian rivalries and made it impossible for the state (as well as the Church) to act as a neutral arbiter or enforcer of the public peace.[13] Even the court system was generally held to be partisan and ineffective in bringing culprits to justice or holding them in prison once convicted.

Beyond such political conflicts and institutional weaknesses, *la violencia* was also fed to an undetermined but probably significant extent by changes in the countryside. It was not the areas of latifundio (such as the Atlantic coast departments) or greatest poverty where the violence was most evident, but in the central Andean regions. Characterized by small farms and cash-crop farming, such areas in recent years had been most susceptible to the pressures of population growth, rural migration, and the uncertainties of land titles and the market economy. "The 'violence' seems to have been especially virulent in those human groups which by their contacts or migratory origins had begun to aspire to a better condition."[14]

Two points concerning the causes of *la violencia* need reiteration. First, although there were at times guerrilla bands that sought genuine social revolution, and although after the mid-1960s such motivations became predominant among the guerrilla bands that remained, during its heyday from the late 1940s to the mid–1960s, the conflict was above all one of peasant versus peasant, village versus village, Liberal versus Conservative, and not, in the main, class warfare. Second, *la violencia* was a complex phenomenon with varying motives and different manifestations at different times and in different localities or regions.

The years of violence were of course highly destructive of lives and property. They also were a major contributor to the onset of Colombia's first military government in decades. Yet the impact was not entirely negative. The formation of a so-called National Front coalition of the two major parties and the eventual assuaging of partisan political passions were one consequence. The National Front's efforts at agrarian reform, however tenuous they would prove to be, were in part a response to the violence and its disruptive impact on the countryside. There is also some evidence that while *la violencia* contributed to personality disorganization in those most directly affected, it helped to promote new kinds of leadership and social solidarity in some communities and, in that sense at least, to erode traditional in favor of more "modern" values.[15] Surprisingly, *la violencia* evidently did not notably interfere with the country's rather rapid rate of economic growth; it may even have stimulated industrialization by swelling the urban labor force and diminishing the propensity to invest in land.[16] Finally, it has been argued that the violence had the effect (negative or positive, depending on one's point of view) of aborting or diverting an otherwise incipient social revolution in Colombia; some even argue that promoting such an effect was deliberate on the part of the country's elite.[17]

That Colombia would have experienced a genuine social revolution without the outbreak of *la violencia* may be doubted; after all, its political Left had always been weak, both organizationally and electorally, and there was no real symbol in terms of a cause—say, nationalism, or a particularly harsh dictatorship—to rally broad support. Yet *la violencia*, together with the loyalties to the traditional parties which initially sparked it, undoubtedly did help to direct Colombians from issues of economic and social policy, and to make it more difficult to generate support for the kind of populist party that rose to power at one time or another in most other Latin American countries in the decades following World War II. In this sense, whether deliberately or not, the long-run impact of *la violencia* may have been to reinforce Colombia's elitist democracy and even, with the ensuing National Front, to impel its rejuvenation.

THE NATIONAL FRONT

It was a bipartisan coalition that finally brought an effective end to *la violencia*. Occasional coalitions between Liberals and Conservatives, or factions thereof, were hardly new, dating from shortly after the crystallization of the parties in the mid-19th century.[18] The most recent examples had been the so-called National Concentration regime of 1930–34, formed in the wake of Conservative electoral defeat in 1930, and the several ultimately failed National Union coalitions of the late 1940s. Essentially, these coalitions were founded on "understandings among gentlemen"; generally lacking a constitutional basis or an institutionalized framework, they were inordinately subject to the pulls of personal and political rivalries, and calls from political partisans to place party advantage above any attractions of shared power.[19]

With military rule in full swing in the mid–1950s, some of Colombia's political leaders, notably former president López, began to call for alterations in Colombia's political institutions that would restore political peace by guaranteeing a share in government for both major parties. A series of consultations and negotiations ensued among party leaders (Alberto Lleras and Laureano Gómez prominent among them) that eventually led, following the fall of Rojas and a year of interim rule by a military junta, to the institutionalized coalition arrangement called the National Front. As incorporated into the constitution by a plebiscite held on December 1, 1957, and as shortly thereafter amended by interparty agreement (and formally by Congress), the central provisions of the agreement called for the following:

1. An equal division (parity) between Liberals and Conservatives, and only those parties, of all seats in legislative bodies, from municipal councils to the national Congress

2. All appointive positions (apart from the military and the small civil service) to be similarly distributed between the parties, again at all levels of government

3. Mandatory alternation in the presidency between the two parties every four years

4. The approval of nonprocedural measures within all elective bodies by a two-thirds vote (thus obviously requiring support for legislation from portions of both parties).[20]

The period of bipartisan government was to last for 16 years, until 1974, at which time Colombian politics would revert to open competition involving all parties.

The return to civilian government was therefore very much in the form of a constrained democracy whereby a variety of antimajoritarian devices assured that neither party could win an election, or lose one. One of the principal motives for partisan violence—the conflict over government offices and their attendant perquisites—would thus presumably be diminished, and the stimulus to military intervention removed. Such a prolonged and institutionalized period of power sharing would also afford Colombia's political and economic elites the opportunity to promote the country's economic development, and even to carry out certain reforms, while minimizing the dangers of counter-elite mobilization.

The institutions of the National Front did not go unaltered for 16 years. A 1968 reform abrogated the two-thirds requirement for the passage of legislation; it also ended the parity requirement for legislative seats at the municipal and departmental levels beginning in 1970, four years ahead of the original schedule, and reopened political competition to all parties.

The functioning of the National Front was not without its inherent problems and limitations. For one thing, the absence of partisan competition diminished political interest among the electorate, and may have helped to produce the high rates of voter abstention, leading some to deplore the declining legitimacy of the political system.[21] Furthermore, while competition between parties was precluded by the stipulations of parity, competition among party factions was not. Certain of these factions challenged aspects of the coalitional arrangement. The most important of these opposition movements was the National Popular Alliance (ANAPO), which purported to embrace both Liberal and Conservative factions; it ran candidates under one or the other banner as circumstances dictated. Its leader was former dictator Rojas Pinilla. In the 1970 presidential race Rojas, running as a Conservative, challenged the Front's political arrangements and made a populist appeal to the urban masses. Nearly elected in a multicandidate race, and perhaps denied victory by fraud,[22] his was the foremost challenge to the National Front during its 16 years of life. Finally, while some reforms were instituted (an agrarian reform, for example, and a substantial expansion of access to education), the overall pattern of income distribution was little affected and the agrarian reform (Law 135 of 1961) had only a modest impact, little more than Law 200 of 1936.[23] In short, the governments of the Front proved essentially immobilist in addressing many of the fundamental problems of the country, with their coalitional nature enhancing the ability of powerful private interests or minority political factions to prevent reform.

Still, the achievements of the National Front were many, and corresponded essentially to its original objectives. Above all, it had kept the political peace between the parties for a decade and a half, and left the experience of partisan comity as a legacy to the years that followed its formal termination in 1974. The old-style *violencia*, by now reduced largely to banditry, revenge, and economic extortion (albeit often in the name of politics), was brought virtually to an end by the mid-1960s. Both in attitudes and in behavior the old pattern of hostilities between the parties declined markedly, and dialogue among their leaders became a common occurrence. Post-National Front elections have taken place without the rancor or violent conflict of the 1940s, the last previous period of truly partisan electoral contests. Central to these changes was the end of the old partisan hegemonies, and of the traditional perception that the state was the exclusive preserve of the party that had captured control of the executive branch.

The military, too, had been kept on the political sidelines for 16 years, even though in cabinets otherwise divided equally between the parties a governmental role for the military was institutionalized by allotting the Ministry of Defense to a military man. The newly created Superior Council of National Defense, designed to oversee the policies of the ministry and including the commander in chief of the armed forces, further tended to institutionalize access for the military. No longer invoked to keep order between the parties and no longer invited to side with one or the other, it became more directly involved in combatting would-be social revolution and in programs of civic-military action that had the intended effect of drawing the state and its rural populace closer together. In the process the military during the National Front years saw its size tripled, its budget doubled, and its professionalization measurably enhanced.[24]

The country made significant strides economically. Fueled by a rapid expansion in "minor" exports (other than coffee and petroleum), the average annual growth rate of output rose from a creditable 5 percent in the years 1958–66 to well over 6 percent thereafter.[25] Overt social unrest was kept to a minimum, in part because of the modest reforms undertaken by the National Front governments, as well as by a generally expanding economic pie. Moreover, levels of mobilization were kept low by the structures of the coalition government, which eliminated the need to appeal to the masses to contest the parties' claims to bureaucratic booty. The high levels of electoral abstention during the National Front years were, at least in part, reflective of that circumstance. In any case, the elite-directed consociational mechanisms of the Front had the effect of mitigating class, as well as partisan, conflict.

The governments of the National Front had a major impact in other ways as well. The stipulation in the plebiscitary reform of December 1957 that the Roman Catholic religion was that of the nation and was to be protected by the state "as an essential element of social order" has, at long last, seemingly removed the question of the appropriate role of the Church from partisan politics. The Church has become a supporter of the political system and of the democratic order regardless of which traditional party holds the presidency. This has freed the Church to address instead the questions of social change that confront both it and society as a whole.[26]

The machinery of the state was also modernized during the National Front years, considerably enhancing the state's capacity to manage both economic development and social reform. Granting power to the president to legislate on such questions was made easier when the fear of partisan hegemony was eliminated, and the inputs of a growing group of technocrats, along with a more technocratic style, became more evident in policy making. A good example was the area of population policy, which was largely taken out of the arena of interparty conflict, thereby giving technocrats (both national and international) a freer hand. Thus Colombia, though having perhaps the most politically influential Church in the region, and one of the most conservative, was the only country in South America to have an officially sanctioned (albeit discretely promoted) birth-control policy during this period.[27] The bipartisan aura of the National Front and its technocratic style likewise provided a congenial enviromnent for international agencies and foreign aid, with Colombia becoming a "showcase" of the Alliance for Progress.

Programs such as *acción comunal*, which promoted community organizations and projects throughout the country, and civic-military action, which involved the military in community action and infrastructure projects in rural areas where the violence had been most endemic, furthered the integration of the nation in quite tangible ways.

By making the traditional ties to parties less relevant, and by making elections less meaingful, the National Front, even while it contributed to political stability, may have played its part in eroding the old, virtually hereditary ties to the parties, as well as in enhancing cynicism toward the significance of the electoral process. The augmented power of the president and the rise of a more technocratic style of policymaking likewise had a tendency to diminish the role of the parties. Organized interest groups proliferated in the climate of bipartisanship and of increased government involvement in economic affairs. The need for top-level negotiations between the parties (for instance, to agree on the coalition's candidates for president) probably also had the effect of accentuating the centralization of power within the parties. Finally, the National Front may have diminished expectations that benefits for certain groups or regions could best be obtained by the traditional route of political clientelism, enhancing instead a sense that linkages with government agencies or officials (perhaps of the opposite political persuasion) was a more effective way to achieve their ends. This occurred as bureaucrats in various government agencies began increasingly to take on such tasks as road building, school construction, pest control, land surveying, and similar tasks not previously performed by the national government, or performed only with the intervention of the local *cacique* or *gamonal* (political boss). Put succinctly, the concept of the public servant at least began to replace that of the political broker.[28]

Meanwhile, some profound changes were occurring in Colombian society. Urbanization, in particular, advanced apace, with the share of the population living in places with more than 1,500 persons increasing from about 47 percent to some 58 percent and the largest cities growing most rapidly of all. The share of the labor force employed in agriculture similarly declined.[29]

The aforementioned changes cannot, of course, be wholly attributed to the 16-year truce between the parties. In fact, in a sense the National Front was merely the formal instrument of an increasing coalescence among the segments of the Colombian elite that, to their cost, had diverged during the 1930s and 1940s, not only over who should control the traditional perquisites of power but also over the issues posed by industrialization and mass mobilization. Yet it seems fair to say that during the years of the National Front, and at least partly because of its particular political arrangements, Colombian politics was altered in significant ways—in the nature of relationships between the parties, in the roles of the military and the Church, and in the strengthening of the state as an instrument of economic development and (potentially, at least) social reform. At the same time, the pattern of elitist democracy remained unchanged in its fundamentals.

Once again, as they had after the War of the Thousand Days at the turn of the century, Colombia's leaders, through concerted effort and bipartisan accord, had pulled the country out of an era of unparalleled violence and consequent military dictatorship, and into an era of political peace and economic growth without finding it necessary to disturb the essentials of the political or social system.

AFTER THE NATIONAL FRONT

The years following the end of the National Front proper have seen the continuation of much of the spirit, and even some of the letter, of the Front agreements. At the same time, the political system has left unresolved some of the familiar problems inherited from the past while acquiring one or two new ones.

To ease the transition to open political competition, the 1968 constitutional reform had stipulated four more years of parity in both cabinet and administrative posts beyond 1974; after 1978 such offices were to be allotted so as to ensure "adequate and equitable participation to the major party other than that of the president." Thus each of the three presidents since 1974—two Liberal and one Conservative—has included members of one or more factions of the rival party in his cabinet on a basis roughly proportional to the outcome of the most recent election.[30] In fact, as during the National Front years, interparty collaboration sometimes seems greater than cooperation between factions of the same party.

TABLE 3.2. Presidents of Colombia, 1930–86

President	Type of Government	Years
Enrique Olaya Herrera	Liberal (National Concentration coalition)	1930–34
Alfonso López Pumarejo	Liberal	1934–38
Eduardo Santos	Liberal	1938–42
Alfonso López Pumarejo	Liberal	1942–45
Alberto Lleras Camargo (*designado*)*	Liberal	1945–46
Mariano Ospina Pérez	Conservative (initially with a National Union coalition)	1946–50
Laureano Gómez-Roberto Urdaneta (*designado*)*	Conservative	1950–53
General Gustavo Rojas Pinilla	Military government with Conservative (Ospinista) collaboration	1953–57
Military junta	Transition to National Front coalition	1957–58
Alberto Lleras Camargo	Liberal (National Front)	1958–62
Guillermo León Valencia	Conservative (National Front)	1962–66
Carlos Lleras Restrepo	Liberal (National Front)	1966–70
Misael Pastrana Borrero	Conservative (National Front)	1970–74
Alfonso López Michelsen	Liberal	1974–78
Julio César Turbay Ayala	Liberal	1978–82
Belisario Betancur	Conservative	1982–86
Virgilio Barco	Liberal	1986–

*The *designado* is elected by Congress to serve as president in the absence or incapacitation of the elected president.

The first two post-National Front presidents were Liberals, in keeping with the evident Liberal majority in the country that has held for half a century: Alfonso López Michelsen (1974–78), son of former president Alfonso López Pumarejo and himself briefly head of a dissident Liberal movement, the Revolutionary Liberal Movement (MRL) during the 1960s; and Julio César Turbay (1978–82), son of the official 1946 Liberal candidate for president, Gabriel Turbay. In 1982, with the Liberals split between two candidates, López Michelsen and Luis Carlos Galán, Conservative Belisario Betancur won the presidency. Once again, party turnover occurred when the majority party split. Betancur, at one time a protégé of Laureano Gómez, had lost a close election in 1978 and had also run (as a dissident Conservative) in 1970. Though backed by a unified party in 1982, he had long since become something of a populist in program and political style.[31] He downplayed the designation Conservative and ran under the rubric National Movement.[32]

Betancur experienced an unusually long political honeymoon; by the end of his first year his prestige was adjudged to be "superior to that of his government." That the president's personal popularity did not translate into support for his party was evident from the midterm elections (municipal and departmental legislative posts) in the spring of 1984: the Conservatives received only 42 percent of the vote (about their usual proportion), with some 58 percent going to the still-divided Liberals. Soon, persistent problems with inflation, deficits, and the public services brought a ground swell of criticism of the president himself, and foreshortened such programs as construction of 400,000 new homes and the provision of houses without down payment for the urban poor.[33] Additional criticism centered on the president's allegedly excessive involvement in hemisphere politics—especially on his role as a would-be mediator in Central American political conflicts—at the expense of domestic issues. In the 1986 elections (March for congressional, municipal, and departmental offices, May for the presidency) the Liberals swept the boards. Virgilio Barco, the Liberals' single candidate for president, won some 58 percent of the vote to 36 percent for the Conservatives' Alvaro Gómez.

Perhaps most important in undermining confidence in the president, and even the legitimacy of his government in the eyes of some, was his policy toward the guerrillas. While there has been no sign of a resumption of the interparty violence of the pre-National Front years, *la violencia* of the old style has been superseded by a variety of revolutionary groups purporting to seek a new social order, several of them having their inception in the 1960s, others of more recent origin. There are numerous such groups, operating primarily in the countryside and most of them quite small.[34]

The largest such organization is the Revolutionary Armed Forces of Colombia (FARC), probably numbering several thousand members. Some of its leaders have from time to time sat on the Central Committee of the Communist Party. Unusual among Colombian (and Latin American) guerrilla bands, most of the leaders and members of the FARC are campesinos. The FARC has had at least some kind of operation in a number of Colombia's departments, but the zone of its greatest strength appears to be in south-central Colombia and the adjacent fringes of the eastern *llanos* (plains). In mid-1985 it constituted the Patriotic Union (UP) in a move to contest the 1986 elections under the conditions of a truce proffered by President Betancur. The UP thereupon garnered some 4 percent of the presidential vote.

The Movimiento 19 de Abril (M-19) is a rather different kind of group. It originated as a reaction to Rojas Pinilla's defeat in 1970, and for most of its history has concentrated on urban terrorism. It was responsible for the abortive seizure of the Palace of Justice in November 1985 that resulted in the deaths of more than 100 people, including members of the Supreme Court and all of the guerrillas involved. In recent years it has developed a rural dimension as well, operating primarily in jungle areas of southern and western Colombia. Ideologically eclectic, the M-19 is composed principally of youth of urban origin.

The Army of National Liberation (ELN) is one of the oldest of the extant guerrilla bands, although it is apparently smaller than the FARC or the M-19. Its site of operations has been primarily in northeastern Colombia, especially in Norte de Santander. Composed largely of urban youth, it was the band that in late 1965 recruited Father Camilo Torres, who shortly thereafter was killed in a skirmish with the army.

A fourth small group, less visible than the others in recent years, has been the Popular Army of Liberation (EPL), which has had its principal base of operations in northern Colombia. Still other small bands have led sporadic or shadowy existences.

There have been some indications that certain of the guerrilla groups have coordinated their activities on occasion, but on the whole they seem to have acted quite independently and, at times, at logger-heads. They also have not been immune from internal dissension, stemming at least in part from personal rivalries among their leaders. While the FARC has usually been considered Moscow-line Communist, the ELN Castroite, and the EPL Maoist, their degree of external support is difficult to determine. The Colombian government charged that Cuba had aided and abetted the M-19 in an "invasion" of southern Colombia in 1981, but the charges were denied by both Cuba and the M-19.

Guerrilla organizations have waxed and waned in Colombia over the years, with the army quite successful against one or another for a time, only to see a subsequent comeback. Similarly, several "independent republics"—remote areas for most practical purposes controlled and governed by guerrilla bands or by peasant "self-defense" groups—have been broken up by the army since the mid-1960s, but they often have succeeded in reconstituting themselves elsewhere.[35] While none of Colombia's guerrilla groups has ever been very successful at mass mobilization, or at posing a real threat to the stability of the government, collectively they have been a significant thorn in the side of the country's elitist democracy. In November 1983 guerrillas were able to kidnap the brother of President Betancur (he was released within a few weeks). Not only has the combatting of the guerrillas absorbed resources and energies needed elsewhere, but the guerrillas' actions have helped to undermine public order—and the public's confidence in the government's abilities to maintain it.

A further impact of these guerrillas may have been to strengthen the role of the military. A security statute decreed by President Julio César Turbay in 1978 gave the military enhanced powers of arrest and expanded the kinds of crimes eligible for trial by military courts. Radio and television news relating to disturbances of public order, illegal strikes, and the like were made subject to censorship. The tough new law led, among other things, to the arrest of many with leftist sympathies who were accused of aiding the guerrillas. While the security law was effectively nullified in June 1982 when President Turbay lifted the state of siege just prior to the inauguration of President Betancur, one consequence was widespread accusations of human rights abuses (arbitrary arrests, torture, and "disappearances") by Amnesty International, as well as by a number of Colombian intellectuals and politicians.[36] In any case, it is fairly clear that the domestic role of the military has increased since the mid-1970s and that its spokesmen have become increasingly vocal on matters of internal security.

Nonetheless, by August 1984 the government of President Betancur had reached an accord with most of the major guerrilla groups, allowing them to return to "legality" without laying down their arms, and promising political reforms (such as direct election of mayors) as well as a "national dialogue" concerning a variety of social and political questions in return for a cessation of hostilities. Not all the guerrillas agreed to the truce, and still others subsequently resumed combat, alleging failure of the government to live up to its side of the bargain. However, the FARC, in particular, continued to adhere to the truce, and Betancur continued to express the hope of integrating the guerrillas into the regular political process.

Congressmen from the president's own party were among the many Colombian political, economic, and military leaders who vociferously opposed any such dealings with the guerrillas, enough so to provoke rumors of a coup during the latter months of 1984. Nonetheless, while the president's popularity and political support had noticeably declined since the early part of his administration, he remained firmly in control as the campaign got under way for the May 1986 presidential election.

A burgeoning drug "industry" added a significant new dimension to Colombian economic, social, and political life beginning in the mid-1970s, when the country experienced a "rise to prominence as the world's drug-smuggling capital [that] has been nothing short of meteoric."[37] By the late 1970s Colombia was exporting an estimated 30 or so metric tons of cocaine and in excess of 20,000 tons of marijuana to the United States. Earnings were similarly high, though equally difficult to determine with any exactness, perhaps amounting to several billion dollars as of 1979 and directly or indirectly supporting as many as 100,000 Colombian families. The marijuana is grown largely in Colombia's northern departments. The cocaine base is for the most part imported from Bolivia and Peru via Ecuador, and processed in laboratories in southern and western Colombia. Colombia is beginning to grow its own coca as well, though it is apparently of an inferior grade. Partly responsible for such a quantum leap in the drug trade was the destruction by the Mexican government of marijuana plots in that country. Colombia's topography and climate are ideally suited to the raising, processing, and smuggling of clandestine drugs. Furthermore, Colombia has long been used to extensive contraband in goods such as coffee and cattle, and the extensive low-level administrative corruption that accompanies it, not to mention the climate of violence fostered by guerrilla and terrorist attacks, and by common crime. The drug traffickers both personify and amplify this general ambiance.

The full ramifications of the drug underworld are, for obvious reasons, difficult to assess. It has contributed to corruption of unprecedented extent among the police, the military, and bureaucrats in some regions of the country, and has even touched diplomats, an aide to the president, and, allegedly, high-ranking army officers. Another by-product has been violence. In late 1981 the leaders of Colombia's drug "mafia" apparently created an organization called Death to Kidnappers (MAS), whose ostensible objective was to kill the guerrillas who were kidnapping drug dealers and holding them for ransom in order to finance their activities. Both the tactics and the functions of MAS have at times resembled those of the "death squads" of Central America, including the evident collusion of elements in the army.[38] Several public officials were assassinated at the behest of the drug traffickers, including, in April 1984, the minister of justice, who had launched a stepped-up campaign against them. By late 1984 they were threatening U.S. personnel and installations in retaliation for the extradition of several of their number for trial in the United States. Drug money was apparently being employed to support (and oppose) political candidates.

For some years the Colombian government took the drug trade rather lightly. As former president López Michelsen put it, the problem was one for the United States with its "permanent number of customers," not for Colombia. By early 1978 even López had begun to consider the problem a serious one, and the ensuing Turbay administration proceeded to wage a major campaign against drug traffickers, as well as against guerrillas and an increasingly active criminal element. Reasons for the change in policy included pressure from the U.S. government and chagrin over Colombia's mounting international reputation as a center for the trade in drugs. More important, it became increasingly clear that the traffic in drugs, with its accompanying lawlessness and corruption, was beginning to erode the foundations of Colombian society and politics. The murder of the minister of justice subsequently led to a much more serious and widespread campaign against the drug dealers (including the reimposition of a state of siege), with many of them at least temporarily fleeing the country.

Rooted in the economic, social, and political changes of the 1930s and before, the years following 1946 had witnessed a prolonged period of endemic violence and military dictatorship, both exceptional in 20th-century Colombia. Yet beginning in 1958 and continuing to the present, Colombia has resumed the course of relative political peace and partial democracy on which it had embarked following the War of the Thousand Days. Indeed, remarkably little has changed since the early 1950s, despite the interludes of violence, dictatorship, and the unique institutional arrangement of the National Front era and its attendant reforms. The constitution of 1886, though amended, is still in force; the Conservative and Liberal parties still dominate the political scene; and the country's elites appear to have been remarkably successful in making considerable progress toward economic development without major structural change and while containing within manageable limits the manifestations of discontent. The onset of a major traffic in drugs, with all its political and economic implications; the increased salience of the military in reaction to the persistence of revolutionary guerrilla war and terrorism; a tenuous truce with the guerrillas; and an expanded Colombian role in hemisphere affairs were the major new developments of the post-National Front decade. Some of these changes have helped to create a climate of profound malaise in the country, but none has so far fundamentally challenged the economic, social, and political patterns that prevailed in 1958 and that the National Front was instituted, essentially, to conserve.

NOTES

1. Alberto Lleras Camargo, Carlos Lleras Restrepo, Alvaro Gómez Hurtado, Julio César Turbay Ayala, and Alfonso López Michelsen are some of those whose names come immediately to mind. The two Llerases have been in politics since the 1930s; both are former presidents. The others—all former presidents or presidential candidates—are sons of former presidents or of presidential candidates.

2. Coffee exports increased some 4-fold in volume and some 13-fold in value between 1905 and 1925; Charles W. Berquist, *Coffee and Conflict in Colombia, 1886-1910* (Durham, N.C.: Duke University Press, 1978), p. 255. See also Marco Palacios, *Coffee in Colombia, 1850-1970* (Cambridge: Cambridge Univer-

sity Press, 1980); and William P. McGreevey, *An Economic History of Colombia, 1845–1930* (Cambridge: Cambridge University Press, 1971).

3. For data on U.S. loans and trade in this period, see J. Fred Rippy, *The Capitalists and Colombia* (New York: Vanguard Press, 1931), pp. 12–13. Despite such increases, Colombia was rated as one of the least dependent (16th of 18) Spanish American countries during this period; see David Scott Palmer, *Peru: The Authoritarian Tradition* (New York: Praeger, 1980), pp. 72–73.

4. Economic Commission for Latin America (ECLA), *Analyses and Projections of Economic Development*, vol. 3, *The Economic Development of Colombia* (Geneva: United Nations, Department of Economic and Social Affairs, 1957), pp. 14–16.

5. Misión "Economía y Humanismo" (Louis J. Lebret, O. P., director), *Estudio sobre las Condiciones del Desarrollo en Colombia* (Bogotá: Aedita, 1958), pp. 23–24.

6. See McGreevey, *Economic History of Colombia*, pp. 238, 296. Interestingly, political stability was maintained despite the highest levels of social mobilization in all of Latin America during the 1920s and a comparatively severe impact of the depression on government revenues during the 1930s; Palmer, *Peru*, pp. 72–73.

7. See Robert H. Dix, *Colombia: The Political Dimensions of Change* (New Haven: Yale University Press, 1967), pp. 82–91, for a fuller description of the *revolución en marcha*.

8. For a good biography of Gaitán that, however, does not fully agree with this characterization (it views him as more revolutionary), see Richard E. Sharpless, *Gaitán of Colombia, a Political Biography* (Pittsburgh: University of Pittsburgh Press, 1978).

9. Antonio García, *Gaitán y el Problema de la Revolución Colombiana* (Bogotá: M. S. C. 1955), p. 19.

10. For a favorable view of the Rojas regime, see Vernon Lee Fluharty, *Dance of the Millions* (Pittsburgh: University of Pittsburgh Press, 1957); for other views see John D. Martz, *Colombia, a Contemporary Political Survey* (Chapel Hill: University of North Carolina Press, 1962), chaps. 11–14; Dix, *Colombia*, pp. 115–26; and Tad Szulc, *Twilight of the Tyrants* (New York: Henry Holt, 1959), chap. 6.

11. Eric J. Hobsbawm, "The Anatomy of Violence," *New Society*, Apr. 11, 1963, p. 16.

12. See Paul W. Oquist, *Violence, Conflict and Politics in Colombia* (New York: Academic Press, 1980), pp. 4–11, for a thoroughgoing attempt to estimate the human cost of *la violencia*. The most thorough compilation of data on *la violencia* is Monseñor Germán Guzmán, Orlando Fals Borda, and Eduardo Umaña Luna, *La Violencia en Colombia*, 2 vols. (Bogotá: Ediciones Tercer Mundo, 1963–64). A very useful critical bibliography is Russell W. Ramsey, "Critical Bibliography on La Violencia in Colombia," *Latin American Research Review* 8, no. 1 (Spring 1973): 3–44.

13. See Oquist, *Violence, Conflict and Politics* for this interpretation.

14. Orlando Fals Borda in Guzmán et al., *La Violencia en Colombia*, vol. 1,

p. 414. A factor analysis by John A. Booth showed the intensity of the violence to be most closely related to the relative parity of support for the two traditional parties (that is, the more nearly equal the support at the departmental level, the more intense the violence). The persistence of the violence over time in a given department was, on the other hand, more closely associated with the magnitude of economic and social change. See his "Rural Violence in Colombia: 1948–1963," *Western Political Quarterly* 17, no. 4 (December 1974): 657–79.

15. See Aaron Lipman and A. Eugene Havens, "The Colombian Violencia: An Ex Post Facto Experiment," *Social Forces* 44, no. 2 (December 1965): 238–45; see also Orlando Fals Borda, "Violence and the Break-up of Tradition in Colombia," in Claudio Veliz, ed., *Obstacles to Change in Latin America* (London: Oxford University Press, 1965), pp. 199–201. Richard S. Weinert, "Violence in Pre-modern Societies: Rural Colombia," *American Political Science Review* 60, no. 2 (June 1966): 340–47, interprets *la violencia* largely as a struggle between traditionalism and modernization. The erosion of traditional bonds by *la violencia* may have contributed to an increased peasant rebelliousness that manifested itself in the 1960s and 1970s.

16. Albert O. Hirschman, *Journeys Toward Progress* (New York: Twentieth Century Fund, 1963), p. 160.

17. For interpretations along these lines, see Eric J. Hobsbawm, "The Revolutionary Situation in Colombia," *The World Today* 19 (June 1963): 248–58; and Fals Borda, "Violence and the Break-up of Tradition."

18. For a good review of these precedents, see Harvey F. Kline, "The National Front: Historical Perspective and Overview," in R. Albert Berry, Ronald G. Hellman, and Mauricio Solaún, eds., *Politics of Compromise* (New Brunswick, N.J.: Transaction Books, 1980), pp. 63–69.

19. Cf. Alexander W. Wilde, "Conversations Among Gentlemen: Oligarchical Democracy in Colombia," in Juan Linz and Alfred Stepan, eds., *The Breakdown of Democratic Regimes*, vol. 3, *Latin America* (Baltimore: Johns Hopkins University Press, 1978), pp. 28–81.

20. Kline, "The National Front," pp. 69–74, contains a full discussion of the provisions and initiation of the Front. The Uruguayan *colegiado* of 1952–66 was a somewhat comparable, though less successful, Latin American example of such an arrangement, though it involved a plural executive.

21. See in particular Rodrigo Losada, "Electoral Participation," in Berry et al., *Politics of Compromise*, pp. 87–103. The National Front was hardly the sole cause of abstention, however; see chap. 5 below.

22. At any rate, there appeared to be irregularities in the early reporting of returns. For a description and an analysis of ANAPO and other oppositions under the National Front, see Robert H. Dix, "Oppositions Under the National Front," in Berry et al., *Politics of Compromise*, pp. 131–79.

23. For this assessment, see R. Albert Berry, "The National Front and Colombia's Economic Development," in Berry et al., *Politics of Compromise*, esp. pp. 296, 299. According to Berry, a number of the policies of the Front probably had a negative distributional impact, including import substitution in capital-intensive industries and various aspects of monetary policy. Berry further sug-

gests that by forcing the majority Liberals into coalition with Conservatives, the National Front "helped to prevent rather than foster the advent of presidents with a high social content in their programs" (p. 313).

24. For the role of the military under the National Front, see J. Mark Ruhl, "The Military," in Berry et al., *Politics of Compromise*, pp. 181–206.

25. Berry, "The National Front," p. 296.

26. For an assessment of the Church's role during the National Front, see Alexander Wilde, "The Contemporary Church: The Political and the Pastoral," in Berry et al., *Politics of Compromise*, pp. 207–35.

27. Cf. William Paul McGreevey, "Population Policy Under the National Front," in Berry et al., *Politics of Compromise*, pp. 413–32.

28. Steffen W. Schmidt, "Bureaucrats as Modernizing Brokers? Clientelism in Colombia," *Comparative Politics* 6, no. 3 (April 1974): 425–50. This was obviously a tendency only, and hardly an absolute, or irreversible, as indicated by the highly "political" presidency of Julio César Turbay (1974–78).

29. Berry, "The National Front," pp. 290–91.

30. President Belisario Betancur began his administration in 1982 (following an election in which he received less than 50 percent of the vote) by dividing his cabinet equally between Liberals and Conservatives. For a delineation of the 1968 constitutional changes, see Jaime Vidal Perdomo, *Historia de la Reforma Constitucional y sus Alcances Jurídicos* (Bogotá: Universidad Externado de Colombia, 1970), pp. 159–67.

31. Betancur is a good example of the possibilities for individual mobility within the Colombian social system. His father was a mule driver who subsequently opened a cantina (tavern) in a small town in Antioquia. Betancur was one of 22 children, only 5 of whom survived infancy. He eventually attended Bolivarian University in Medellín on a scholarship, and became a lawyer and dean of the Law School at the National University.

32. Other components of the National Movement included the tiny Christian Democratic Party, the remnants of the National Popular Alliance (ANAPO), the party led by María Eugenia Rojas, the daughter of the former dictator, and dissident Liberals including Gloria Gaitán, daughter of the late populist Liberal, Jorge Eliécer Gaitán.

33. Surveys sponsored by the Liberal Party claimed that Betancur had declined from an 81.9 percent approval rating in October 1982 to 12.5 percent some two years later; *Latin America Regional Reports. Andean Group Report* (London), November 9, 1984, p. 8.

34. For a good overview of Colombian guerrilla movements as of November 1983, see *Visión*, 61, no. 10 (November 21, 1983): 304; see also Bruce Bagley, "The State and the Peasantry in Contemporary Colombia" (paper prepared for the March 1982 meeting of the Latin American Studies Association, Washington, D.C.), pp. 67–74; and, for the early years of the guerrilla movement, Richard Gott, *Guerrilla Movements in Latin America* (Garden City, N.Y.: Doubleday, 1971), pt. III. *Latin American Weekly Report* (London) carries good current coverage.

35. The longest lasting of these "independent republics" was Viotá, a region of coffee estates not far from Bogotá. It took form in the late 1920s, when

peasants spurred on by "revolutionary socialists" (soon to become Communists) invaded several haciendas and formed self-defense groups to protect their lands. These settlers set up an effectively autonomous zone of some 500 square kilometers that kept the government at bay for many years; see Miguel Urrutia, *The Development of the Colombian Labor Movement* (New Haven: Yale University Press, 1969), p. 130.

36. For a detailed report on human rights abuses during this period, mostly by the military, see Americas Watch, *Human Rights in the Two Colombias: Functioning Democracy, Militarized Society* (New York: Americas Watch, 1982). The Colombian Committee for the Defense of Human Rights reported 311 "disappearances" between January 1981 and 1984; *Latin America Weekly Report* (London), November 16, 1984, p. 12.

37. Richard B. Craig, "Colombian Narcotics and United States-Colombian Relations," *Journal of Interamerican Studies and World Affairs* 23, no. 3 (August 1981): 244. The data below derive from the same source unless otherwise noted. See also Peter A. Lupsha, "Drug Trafficking: Mexico and Colombia in Comparative Perspective," *Journal of International Affairs* 35, no. 1 (Spring–Summer 1981): pp. 95–115.

38. There was some indication that, rather than an organization, the MAS might be a label used for various death squad activities by members of the armed forces and civilians working with them. In any case, its real nature and its links to the military remain somewhat nebulous; See Americas Watch, *The "MAS Case" in Colombia: Taking on the Death Squads* (New York: Americas Watch, 1983), esp. p. 13n, and its *Human Rights*, pp. 29–31.

4

THE CONTEXTS OF POLITICS

Any political system is part of a wider web that includes a country's terrain, and the possibilities and problems it sets for human organization; the number and distribution of its people; the economic resources available and the use made of them; the structure of social relationships; and the beliefs and attitudes its people bring to the political dimension of their lives. While some or all of this is implied by—indeed, derives from—a country's historical experience, more explicit attention to such matters is called for prior to embarking on the analysis of politics and government more strictly considered. In a number of respects Colombia's economic, social, and cultural patterns parallel those of other Latin American countries. The numerous differences, on the other hand, may help to account for some of the unique aspects of Colombian political life.

THE GEOGRAPHICAL CONTEXT

Topography does not determine political behavior, but it strongly conditions the shape of the economy, the society, and the polity—in Colombia at least as much as anywhere else. Colombia lies entirely within the tropical zone. But the fact that the center and west of the country are divided three times over in a roughly north-south direction by parallel spurs of the Andean mountain chain (cordillera) means that climate, crops, and population density are more dependent on altitude than on latitude. The capital, Bogotá, located on a high plateau of the easternmost mountain chain at some 8,500 feet above sea level, is temperate in climate; Cali, a western city located at about 3,000 feet, is subtropical; and Barranquilla, on the Atlantic (Caribbean) coast and virtually at sea level, has a tropical climate and vegetation. Much of the population and economic life of the country is contained in the plateaus and valleys of the Andes. Surrounding, as it were, this mountainous core are lowland areas: the relatively populous northern (Caribbean) coastal plain, the relatively unpopulated western (Pacific) coastal fringe, and the eastern plains (llanos) and southeastern jungle, which together contain almost 60 percent of the land surface of the country, but less than 3 percent of its people.[1]

Colombia therefore has a wide variety of topographies, climates, and crops. Its people have been diverse as well, and often effectively isolated from each other by barriers of mountain or jungle. It is only within the last two or three decades that the airplane, which can overleap such obstacles; the railroad from the capital to the Atlantic coast (completed in 1961); and a national road network have effectively integrated at least the principal regions of the country. Even so, much of the east and southeast, the west coast, and numerous pockets remain fairly inaccessible and relatively untouched by the amenities of modern life. Such geographic splintering, and the attendant difficulties of transport and communication, long hampered the development of a national economic market. They also formed the basis for Colombia's historically virulent regionalism, which, though attenuated today, persists as a major influence on Colombian political life. Over the years local and regional isolation also afforded ample opportunities for the survival of political chieftains (*caciques* or *gamonales*) who controlled particular regions or "city-states," and were able to trade on that control to acquire benefits both for themselves and for their localities.

Regionalism and localism are of course not unique to Colombia. There are also wide disparities between the most populous and most industrialized regions, on the one hand, and those that have fewer people and/or less industry, on the other. Almost half of all Colombians, and 80 percent of the country's industry, are concentrated in 4 (of 23) departments: Cundinamarca (the capital of which is Bogotá), Antioquia (Medellín), Valle del Cauca (Cali), and Atlántico (Barranquilla).[2]

What does stand out with regard to Colombian regionalism, in contrast with at least most other Latin American nations, is the comparatively high degree of regional dispersion of population, income, industry, and even universities. Thus regional inequalities appear to be of lesser dimension than in most Third World countries.[3] Perhaps most important in terms of its political implications is that, instead of the concentration of people and economic resources in one or two cities, usually the capital and perhaps one other, Colombia has four geographically dispersed regions each of which contains a city with more than, or nearly, a million persons, along with a significant concentration of industry and commerce. Notably, the gap in size between the largest city (Bogotá, with a population of 4,584,000 people) and the second largest (Medellín, with 1,664,000 people) is narrower than usual. In addition to the country's four largest urban centers, there are a number of lesser centers of some significance, most particularly Bucaramanga, the capital of the department of Santander in eastern Colombia, and Cartagena, on the Atlantic coast. Each of the latter has a population of well over 400,000. Colombian regionalism is therefore one of multiple balances: "A functional map of Colombia would not resemble a wheel with all the spokes leading to Bogotá (as Venezuela is dominated by Caracas, for example) but a series of wheels with complex interrelations between them."[4] During the 19th century the degree of economic and demographic balance among several regions, together with their relative mutual isolation, may have helped to fuel the pervasive civil wars, and today may at times hinder "rational" economic development by forcing the government to allocate scarce resources among multiple regional claimants. Nonetheless, such a degree of regional balance may have helped to ensure more symmetrical economic development than in most countries, and may have served to assure a greater degree of pluralistic access to the political system.

There is evidence that the regional concentration of both industry and income has been increasing over time, and that the gap between Bogotá and the rest of the country may be widening somewhat.[5] Yet it remains true that Colombia, more than most other countries of the Third World, sustains a relative measure of dispersion of resources and population, with all of the attendant economic and political implications.

The geographical context of politics includes not solely a nation's internal configuration, but its place in its hemisphere and the larger world as well. In its immediate environment Colombia borders on five countries and perforce looks in several directions: south along the Andean chain to Ecuador, one of the erstwhile components of Gran Colombia; southeast toward the Amazon basin and little-populated frontiers with Peru and Brazil; east to another former component of Gran Colombia, Venezuela, the neighbor with which it is most closely related in a variety of ways; and finally, northwest to Panama, over which Colombia was formerly suzerain. Colombia also fronts on both the Atlantic and the Pacific oceans, the only South American country to do so, with the exception of the southernmost tip of Chile. Most important, Colombia exists in the same hemisphere as the United States, with its northern coast only a little more than two hours by air from Miami, closer geographically than any foreign country to the Panama Canal, and proximate as well to a Central America in upheaval, where the United States is currently deeply engaged. There are of course economic and cultural ties with countries beyond the western hemisphere, but as powers with the potential for a major influence on Colombian politics, their presence is remote and marginal. For better or for worse, it is its placement well within the sphere of influence of one of the world's great powers that poses the fundamental constraints on Colombia's international actions and, in a sense, on its domestic policies and behavior as well.

THE DEMOGRAPHIC CONTEXT

In 1900 Colombia had a population of only a little more than 4 million; in the next half century it reached the 11 million-plus level; by the early 1980s, its population was estimated at 27 million, with 38 million projected for the year 2000. On the other hand, an annual rate of population growth that had averaged 3 percent or more during 1960–70 had declined to a 1.9 percent between 1970 and 1982.[6] Thus, while Colombia's population is still growing rapidly, the growth rate has slowed significantly in recent years, undoubtedly as a consequence of increasing urbanization and literacy, as well as of government population policy. Nationwide, population pressures do not approach those of South Asia, or even of El Salvador. Population growth over the last several decades has nonetheless left Colombia's population a young one, thereby increasing the need to commit resources to education; it has also had implications for both voting rates and voting patterns (see chapter 5). Perhaps most important, the growth of Colombia's population continues to exceed the economy's capacity to employ and feed it adequately.

Of at least equal relevance has been the very rapid rate of urbanization. Population pressure on the land in areas where very small plots (minifundios) predominate, the increasing commercialization of agriculture, and the presumed attractions of city life—including hoped-for employment and increased educational opportunities for one's children—all help to account for the cityward movement. Violence in the countryside may for a time also have contributed to the accelerated pace of migration. In any case, by 1982 some 65 percent of the population was considered urban; significantly, Colombia was no longer largely a rural country in terms of the place of residence of the majority of its citizens. The rate of urban growth, while still rapid, has nonetheless slowed markedly, from a 5.2 percent annual rate for 1960–70 to 2.7 percent between 1970 and 1982.[7]

Just as striking as the broad movement to towns and cities was the fact that by 1980, half of all urban Colombians lived in cities of more than 500,000 persons (compared with 28 percent only 20 years earlier).[8] In addition to its 4 largest cities—3 of them (Bogotá, Medellín, and Cali) well over a million in population and the fourth (Barranquilla) approaching that figure—Colombia has some 15 other cities with at least 100,000 persons. Whether judged by a minimal definition of the term "urban," or by the numbers living in large cities, Colombia was by the 1980s substantially, and increasingly, an urban society. The "typical" Colombian was no longer a *campesino*, but a town or city dweller.[9]

The rate of urban growth has considerably outrun the capacity of the cities to gainfully employ the new migrants. As a result, many migrants have moved not to the cities but across the border to Venezuela, where hundreds of thousands, if not millions, of Colombians are now thought to reside,[10] or to other countries, including the United States. Many thousands more regularly cross the Venezuelan border for seasonal agricultural work.

Meanwhile, in the expanding urban centers the strain on housing and urban services has been great, posing a problem for public policy. Although some public housing has been constructed, much of it with U.S. financial assistance during the days of the Alliance for Progress, many of the urban newcomers have simply squatted on undeveloped public or private lands. These "clandestine" communities include both settlements that are developed through the illegal taking of land and those that are not legally recognized because they entail sales of lots in areas lacking in urban services. These new settlers, acting individually or in groups sometimes numbering in the thousands, immediately construct rudimentary shelters, making it at least politically difficult to expel them. By condoning such settlements, politicians and government authorities hope to acquire the support of the occupants; moreover, the burgeoning of such settlements reduces the pressure to provide government-built housing for the urban poor and acts as a "safety valve" for the dissatisfaction of this stratum of the population. As time goes on, many of the new settlers improve and expand their original flimsy dwellings, thus creating communities with a sense of permanence, and even something of an entrepreneurial spirit.[11]

Rapid population growth and an even more rapid growth of urban centers have therefore together been instrumental in creating a sociologically new Colombia since the 1950s. Even though both trends have apparently passed their peaks, their impact will continue to have important consequences for Colombian society, economy, and politics.

THE ECONOMIC CONTEXT

Colombia is fundamentally a capitalist, free-market economy coupled with state ownership of such infrastructure facilities as roads, railroads, telecommunications, and electric utilities. The government is also deeply involved in the development of energy resources, including petroleum, coal, and hydroelectric power; in regional development; and in development planning and financing. Yet even in such basic areas as energy and steel, the government has often relied on the private sector (foreign or domestic) through joint-venture arrangements or by selling back to the private sector enterprises initially developed by the state. In all, as a percentage of the gross national product (GNP), both government revenues and government expenditures are relatively low compared with most other Latin American countries—indeed, compared with most other countries worldwide.[12]

High-grade, mountain-grown coffee is still in many ways king in Colombia, providing roughly half of the country's (legal) export earnings in a typical year, although only a much smaller percentage of the gross domestic product (GDP). Prior to the 1960s, coffee's share of Colombian exports was considerably higher, accounting for more than 80 percent of the country's foreign exchange in some years. Increases in other agricultural exports, as well as some industrial exports, such as textiles, have lowered that percentage since the mid-1960s.[13] One of the notable economic changes since about 1960 has been the increase in the cultivation of rice, cotton, and sugar, usually on large commercial farms. This is a marked shift from the use of much of the best farmland as extensive pasturage, a practice that dated from colonial days.

Income from the drug trade has contributed more to the Colombian economy in some years than coffee, though that income does not appear in most compilations of official statistics. In the early 1980s it was said to add some 15–18 percent to the growth of the money supply, thus helping to fuel inflation. The drug "industry" diverts needed agricultural land to other purposes, as well as absorbing government funds for its attempted control. It likewise makes difficult government economic planning, penetrates or controls legitimate business enterprises, and heightens the climate of tax evasion and general lawlessness. At the same time it has provided employment and enhanced income for many Colombians, including peasants in impoverished areas of the country.[14]

Once an oil exporter, by the 1970s Colombia had become an oil importer. However, recent discoveries and investments have made it possible for the country to again become an exporter in 1986. Meanwhile, the development of large coal reserves, especially at El Cerrejón in northeastern Colombia, under a joint venture contract with an Exxon subsidiary, as well as the expansion of the substantial hydroelectric potential, should before long make Colombia a significant exporter of energy resources.[15]

Colombia's basic agricultural and mineral resources have remained largely in the hands of Colombians, as have its politically sensitive public utilities. Foreign capital has played a major role in the petroleum industry, which has not been Colombia's major earner of foreign exchange and employs rather few workers. The United Fruit Company for years controlled banana production, but that was essentially confined to the Atlantic coast region. Coffee, on the other hand, which for many decades has been Colombia's principal export earner, and the direct and indirect employer of hundreds of thousands of Colombians, has been primarily in Colombian hands.[16] For the most part, both land and entrepreneurship have always been mainly Colombian.

While agriculture still makes up an important though declining sector of the economy—accounting for 26 percent of the GDP in 1982, down from 34 percent in 1960—manufacturing accounts for 21 percent, other "industry" (including construction and mining) another 10 percent, and "services" (including commerce and transportation) 42 percent.[17] The long-term trend has clearly been toward an industrial and service economy. Although Colombia is hardly a fully industrialized country, as early as the late 1950s most domestic consumption of consumer goods such as shoes, textiles, processed foods, cosmetics, and furniture was being supplied by Colombian industry, and some heavier industrial production had already begun (in cement, steel, and tires, for example).

Foreign investment has played an important role in the recent expansion of manufacturing in Colombia. In fact, "by the end of the National Front, industries which contained some foreign investment contributed close to half of total value added in manufacturing."[18] In 1975, of the country's 100 largest enterprises, a third derived at least half their capital from foreign parent companies, with the heaviest concentration in the fast-growing intermediate-goods sector.[19] Direct participation of foreigners in financial and industrial management was, by comparative standards, quite low;[20] in fact, at least until quite recently, most of the capital for Colombian industrialization derived from domestic sources (notably from coffee). Moreover, since 1975 foreign banks have been "colombianized" (that is, majority ownership by Colombian nationals is required). Major investments are subject to government approval, and the exploitation of mineral resources is by contract with the government, rather than by concession (as formerly).

Colombia's financial and industrial sectors have become increasingly oligopolized, notably in the form of financial-industrial conglomerates such as the Santodomingo complex and the Grupo Suramericano.[21] Including a variety of enterprises and, usually, one or more major financial institutions, they have been able to wield considerable economic power beyond that of the individual firm. Their political weight, too, has in some instances come to overshadow that of the producers' associations. At times closely linked to the state or, at least indirectly, to particular presidents (the head of the Grupo Grancolombiano was a cousin of former president Alfonso López Michelsen), conglomerates have in some instances found themselves subject to attempts by the state to limit their power.

In 1983 the Grupo Grancolombiano saw several of its executives arrested (including López Michelsen's cousin) and its principal bank (the Banco de Colombia) taken over by the government, on grounds of irregularities in financial dealings.

The Colombian economy has been notable for its steady, if unspectacular, growth in recent decades. While it has not experienced the kind of boom that occurred in Brazil during the 1960s, neither has it suffered, until very recently, the pronounced economic downturns (even negative growth rates in some years) of some of the countries to the south. Overall, between 1960 and 1970, Colombia's GDP grew at an annual rate of 5.1 percent, and between 1970 and 1982 the rate was 5.4 percent.[22] In the last several years, however, Colombia has experienced a recession, along with much of Latin America (and the world). The GDP grew only 4.1 percent in 1980, 2.3 percent in 1981, and at a rate of just under 1 percent in both 1982 and 1983. Recession has been accompanied by trade and budget deficits, capital flight, and an inability of some companies, especially in textiles and steel, to pay their creditors. However, 1984 showed a return to 3 percent growth, and preliminary data for 1985 promised a similar rate, thus indicating that the economy might be on the way up again, although serious problems remained.[23]

Colombia has experienced historically high rates of inflation since the mid-1970s, in the range of 20–30 percent on an annual basis, although the rates for 1983 and 1984 were about 18 percent. While higher than those of the majority of Latin American countries, such rates have remained well below the levels of inflation in Argentina, Brazil, Chile, and Uruguay since at least the 1950s.[24] Moreover, although inflation has had a markedly adverse effect on real wages at certain times (for instance, during the early 1970s) and in certain sectors (such as government employment), the overall trend for the period 1962–81 has been a slow increase in real wages.[25] At the same time, the rate of unemployment surged to 14 percent by mid-1985; underemployment was perhaps another 20 percent.

By 1984 Colombia was experiencing something of a credit squeeze, and it hosted a Latin American debtors' conference at Cartagena in June. Its currency reserves showed a marked decline from the late 1970s, when high world coffee prices brought a highly favorable balance in its international accounts, although by the mid-1980s they showed signs of an upturn. Still, in comparison with other Latin American debtors, Colombia has fared quite well in

TABLE 4.1. Indicators of Latin American
Economic Performance

	Inflation (percent)		Average Annual Growth of GNP per Capita
	1960–70	1970–82	1960–82
Argentina	21.4	136.0	1.6
Bolivia	3.5	25.9	1.7
Brazil	46.1	42.1	4.8
Chile	33.0	144.3	0.6
Colombia	**11.9**	**22.7**	**3.1**
Costa Rica	1.9	18.4	2.8
Cuba	n.a.	n.a.	n.a.
Dominican Rep.	2.1	8.8	3.2
Ecuador	6.1	14.5	4.8
El Salvador	0.5	10.8	0.9
Guatemala	0.3	10.1	2.4
Honduras	2.9	8.7	1.0
Mexico	3.5	20.9	3.7
Nicaragua	1.8	14.3	0.2
Panama	1.5	7.5	3.4
Paraguay	3.1	12.7	3.7
Peru	10.4	37.0	1.0
Uruguay	50.2	59.3	1.7
Venezuela	1.3	12.4	1.9

Source: World Bank, *World Development Report 1984* (New York: Oxford University Press, 1984), pp. 218–19.

recent years. As of 1982 its foreign debt was the second lowest in Latin America (Cuba omitted), and its debt service the fourth lowest as a percentage of its GNP.[26] There were, on the other hand, a number of major and smaller private companies in considerable financial difficulty that were being forced to renegotiate their foreign loans, for which the government refused to assume liability. Indicative of external confidence in the Colombian economy was a credit agreement signed in December 1985 with a consortium of private banks providing some $1 billion in loans, largely for the production of coal and petroleum.

Colombia's GNP per capita was $1,460 in 1982, ranking it ninth highest, and therefore just about at the median point, among the 18 Latin American countries on which there were data.[27] The Colombian economy shares with its continental neighbors many familiar patterns and problems of late-late industrialization: increasing industrialization and, in particular, rapid growth of the urban service sector, with a concomitant decline in agriculture's share of GNP; a tendency toward oligopoly in finance and industry; excessive dependence on a single export crop; problems of inflation, unemployment/underemployment, and a recently slowed rate of growth; continued low levels of health, education, and productivity; seemingly chronic depression in a major industry (textiles); and the dilemma of how to attract needed foreign investment while limiting foreign control over the most dynamic sectors of industry.

On the other hand, in several ways potentially quite relevant to politics, the Colombian economy is significantly divergent or atypical:

1. The state's involvement in the country's economic life, while substantial, is among the lowest in the hemisphere.

2. Rates of economic growth, though unexceptional, have been steadier than in most countries (at least until the recession of the 1980s that hit virtually all of Latin America).

3. Inflation, while higher recently than before, has remained well short of the "runaway" stage with its attendant potential consequences.

4. The country's external public debt is among the lowest in the region.

5. The country is, or soon will be, at least self-sufficient in energy resources.

6. Foreign investment, while today substantial in manufacturing and energy, has never dominated the key area of the country's economy (coffee production).

7. Drugs have become an important, if clandestine, export sector, the size, ramifications, and future of which are difficult to determine but are surely considerable.

THE SOCIAL CONTEXT

Wide differences in income, occupation, education, and life-style—differences that tend to be cumulative—suggest that distinctions of social class are highly salient in the lives of Colombians. Income distribution is strongly skewed. As of 1970, Colombia ranked fourth highest among the 13 Latin American countries on which there were data (and 11th of 69 worldwide) in terms of total income going to the top 10 percent of the working population.[28] Although income inequalities had seemed to lessen somewhat from the mid-1950s to the mid-1960s, since that time they have apparently increased even further.[29] Concomitantly, less than 1 percent of the stockholders hold almost half the shares on the Bogotá Stock Exchange, and more than half the credit in the banking system is in the hands of only 1 percent of the debtors.[30] An empirical study of the concentration of economic power in Colombia concluded that some 64 individuals (9 percent) of a group of executives of banks, cement companies, and firms worth more than 100 million pesos listed on the Bogotá Stock Exchange, controlled 80 percent of that power.[31]

Landownership, too, has been highly concentrated in Colombia and has changed little in this respect in recent years. According to the 1970 agricultural census, in a still substantially agricultural country only 8.42 percent of the farms contained 77.77 of the farmland.[32] In fact, as of the 1970s, Colombia ranked fifth highest in the world in terms of land concentration, despite the fact that landownership was rather widespread (more than two-thirds of all farms were worked by their owners).[33] Moreover, since at least the middle of the 19th century, there has been substantial overlap among the holders of landed and mercantile-industrial wealth in Colombia.[34]

Higher education is highly selective, with only 2 percent of the relevant age group (20–24 years) even enrolled (let alone graduated), although that percentage has increased dramatically in recent years (see below).[35] There is also a pronounced overlap between education and economic power. Two-thirds of the economic power holders in one study had pursued university studies, and almost all of the other third had attained at least a secondary school education, heretofore also a relatively scarce commodity in Colombia.[36]

The media—the press, radio, and television—are closely linked to a variety of economic interests, although the state plays a major role in television.[37]

Critical for our purposes is, finally, the very considerable inter-penetration between the holders of political power and those in whom other resources are concentrated. Colombian presidents have often been prominent business leaders and managers or directors of major economic groups. Mariano Ospina Pérez was for several years manager of the National Federation of Coffee Growers (FEDECAFE) and was prominent in real estate, publishing, agriculture, and mining. Both Carlos Lleras Restrepo and Misael Pastrana Borrero had been president of Celanese Colombiana, one of the country's large textile enterprises, among their other economic interests. A study of the cabinet ministers who held office during 1930–70 showed that over 90 percent had earned university degrees (in a society where fewer than 1 percent had done so).[38] Almost all of Colombia's congress-men are professional men (usually lawyers) and/or owners of sub-stantial property,[39] again in a society where both are scarce. In fact, the constitution stipulates that senators must already have held high public office, or have practiced a profession requiring a university degree for at least five years.

This concentration of resources—of wealth, land, education, con-trol of the press, and political position—has helped to forge an upper class that has been characterized as follows:

> As a young man, this upper-class Colombian was probably educated in a Colombian prep school or university, and later went to the United States or Europe for further study. . . . Quite often he is highly literate, having gone through a youthful period writing doggerel, although now he prefers the stock reports. . . . His interest in politics may take him to Congress or to a cabinet post, or to service on the directorate of his party, even while he heads his own company or runs his coffee business or hovers over his investments.
>
> This upper-class Colombian has made his mistakes, but he has also done a first-class job of building the national economy and the national culture into a respectable edifice worthy of admiration. In brief, he is quite a fellow. His one "blind spot" is that he has always felt that the economy was for *him*; that culture (not necessarily esthetics) was for his sole consumption.[40]

Mobility upward and into this Colombian upper class has not been impossible. Individual examples, like that of President Betancur, whose father was a mule driver and small-town tavern owner, make the point. Similarly, former president López Michelsen, like his father Alfonso López Pumarejo a scion of Colombia's elite, is the great-grandson of a tailor. The Colombian elite is hardly rigid; it is open to individual upward (and downward) mobility even while basic social alignments and the distances among classes remain about the same. Such co-optation of the ambitious and the talented is undoubtedly one of the secrets of the longevity of Colombia's upper class and of its continued hold on economic, social, and political power: the occasional admission of new elements to elite status permits adaptation to changing circumstances. Thus, the number of businessmen and engineers in the ranks of the elite has increased over the years as the economy has become more industrial; the weight of landowners in the upper class has correspondingly declined.[41]

It is no longer possible to say, as it may have been in the 1950s, that "the most difficult task in studying the Colombian middle class is to find it,"[42] although its extent, its boundaries, and even its nature may be hard to delineate precisely. Numbering roughly 20 percent of the population, the middle class includes professionals such as lawyers, doctors, and architects without other bases of wealth; teachers; white-collar employees in both the public and the private sectors; and small businessmen. Most are urban, although Colombia has long had a rural middle class in such departments as Antioquia and Caldas. Some members of Colombia's middle sectors are downwardly mobile members of formerly upper-class families who have fallen on hard times; their values and aspirations tend to be imitative of the upper class. An increasing number are upwardly mobile, however, spurred on by Colombia's growing economy and by the rapid expansion in educational enrollments. The latter phenomenon has been extraordinary in recent years. Between 1960 and 1981 the numbers enrolled in secondary school as a percentage of the relevant age group increased from 12 to 48 percent. The comparable enrollment increase at the university level was from 2 to 13 percent.[43] Many of those enrolled do not go on to graduate; nonetheless, with access to education much greater than only a generation ago, the implications for the future evolution of Colombia society would appear to be far-reaching.

Not coincidentally, the latter trend has witnessed an increasing percentage of educated women and of women professionals. In fact, as of 1981, a higher percentage of women than of men were enrolled in secondary schools. Women were also increasingly active in the urban work force (38 percent in 1978, compared with 72 percent of men), with much of the change coming among the middle class.[44]

The Colombian (and other Latin American) middle class has a smaller component of entrepreneurs (including salesmen and the like) and self-employed professionals, and a higher proportion of employees, than at a comparable stage of middle-class development in North America or western Europe. In particular, the Colombian middle class is highly dependent on the state, both for employment and for public policies favoring its interests and claims. Those who have elsewhere provided the middle class with much of its economic power and often political leadership—the "upper bourgeoisie"—have tended to fuse with the landed upper class. The middle class, in turn, has tended to lack the kind of independent political definition it has often had elsewhere. The pressures of inflation and constrained government budgets in recent years have thus placed unusual pressures on this sector and have led to increasing alienation (for instance, voter abstention) and outright direct action (in the form of strikes and the like) by the unionized among them (such as bank employees).

Virtually anyone who does manual labor in Colombia, whether rural or urban, is deemed lower class. The principal exceptions are those who, like some farmers, work the land but are able to hire others to assist them. Among Colombia's lower classes—altogether some three-quarters of the population—the campesinos (broadly, peasants) are still a substantial, though declining, percentage. By 1980 the agricultural portion of the work force had dropped sharply to 26 percent from just over half (51 percent) 20 years earlier.[45]

Included under the broad rubric "campesino" are squatters, tenants, sharecroppers, day laborers, and *minifundistas* (those who own tiny plots of land that barely provide subsistence). Their material and social circumstances therefore differ, but they share conditions of poverty and low levels of education and health compared with the rest of the country. Typically the campesino has been economically at the mercy of the moneylender, the middleman, and the hacendado (hacienda owner).

Yet significant changes have been under way in rural Colombia in recent decades, some of them favorable, and some not so favorable, to the conditions of life of the campesino. Real wages in the rural sector may have risen by as much as a third between the mid-1920s and the mid-1960s, while levels of education and health showed some modest improvement. Yet the decade 1965–75 brought a sharp

downturn (17 percent) in real agricultural wages, leading to the conclusion that "the present situation remains very bad in many respects,
and the indication of wage stagnation, and even decline over the last
10 years is worrisome."[46] Meanwhile, there are indications that the
rapid commercialization of agriculture since the 1960s has accelerated the rate of land concentration and augmented the ranks of the
landless even as it has enhanced the ranks of Colombia's rural middle
class.[47]

However, this is only the latest of the economic and social
changes to leave its mark on rural Colombia. Historically, perhaps the
most important such change was the shift to coffee production for
export, and the attendant involvement in the market economy of
thousands of peasant smallholders beginning in the latter part of the
19th century. In more recent decades, the penetration of roads, the
expansion of cities into surrounding farmlands, the impact of *la violencia*, and the attractions of urban life have all served to loosen traditional attitudes and attachments in the countryside, as well as to
contribute to massive cityward migration.

By 1980 the Colombian labor force was predominantly urban,
with 21 percent employed in industry and 53 percent in services,
compared with 19 and 30 percent, respectively, only two decades before.[48] In a sense, blue-collar industrial workers (*obreros*) form a
privileged stratum among the loosely delineated urban lower class.
They tend to have regular employment; their wages are relatively
high, sometimes placing them above individual members of the lower
middle class (white-collar workers or *empleados*) in earnings; and
they generally come under the provisions of the labor code regarding
sickness and vacation benefits, severance pay, and the like. Service
workers are, as a group, less steadily employed, work at generally
lower wages, and are less consistently protected by the labor code.

The burgeoning service sector, in particular, as well as the many
unemployed and underemployed, are often results of the massive
migration to the cities in recent decades. Removal to the city may
not have done much to change the relative social position of most
migrants; their mobility has usually been more geographical and
horizontal than vertical. Job opportunities are scarce, and housing is
frequently a shack on a hillside in a district that lacks running water
and other municipal facilities. All of Colombia's larger cities have
such shantytowns, or erstwhile shantytowns. Although there is considerable variation in income levels and occupations both within and

among such communities, they house the majority of Colombia's urban poor.[49]

There is a strong correlation between race and social class in Colombia, although race and ethnicity play almost no identifiable independent political role. Rather, the historic alignment of low status with the black slave, and the Indian servant and agricultural laborer, has persisted in the form of a general identification of darker skin with lower social status. There are no rigid color lines, however, and it is life-style rather than ethnic origin per se that perpetuates such gradation. Very rough estimates describe Colombia's population as 20 percent white (though not many of these would be genetically "pure" white), 50 to 60 percent mestizo (white-Indian mix), 15 to 25 percent mulatto (black-white mix), 4 percent black, and 1 percent or so Indian.[50] There are also white-black-Indian racial mixtures. Here again, however, regional distinctions are apparent. The Atlantic and Pacific coastal regions, and some interior river valleys, are predominantly mulatto and black;[51] mestizos predominate in the mountainous and interior sections of the country.

Since colonial days, immigration into Colombia has been quite small, despite sporadic attempts to encourage it. Individual immigrants and their descendants, mainly European in origin, although also Lebanese, Jewish, and North American, have occasionally had an impact on business or politics (for instance, the Eder family in the Cauca Valley), but a massive flow of immigrants like those to Argentina, Uruguay, Brazil, or, in more recent years, Venezuela, has not occurred.

Modern Colombia has therefore not had the problem of assimilating European enclaves faced by Argentina or, at times, Brazil. Nor has it had an Indian subculture of any appreciable size, as in Mexico, Guatemala, or some of its Andean neighbors. Nor have blacks retained the degree of cultural identity characteristic of some other Latin American countries. Rather, the principal effect of ethnic and racial differences in Colombia has been to accentuate distinctions among social strata that are largely based on other grounds.

The foregoing depiction of the Colombia social order shows that it has much in common with that of many other Latin American countries, including wide gaps in wealth, education, and life-style among the social classes. As elsewhere, the pace of social change has been extraordinarily rapid since the 1960s. Whether it is the decline in the percentage of the work force employed in agriculture and the attendant rise in the service sector, the increase in the numbers attending school or university, or the expansion of the cities, including those living in shantytowns, the percentage change between 1960 and the early 1980s—often paralleled by Brazil, Mexico, and Venezuela—is notable. Given such facts, the degree of social unrest and tension in the country, as in other parts of Latin America, is perhaps not remarkable. It is reflected in the increasing frequency of strikes and land invasions, and of guerrilla warfare and occasional urban terrorism; the prevalence of common crime; and a general climate of lawlessness. At the same time, it raises even more strikingly the question of how, in the face of such manifestations of apparent social malaise, Colombia has been able to maintain its relative political stability.

In conclusion, whatever the similarities with the rest of Latin America, several variations from the usual Latin American patterns are worth reiterating. Colombia ranks among those Latin American countries with the most highly skewed patterns of income distribution and land concentration. Despite this fact, and in seeming contradiction, there has existed, at least since the southward Antioqueño colonization and the widespread growth of coffee cultivation in the 19th century, a significant rural middle class in certain parts of the country. There has been little foreign immigration since independence, nor anything but isolated remaining traces of separate Indian or African cultural enclaves. Taken together, such characteristics have helped to distinguish Colombian society from most others of the hemisphere.

POLITICAL CULTURE

The hazards are great in attempting to generalize about any people's political attitudes, beliefs, and styles of behavior—its political culture—and nowhere greater than in a nation undergoing rapid socioeconomic change and marked by such diverse regions and social strata as is Colombia. Nonetheless, some attempt to do so seems indicated, although important exceptions to the overall characterizations will be noted.

In key respects, Colombian political culture resembles the "typical" Latin American pattern. Central among the attributes that Colombians share with their fellow Latin Americans are the ties between patrons and clients. This is essentially an exchange relationship, applicable to a wide range of political and nonpolitical situations, between two individuals of unequal status. Thus, a landlord or a political boss (*gamonal*) may offer protection, a gratuity, or a job in exchange for the vote (or other political service) of a peasant or an employee. The political boss (*patrón*) in this sense, and by these means, seeks to build a network of two-person relationships, centered on himself, in which payment on his part consists of particular favors for different individuals rather than benefits for categories of persons (such as peasants); such networks can be pyramided from the local to the national level. "Small *patrones* usually have *patrones* of their own—'bigger' and more powerful men who serve them as protectors and as contacts in communicating with the higher political, social or economic powers."[52]

Such relationships are necessarily quite personal in nature; they also entail a distinct attribution of superiority and subordination (that is, it is clearly understood who is to defer to whom in the relationship, although that relationship is in principle reciprocal and mandates the requisite courtesies and attentions on both sides).[53] The patron-client relationship may be further strengthened through the system of *compadrazgo*, a kind of ritualized kinship relationship in which there are mutual obligations, again often of an unequal nature. Thus a campesino's *compadre*—a landowner, say, or a local merchant—may advance him credit to pay for seeds or a fiesta, but the campesino will be obligated to sell his crops to or buy his goods from his *compadre* (at, of course, the *compadre*'s prices).

Implicit in the patron-client relationship are other key aspects of Colombian (and Latin American) political culture. An emphasis on hierarchy, deference, and paternalism is one. Colombians tend to be born into a rank or status that makes them rather clearly superior or subordinate to those born to other social positions, positions that it is difficult, although not impossible, to alter during one's lifetime. The social, political, and religious realms have historically been built on such principles. Authority in such a system is expected (by all) to "trickle down," not "bubble up" from below; authority also tends to be externalized in such a culture, not internalized as in Protestant cultures.[54] Nor are such perspectives confined to the upper class. Not only does the campesino expect to defer to his "betters," but a peasant who achieves a measure of education or wealth expects deference from those of lesser attainments. Similar tendencies to *caciquismo* appear in urban shantytowns.[55]

Characteristically, such a culture is a "subject" one, in which government is seen in terms of its policy outputs (and perhaps the possibility of averting the consequences of government policy for oneself), rather than in terms of citizen participation and input in the formulation of policy. Ideally, the reciprocal of such paternalistic authority is an attitude of noblesse oblige, by which those in positions of power or authority show a benign concern for those whose deference they are accorded. Such traits are not merely a part of the traditional landlord-peasant relationship on the hacienda, although that has been perhaps their preeminent home. They also permeate Colombia's political parties and, often, such ostensibly modern entities as factories, labor unions, and government bureaucracies. While the emphasis on hierarchy and paternalism in Colombian political culture may gradually be giving way to more "open" or egalitarian perspectives, its hold is still very strong. Among the consequences of such a syndrome is a tendency to defer to the *patrón*—whether landlord, boss, priest, or *gamonal*—in matters political.

The attainment or assertion of status seems especially important for Colombians, perhaps even more so than for many other Latin Americans. Arguably, status considerations constitute the overriding incentives for Colombians to seek political office, and explain a good deal about the Colombian political system, including the parties' seeming lack of interest in programs or questions of public policy, and their persistent factionalism.[56]

Another feature of Colombian political culture, again implicit in the patron-client relationship, is the importance of face-to-face relationships (with extended family, *compadres*, or those from one's own *patria chica* or "little fatherland," that is, one's neighborhood or home town) and the attendant lack of trust toward those "anonymous" others not so connected or so intimately known. Traditionally, it is to this circle of intimates, rather than to an abstraction such as the public service, that a Colombian (Latin American) owes his first loyalties even when holding government office. Thus, the use of *palancas* (pull)—that is, the use of relatives, patrons, or *compadres* to intercede on one's behalf with government authorities—is both widespread and legitimate. Who one is, then, is more important than what one does. The syndrome is comparable, although perhaps not so extreme, with that depicted by Edward Banfield in regard to a small town in southern Italy, a syndrome that he called "amoral familism": "Maximize the material, short-run advantage of the nuclear family [the extended family in the Colombian case]; assume that all others will do the same." The corollary of such a posture is the assumption that "no one will further the interest of the group or community except as it is to his private advantage to do so."[57] Personal and particularistic relationships, in short, tend to be valued and trusted well above institutions and interpersonal loyalties.

Personalismo is yet another prominent attribute of the political culture of Colombians. It is a version of individualism that places great emphasis on the inherent uniqueness of the person and an exaggerated sense of personal honor and dignity, in contrast with the North American version of individualism that emphasizes the external or social equality of persons and the individual's equal chance with every other to achieve success. For Latin Americans there is an "exaltation of the I, which does not perceive itself as a unit in the group, but as the whole group itself. Pride and *dignidad* [dignity] are exaggerated, and the group serves as a pedestal for the self."[58] Thus it is not by chance that political factions in Colombia almost invariably carry the name of their leaders (Lleristas, Lopistas, Pastranistas), or that cabinet ministers or mayors like to launch their "own" projects rather than pursue policies or programs inaugurated by a predecessor, often to the detriment of policy continuity and effectiveness. Attendant difficulties in subordinating personal to group interests, and in reaching compromises that might offend personal honor or dignity, may help to account, respectively, for the relative weakness of voluntary associations in Colombia and for the historic difficulties in institutionalizing the concept of legitimate political opposition.

A certain sense of fatalism, especially but not exclusively among campesinos, and an accompanying "ethic of other worldliness"[59] form a further notable facet of Colombian political culture. One's success in life or the success of a crop, for example, is felt to rest largely in the hands of fate or of God, rather than with one's own actions. Such a sense of resignation before powers one cannot control has a tendency to work against what a North American might see as efforts to seek constructive solutions to problems. It also militates against formation of a consciousness of class, and against a willingness to support organizations that promote change. The traditional passivity of rural Colombians has been eroded somewhat in recent years, however, by the years of *la violencia*, by the increasing commercialization of agriculture, and by massive rural-urban migration, with not yet wholly foreseeable consequences.

Colombia's Hispanic legal tradition has also had an important bearing on politics. According to that tradition, "laws are largely viewed as moral ideals not to be enforced if their enforcement is, for some reason, too harsh, impractical, or unjust. . . . Not infrequently, the constitution includes articles or clauses whose implementation is not intended for many years, their impracticality rendering them inapplicable."[60] It is a legal tradition, in other words, with a strong "idealistic" bent in which casuistry or the well-turned legal phrase is likely to take precedence over the practicalities of enforcement. It manifests itself today in an often rather wide gap between the law on paper and its possible or effective implementation, whether the arena is education, health care, or agrarian reform.

In the end, such values as paternalism, particularism, personalism, fatalism, and legalism are characteristic not just of Colombia, although they may well have their particular variants there, nor even of Latin America, but of much of the Third World. There are two significant variants in Colombia's political culture compared with other Latin American nations that nonetheless merit attention. One is the entrepreneurial, yet conservative, spirit of the region (department) of Antioquia. The other is the nature of Colombian nationalism.

Given the geographic, economic, and racial diversity of Colombia's regions, one might well expect a wide range of variation in its culture and behavior, including its political culture. Among *costeños* (people from the Caribbean coast) sexual norms tend to be more permissive, free unions are prevalent, and religious adherence and institutions are weak; among *paisas* (people from the department of Antioquia and neighboring Caldas), on the other hand, the institutions of Catholic marriage, and allegiance to the Church generally, are taken more seriously. In Antioquia, for example, both the number of priests per inhabitant, and the proportion of religious vocations among its people, are the highest in the country.[61]

It is the attitudes and behavior of Antioqueños with respect to economic entrepreneurship, in combination with their deep Catholicism, that sets them apart from other Colombians. Although the myth has at times tended to outrun the reality, Antioquian distinctiveness has played a noteworthy role in Colombia's economic and political development, and therefore calls for some brief attention.

Evidence from literature, folklore, and psychological testing indicates that Antioqueños both are, and are considered by their fellow Colombians to be, especially hardworking, and replete with the entrepreneurial energies and talent relatively scarce among others of their countrymen. Colombia's early industrial development (notably in textiles) took particular hold in Antioquia, and it was Colombians born in that region who frequently assumed the lead in banking, trade, and industry in other parts of the country. "In proportion to population, more than three times as many Antioqueños became entrepreneurs as Old Colombians of non-Antioqueño stock."[62] In this sense Antioquia has been the engine of Colombian economic development, much as have the states of São Paulo in Brazil and Nuevo León in Mexico. However, in Brazil immigrants have been disproportionately represented among the entrepreneurs, and in Mexico it took a social revolution to fully unleash industrial development. In Colombia neither was the case.

The notion that Antioquia's exceptional status is explained by the fact that its citizens are largely of Basque origin or are converted Jews has been largely discredited. The theory that Antioqueño behavior is accounted for by "need-aggression," deriving from felt status deprivation of those provincial Colombians relative to their claimed social superiors in the capital and the Colombian east, may have some substance but fails to confront the fact that historically Antioqueños seem to have been more respected than scorned, and by difficulty in explaining why it was Antioquia among all the provinces that was the site of economic innovation.

Rather, "in Medellín both the composition and values of the local elite were logical reflections of key developments in Antioquia's colonial economic history."[63] The mining of gold as a source of both capital and status, and the relative unavailability of servile labor, which forced Antioqueños to mine and farm their own properties, were among the factors that contributed to an early entrepreneurial disposition on the part of the Antioqueño elite.[64] Above all, however, it was the late-19th-century expansion of coffee cultivation, especially in Antioquia though elsewhere as well, that provided the basis for Colombia's industrial development. "The *Antioqueño's* experience with opening land and employing his own labor in coffee cultivation, as well as the contacts which many established with urban coffee buyers, was an important factor in establishing a set of social and psychological attitudes favorable to development."[65] At least as important as entrepreneurial attitudes was the fact that the rapid growth of coffee exports, and its rather widespread cultivation of coffee on small plots, raised income levels and created a demand for new products such as textiles. Capital and marketing skills were also by-products of the coffee trade. Neither status resentment nor ethnic deviance but, rather, the opportunities and incentives afforded by their economic environment, seem to explain the Antioqueños' leadership role in Colombian economic development.

Finally, the fact that the principal site of Colombian industrialization has been in the most Catholic and conservative (as well as Conservative) departments may help to explain the relative lack of conflict over development strategies. Traditional values have in this sense blended with those of modernization, and elites whose wealth has been founded on agriculture (coffee) have been in the forefront of the industrializing process.[66]

Colombia's divergence from the Latin American universe of political cultures may be even more noteworthy for the relative weakness of its nationalism. To be sure, the nationalist sentiments of Colombians have been temporarily aroused by U.S. actions in Panama in the early years of the 20th century, by the behavior of the Tropical Oil Company or the United Fruit Company during the 1920s, by a brief conflict with Peru during the early 1930s, or by occasional border tensions with Venezuela in more recent times. And cries of "*entreguismo*" (turning over things to foreigners) and "*vendepatrias*" (sellers of the fatherland) were heard during the 1970s debates over coal contracts.[67] Yet for the most part, these outbursts of nationalistic sentiment or resentment have been short-lived or rather localized. With the exception of some students and intellectuals, and small left-wing political groups, nationalist concerns have seldom been major issues in Colombian politics. Even for populists such as Gaitán and Rojas, nationalism played a distinctly secondary role. In contrast, nationalism has been a significant political force at one stage or another in most Latin American countries, often eventuating in the extensive nationalization of foreign enterprises. Overall, although Colombia did "colombianize" foreign banks in 1975 by requiring 51 percent Colombian ownership, its policies have been among the most favorable in the hemisphere toward multinational corporations.

The reasons for such attitudes, which have had profound effects on Colombia's economic and political development, probably rest largely on the fact that most of Colombia's land and economic production have throughout the country's history been in the hands of Colombians. The cases of copper in Chile, petroleum in Venezuela, tin in Bolivia, sugar in Cuba, and the multiple foreign holdings in pre-revolutionary Mexico or pre-Perón Argentina have never been replicated in Colombia. The marked increase in recent years in foreign (especially U.S.) investment in manufacturing, especially in sectors most strategic for the country's economic growth, could stir economic nationalism, but manufacturing would seem less vulnerable in this regard than foreign control of natural resources or of the principal export crop.

Underlying the general weakness of nationalistic attitudes in Colombia may also be the fact that the elites controlling the country's two traditional parties identify the United States as the last line of defense of their position and their values. Moreover, party leaders have had little incentive to mobilize their mass followings along lines other than the traditional ones of jobs and other perquisites for the party faithful, and of hatred for those who would transfer them into the hands of Colombians of the rival partisan persuasion.

In sum, while in many ways similar to those of other Latin American countries, Colombia's political culture has been sufficiently divergent—notably in the nature of the Antioqueños and the weakness of nationalist attitudes—to help at least partially to account for the unique dimensions of its economic and political systems.

Yet it may be well not to make too much of political culture as an explanatory variable. For political culture in Colombia, as in other countries, is probably as much the product of economic, social, and political structures inherited from the past as it is their cause.[68] Likewise, values can and do change; they are not the products of genetic endowment. Last, it may be well to remember, as North Americans look at a culture whose values may in some respects appear unattractive, or irrelevant in the modern world, that this is a culture in which, more perhaps than in their own, "honor is put before gain, the primacy of being is affirmed over the tyranny of doing, [and] human existence is protected from the enslavement of the machine. . . ."[69]

NOTES

1. For an excellent, succinct description of the several Colombian regions, with accompanying data, see Harvey F. Kline, *Colombia: Portrait of Unity and Diversity* (Boulder, Colo.: Westview Press, 1983), pp. 1–12.

2. For population data, see ibid., p. 5; for industrial data, see *Colombia Today* 19, no. 2 (1984). Industrial data for Atlántico include adjacent areas of the Atlantic coast, including Cartagena.

3. John W. Sloan, "Regionalism, Political Parties and Public Policy in Colombia," *Inter-American Economic Affairs* 33, no. 3 (Winter 1979): 39–45. Virtually every Colombian department has its own university.

4. John M. Hunter, *Emerging Colombia* (Washington, D.C.: Public Affairs Press, 1962), p. 10.

5. Such trends were noticeable at least as early as the 1950s; see Robert H. Dix, *Colombia: The Political Dimensions of Change* (New Haven: Yale University Press, 1967), pp. 22–23.

6. World Bank, *World Development Report 1984* (New York: Oxford University Press, 1984), p. 254; and Dix, *Colombia*, p. 38.

7. World Bank, *World Development Report 1984*, p. 261.

8. Ibid.

9. The absolute number of Colombians living in rural areas continues to increase, however, at a rate of some 14,000 families per year (net of rural-urban migration); Robin Ruth Marsh, *Development Strategies in Rural Colombia: The Case of Caquetá* (Los Angeles: University of California, Los Angeles, Latin American Center, 1983), p. 22.

10. For widely varying estimates, see Gabriel Murillo Castaño, *Migrant Workers in the Americas*, trans. Sandra del Castillo (La Jolla, Calif.: University of California, San Diego, Center for U.S.-Mexican Studies, 1984), pp. 41–42.

11. See Stephen O. Bender, "Low Income Housing Development and Income Distribution: The Impact of Growth and Change," in R. Albert Berry and Ronald Soligo, eds., *Economic Policy and Income Distribution in Colombia* (Boulder, Colo.: Westview Press, 1980), pp. 247–63.

12. As of 1973, Colombia ranked 12th out of 18 Latin American countries, and 103rd of 116 worldwide, in this respect; Charles L. Taylor and David Jodice, *World Handbook of Political and Social Indicators*, 3rd ed. (New Haven: Yale University Press, 1981), vol. 1, pp. 5–7.

13. Jonathan Hartlyn, "The Impact of Patterns of Industrialization and of Popular Sector Incorporation on Political Regime Type: A Case Study of Colombia," *Studies in Comparative International Development* 19, no. 1 (Spring 1984): 48. In the late 1970s there was a temporary surge in coffee's share of export income (to roughly two-thirds of the total) due to a boom in coffee prices resulting mainly from weather damage to the Brazilian crop.

14. See Kline, *Colombia*, pp. 114–15, for a listing of these and other consequences, citing Richard B. Craig, "Domestic Implications of Illicit Drug Cultivation, Processing, and Trafficking in Colombia" (MS, 1981).

15. See Kline, *Colombia*, pp. 111–14, for a succinct overview of the history and prospects of the development of Colombia's energy resources. For a report on the most recent oil discoveries in the eastern plains, see *Colombia Today* 19, no. 8 (1984).

16. As of 1933, however, foreign firms carried out almost half of the exporting of coffee, although that proportion declined notably thereafter; Marco Palacios, *Coffee in Colombia, 1850–1970* (Cambridge: Cambridge University Press, 1980), p. 261.

17. World Bank, *World Development Report 1984*, p. 223.

18. Hartlyn, "The Impact of Patterns of Industrialization," p. 43.

19. Raúl A. Fernández, "Imperialist Capitalism in the Third World; Theory and Evidence from Colombia," *Latin American Perspectives* 6, no. 1 (Winter 1979): 46–50.

20. Fabio Hernán Gómez, *Concentración del Poder Económico en Colombia* (Bogotá: Centro de Investigación y Acción Social, 1974), pp. 56–57, 70. Still another source estimated foreign control of the economy to represent some 18 percent of the GDP, slightly below the Latin American average; see Julio Silva Colmenares, *Los Verdaderos Dueños del País* (Bogotá: Fondo Editorial Suramérica, 1977), p. 300.

21. For an exhaustive description of these groups, see Silva Colmenares, *Los Verdaderos Dueños*.

22. World Bank, *World Development Report 1984*, p. 221.

23. See *Colombia Today* 19, nos. 3 and 11 (1984), and 21, no. 1 (1986), for the above data on the GDP.

24. World Bank, *World Development Report 1984*, pp. 218–19; and *Colombia Today* 19, no. 11 (1984); see also Hartlyn, "The Impact of Patterns of Industrialization," p. 50.

25. See R. Albert Berry, "The Effects of Inflation on Income Distribution in Colombia: Some Hypotheses and a Framework for Analysis," in Berry and Soligo, *Economic Policy*, chap. 4; and Miguel Urrutia, *Gremios, Política Económica y Democracia* (Bogotá: Fondo Cultural Cafetero, 1983), p. 38.

26. World Bank, *World Development Report 1984*, pp. 248–49.

27. Ibid., pp. 218–19. There were no data on Cuba.

28. Taylor and Jodice, *World Handbook*, pp. 134–36. Albert Berry and Miguel Urrutia, *Income Distribution in Colombia* (New Haven: Yale University Press, 1976), p. 51, cites several studies for the 1961–70 period showing 42 and 50 percent of the income going to the top 10 percent of the population.

29. R. Albert Berry and Ronald Soligo, "The Distribution of Income in Colombia: An Overview," in their *Economic Policy*, esp. pp. 14–16; for a rather different view of the 1970s, see Urrutia, *Gremios*, pp. 207–08.

30. According to Jaime Michelsen, former head of one of these conglomerates, as cited in Alfredo Vásquez Carrizosa, *El Poder Presidencial en Colombia* (Bogotá: Sociedad Ediciones Internacionales, 1979), p. 390.

31. Gómez, *Concentracion del Poder*, esp. p. 30; see also Silva Colmenares, *Los Verdaderos Dueños*.

32. A. Eugene Havens, William L. Flinn, and Susana Lastarria Cornhill, "Agrarian Reform and the National Front: A Class Analysis," in R. Albert Berry

et al., eds., *Politics of Compromise* (New Brunswick, N.J.: Transaction Books, 1980), p. 358.

33. *Encyclopedia of the Third World* (New York: Facts on File, 1978), vol. 1, p. 326.

34. See Palacios, *Coffee in Colombia*, chap. 2.

35. World Bank, *World Development Report 1984*, p. 267.

36. Gómez, *Concentración del Poder*, pp. 64–65. As of 1960, secondary enrollment was 12 percent of the relevant age group. Although by 1981 that percentage had quadrupled, it was still well below the levels of most "developed" countries; World Bank, *World Development Report 1984*, p. 267.

37. For a detailed description of these connections, see *Latin American Weekly Report*, July 15, 1977, p. 211, and July 29, 1977, p. 227.

38. Richard Hartwig, "Cabinet Instability and the Colombian Political System" (MS, Vanderbilt University, 1971), pp. 6–7.

39. Saturnino Sepúlveda Niño, *Elites Colombianas en Crisis* (Bogotá: 1970); see also Harvey Kline, "Selección de Candidatos," in Gary Hoskin et al., *Estudio del Comportamiento Legislativo en Colombia*, vol. 2 (Bogotá: Universidad de los Andes/Cámara de Comercio, 1975), chap. 5, concerning the sociologically unrepresentative nature of the Colombian Congress.

40. Vernon Lee Fluharty, *Dance of the Millions* (Pittsburgh: University of Pittsburgh Press, 1957), pp. 185–86.

41. Frank Safford, *The Ideal of the Practical: Colombia's Struggle to Form a Technical Elite* (Austin: University of Texas Press, 1976), pp. 237–39.

42. Fluharty, *Dance of the Millions*, p. 187.

43. World Bank, *World Development Report 1984*, p. 267.

44. Ibid., p. 199; see also Kline, *Colombia*, p. 18.

45. World Bank, *World Development Report 1984*, p. 259.

46. R. Albert Berry, "Rural Poverty in Twentieth-Century Colombia," *Journal of Interamerican Studies and World Affairs* 20, no. 4 (November 1978): 373; for data on real income, see ibid., p. 363.

47. Bruce M. Bagley, "The State and the Peasantry in Contemporary Colombia" (paper prepared for the meeting of the Latin American Studies Association, Washington, D.C., March 1982), p. 63.

48. World Bank, *World Development Report 1984*, p. 259.

49. For a good description of the entire process, see Bender, "Low Income Housing." For the wide internal variation within such communities, see Nora de Camacho, "Obreros, Marginados y Participación Electoral," in Rodrigo Parra Sandoval, ed., *Dependencia Externa y Desarrollo Político en Colombia* (Bogotá: Imprenta Nacional, 1970), pp. 209–22. Monthly income ranged from 100 to 1,800 pesos monthly in the barrio (*tugurio*) studied by Camacho.

50. Howard I. Blutstein et al., *Area Handbook for Colombia* (Washington, D.C.: U.S. Government Printing Office, 1977), p. 91. Government statistics indicate that there are fewer than 500,000 Indians (defined both racially and culturally [that is, dressing and otherwise living according to Indian custom]), or 1.5 percent of the population. Most live in the Amazon jungle, in the Guajira pensinsula of northeastern Colombia, or near the Ecuadorian border; see Kline, *Colombia*, p. 13.

51. For a thoroughgoing analysis of racial patterns in one section of Colombia (the city of Cartagena on the Atlantic coast), see Mauricio Solaún and Sidney Kronus, *Discrimination Without Violence* (New York: John Wiley and Sons, 1973).

52. John P. Gillin, "Some Signposts for Policy," in Council on Foreign Relations, *Social Change in Latin America Today* (New York: Vintage Books, 1960), p. 37.

53. For a detailed elaboration of the nature of patron-client relationships in the Colombian context, see Steffen W. Schmidt, "Patrons, Brokers, and Clients: Party Linkages in the Colombian System," in Kay Lawson, ed., *Political Parties and Linkages* (New Haven: Yale University Press, 1980), chap. 12.

54. For an elaboration of this contrast between Catholic and Protestant cultures, see Alfonso López Michelson, *Cuestiones Colombianas (Ensayos)* (México, D.F.: Impresiones Modernas, 1955).

55. A. Eugene Havens and William L. Flinn, eds., *Internal Colonialism and Structural Change in Colombia* (New York: Praeger, 1970), pp. 101-04.

56. James Payne makes a persuasive argument to this effect in *Patterns of Conflict in Colombia* (New Haven: Yale University Press, 1968), although he clearly overstates his case.

57. Edward Banfield, *The Moral Basis of a Backward Society* (New York: The Free Press, 1958), pp. 83-84. A survey in one part of Colombia indicated that 80 percent of Colombians felt it necessary to "beware of others"; Mauricio Solaún, "Colombian Politics: Historical Characteristics and Problems," in Berry et al., *Politics of Compromise*, n. 61.

58. Gillin, "Some Signposts," p. 30.

59. The term is used by Orlando Fals Borda in "Violence and the Break-up of Tradition in Colombia," in Claudio Veliz, ed., *Obstacles to Change in Latin America* (London: Oxford University Press, 1965), pp. 193-94.

60. Solaún, "Colombian Politics," pp. 19-20.

61. For a categorization of Colombian family patterns, see *Anuario de la Iglesia Católica en Colombia, 1961* (Bogotá: Centro de Investigaciones Sociales, 1961), pp. 956-58. For the pattern of priestly vocations, see Gustavo Pérez Ramírez, *El Problema Sacerdotal en Colombia* (Bogotá: Centro de Investigaciones Sociales, 1962), p. 16, chap. 4. Daniel H. Levine found that 47 percent of Colombia's bishops were born either in Antioquia or in its southern "extension," Caldas; see his "Church Elites in Venezuela and Colombia: Context, Background, and Beliefs," *Latin American Research Review* 14, no. 1 (1979): 68.

62. Everett E. Hagen, *On the Theory of Social Change* (Homewood, Ill.: Dorsey Press, 1962), p. 365. Another study showed some 41 percent of directors of economic enterprises to have been born either in Antioquia or in departments populated mainly by Antioqueños during the 19th century; see Gómez, *Concentración del Poder*, p. 59.

63. Ann Twinam, *Miners, Merchants and Farmers in Colonial Colombia* (Austin: University of Texas Press, 1982), p. 147. For the argument concerning "need-aggression" as the psychological basis for entrepreneurship, both in Colombia and in other countries, see Hagen, *On the Theory of Social Change.*

64. For such economic and structural arguments concerning the basis of Antioqueño entrepreneurship, see Twinam, *Miners, Merchants and Farmers*; Stafford, *The Ideal of the Practical*, pp. 31, 40, chap. 9; Luis H. Fajardo, *Social Structure and Personality: The Protestant Ethic of the Antioqueños* (Cali, Colombia: Ediciones Departamento del Valle, n.d.); and Miguel Urrutia, *The Development of the Colombian Labor Movement* (New Haven: Yale University Press, 1969), pp. 48–51.

65. William P. McGreevey, *An Economic History of Colombia, 1845–1930* (Cambridge: Cambridge University Press, 1971), p. 233.

66. Antioquia has generally led other regions of Colombia in literacy and school attendance; see ibid., pp. 233–34. The elites of Medellín, Antioquia's capital, are said elsewhere to have evolved a collaborative civic culture; see Alejandro Portes and John Walton, *Urban Latin America* (Austin: University of Texas Press, 1976), pp. 131–32.

67. Harvey Kline, "The Colombian Debates about Coal, Exxon, and Themselves," *Inter-American Economic Affairs* 36, no. 4 (Spring 1983): 5.

68. For a good discussion of this point in the Colombian context, see the introduction to Frank Safford, *The Ideal of the Practical*.

69. 181st General Assembly of the United Presbyterian Church, U.S.A., "Hispanic Americans and the Crisis in the Nation," Pamphlet (San Antonio, 1969), p. 5.

5

POLITICAL PARTIES AND ELECTIONS

Colombia's two major parties, the Liberal and the Conservative, are among the oldest in the world. Many of the other Latin American countries divided politically along similar lines during the 19th century, but in most cases only vestiges at best remain of that original partisan configuration. In Colombia much of political life since about 1848, whether electoral or violent, has been conducted in the name of the country's two "historic collectivities." Despite persistent factionalism, periodic "union" governments, the occasional appearance of third parties, and long periods of one-party hegemony, the two parties have survived and put down exceedingly deep roots. And, in contrast with the great majority of Latin American countries, elections, while not always strictly competitive, have played a meaningful role throughout most of the history of the republic. Although strongly elitist in the manner of their operation, Colombia's traditional parties have historically evoked the profound psychic attachment of most Colombians—even those who have known and cared little about doctrines and programs. By the same token, parties formed in opposition to the country's elitist democracy—and particularly those that have sought to restructure the electorate along class lines—have fared very poorly. Thus Colombia is exceptional among the major countries of Latin America in not having even one significant party of a democratic socialist, Marxist, Christian Democratic, or, more vaguely, "populist" stripe.

THE TRADITIONAL PARTIES

Neither of Colombia's traditional parties exhibits very well the distinction between cadre and mass parties, for they have attributes of both.[1] On the one hand, they are essentially parties of notables tied together by clientelistic relationships, with weakly articulated organizations and minimal programmatic content. Yet both Liberals and Conservatives have been capable of fairly high levels of mass mobilization in a manner hardly typical of such parties, even though those loyalties are not in the first instance based on differences of class or ideology.

As in Colombian society at large, the parties tend to concentrate power and authority in a small group of leaders who rank high on such measures of social class as income, education, and occupation. No doubt there is something of this in most parties in many political systems. Yet the tendency seems particularly acute in Colombia, and the discrepancy in social background between the top leadership of the parties and the lower-level leaders unusually great. The social gulf between the top party leadership and the bulk of the population is, of course, even greater. For instance, in a society where only a few have a university education, almost every member of the parties' leadership is university educated.[2]

The parties' leadership tends to be self-perpetuating, with the same names recurring in party directorates over long periods of time. Men such as Laureano Gómez and Mariano Ospina Pérez (Conservative), and Carlos Lleras Restrepo and Alfonso López Pumarejo (Liberal), may remain de facto leaders of their parties, or factions thereof, for decades and then pass the mantle of leadership on to their sons or other relatives or protégés. Party conventions reinforce the tendency toward the self-perpetuation of leadership by granting the right of attendance as delegates to former presidents, cabinet ministers, governors, and others who have served the party in the past. In fact, party conventions are typically made up largely of incumbent congressmen and are often held in the halls of Congress.

Informal ties between patrons and clients link party or factional leaders to others at the departmental and municipal levels, and hence to the party masses. These loyalties and exchanges are more personal than organizational, even though they take place under the rubric Conservative or Liberal. In a sense the parties resemble loosely organized constellations of locally and regionally focused patrons with their respective clienteles. Colombia's historic parties are therefore simultaneously elitist and multiclass in nature.

As the country has become more urban and more literate, and something of a middle class has evolved, the role of the traditional cacique and *gamonal* (petty political boss) has eroded somewhat. Party politics in most regions is still highly dependent on them, but in the larger cities the parties have generally failed to develop equivalent mechanisms of partisan mobilization and control.[3] This is undoubtedly one reason for the evident decline of partisan attachments and party mobilization in Colombia's recent elections.

Prior to the 1920s, formal party organization was quite rudimentary, with only occasional party conventions and only intermittently functioning party directorates. In fact, elaborate organization was unnecessary, given the nature of patron-client ties. As the electorate grew in size and sophistication, party assemblies/conventions and directorates proliferated at the departmental and municipal levels, party carnets (membership cards) were issued, and party headquarters became centers of political activity and the dispensing of jobs and other favors. Yet in many localities they have tended to function rather sporadically, at least in recent years, and primarily around election time; on the whole Colombia's parties must be deemed only weakly institutionalized.[4] Such organizational paraphernalia should in any case not be taken as a replacement for the more informal sets of relationships that pervade the parties. Often the real leader of a party (or faction) is not a member of the party directorate, thus underscoring the diminishing importance of party organizations as arenas of political decision making. And while the national party conventions formally select both the party directorates and, every four years, their presidential candidates, the parties' choices are more often than not preselected by party leaders.

The selection of candidates and of party directorates at the departmental and municipal levels also tends to be self-perpetuating, and the "natural chiefs" play a major role behind the scenes at all levels of the party system. Yet they are hardly dictators; they must provide the appropriate favors in the form of jobs or regional benefits in order to retain the devotion of the *gamonales*. The "natural chiefs" would be lost without the ability and the willingness of local powerbrokers to mobilize the vote. Patron-client relationships are, after all, intrinsically two-directional, even if the exchange is between unequals in power and resources.

The parties as such do relatively little fund-raising, though party members holding public employment are expected to contribute to party coffers. Attempts at regular dues collection generally have not prospered. However, the sustaining organizational needs of the parties are modest, with little in the way of a permanent party bureaucracy except perhaps a headquarters where politicians may hold court or receive petitioners for favors. Campaign funds are for the most part directed to individual candidates and derive largely from the candidates themselves; from their friends, relatives, and patrons; and to a lesser extent from private firms or interest groups possibly including, in a few cases, drug dealers. Presidential fund-raising is more structured and more broadly based, and in recent years has involved substantial sums of money.[5]

The Liberal Party in particular has from time to time made some effort to develop affiliated youth, women's, and other mass organizations, but to only limited effect, except perhaps at campaign time. Much more important, although very different, adjuncts to both parties and their various factions are the major organs of the national and regional press. Colombia's newspapers are almost entirely partisan, and serve as major vehicles for debating and transmitting party positions and strategies. Newspaper publishing has proved to be a vehicle to build political careers in both major parties, and the decision by a publisher to back a particular candidate plays an important role in the internal life of the parties. *El Tiempo* and *El Espectador* are the principal Bogotá Liberal dailies, each with about 100,000 daily circulation. *La República* (Bogotá) and *El Colombiano* (Medellín) have close ties to the family of former Conservative president Mariano Ospina Pérez, while *El Siglo* (Bogotá) has been the particular vehicle of the faction of the Conservative Party headed by Alvaro Gómez, son of former president Laureano Gómez and himself a presidential candidate in 1974 and 1986. Most of these papers, and the major regional dailies as well, are economically linked with other industrial and financial enterprises, and are highly dependent on advertising income from the private sector. In all, the nature and role of the press help to strengthen the elitist nature of the established parties.[6]

More parties of notables than genuinely mass parties, and knit together more by the personalized ties of patron-clientelism than by elaborate organization, Colombia's traditional parties are a throwback to the 19th century.

THE "HEREDITARY HATREDS"

Central to party life as a partisan press and networks of patrons and clients may be, it is the parties' ability to mobilize both elites and masses in the name of their respective labels that has, over the years, set Colombia's Conservatives and Liberals apart from typical parties of notables and has enabled them to survive into an era when similar parties elsewhere in Latin America have largely faded away.

At least until very recently Colombians—virtually all Colombians, of whatever social stratum—have been marked by deep attachment to one or the other "hereditary hatred." Historically, Colombians have been socialized early into loyalty toward one and—equally important—enmity toward the other, traditional party. "Among the most remote childhood memories of a Colombian are . . . those of political parties similar to two races which live side by side but hate each other eternally."[7] Colombians have tended to be "born" Liberal or Conservative and to carry this identification throughout their lifetimes. Particularly in small towns and the countryside, these have been more than mere electoral preferences; they have been part of one's attachment to family, community, and the community's patron. They have also been part of a society where, at least in the days before the National Front, one's livelihood, or even access to a hospital or burial in the local cemetery, might well depend on the victory or defeat of one's party. Such attachments were, of course, one of the principal initial sources of *la violencia*.

Yet, other Latin American countries have experienced intense competition for political office and the related perquisites. Others have experienced the close communal attachments of the village and small town, and the ties to politically prominent patrons. Why, in Colombia, should these have taken particular hold and endured so long?

From the beginning of Colombia's independent life, the military was inordinately weak (see chapter 6). Moreover, divisions within the elite and the fact that each segment thereof could count on a more or less secure regional base difficult for any central authority to suppress (or even to reach, due to formidable problems of internal communication) afforded the conditions for genuine competition for political office. Elections, not the military coup, therefore early became the principal means for effecting the transfer of power at the national level. These elections, while often far from free of fraud or intimidation at the local level, were nonetheless usually fairly competitive nationwide. This gave rise to parties in the form of alliances of regional patrons and caudillos as the only practicable means of attaining national power, the more so since no one region (let alone the military) could readily dominate the country.[8]

Since incumbents tended to use the advantages of office to try to control elections, the minority frequently concluded that the only way to avoid permanent exclusion from office was to raise an army of its dependents (mostly campesinos) in order to fight its way to power. As community was pitted against community in the civil wars that ensued between the parties, political allegiances became bonds of community self-defense. "Open warfare caused each locality . . . to strengthen its internal political bond as a means of survival in civil conflicts. In this manner politics became . . . as important as life itself—it was identified with [the] struggle for existence." That is, a cycle of vengence was begun, and hereditary political cohesion became (or was perceived to be) indispensable to family and community survival.[9]

Given that an important dimension of the late-19th-century combat between the parties was between pro-clericals (generally Conservatives) and anti-clericals (generally Liberals)—again, more prominently so than in most of Latin America—a messianic tone was often injected into the political struggles of the day, whether electoral or otherwise.[10] As a popular Conservative couplet put it, "The color blue . . . is the color of heaven, while the color red is the color of the flames of hell."[11]

Rather than parties' serving the purposes of compromise or the aggregation of other interests, the identification of families, communities, and regions with one or the other party became a major basis of conflict. As one Colombian lamented, "Here the whole country is political. The national country has disappeared."[12] It is nonetheless paradoxically true that in a geographically fragmented society, with poor internal communications and a weak central government, the deep loyalties to the parties helped to knit together the disparate parts of the country in a way that almost nothing else could: the parties were the only entities that evoked loyalties beyond the locality or region. Similarly, the multiclass nature of the parties contributed to stability by joining together disparate social elements even while reaffirming, in the parties' internal structures and behaviors, the pattern of social hierarchy.

Over the years many Colombian communities have manifested a strong tendency toward domination by one or the other of the two major parties. Averages of municipal voting for 1930 and 1946 showed that some 36 percent of the *municipios* (townships or counties) gave at least 80 percent of their votes to either the Liberals or the Conservatives, and were thus categorized as hegemonic. Another 41 percent varied between 60 and 79 percent control by either party. Only 23 percent of the *municipios* were genuinely competitive, in that no one party received as much as 60 percent of the vote. By 1978 the percentages of noncompetitive communities had declined somewhat, but not by a great deal.[13] If hamlets and villages incorporated within *municipios* and for which data are unavailable were examined, the percentages of single-party communities would be significantly higher.

Thus the historic prominence of civilian, nationwide competition for political power—whether at the ballot box or on the battlefield— by rival coalitions of patrons and their clients, heightened by the deep attachments to family and community of a traditional society and by the messianic appeals of religion (or opposition to its ministers) created intense, lasting attachments to political labels that were seldom approached in the rest of Latin America. Such attachments are no longer quite what they were but over time they have given Colombia's parties much of their peculiar cast, and account in considerable part for their endurance through almost a century and a half of political life.

PARTY CONTRASTS

If elitism, patron-client networks, and party loyalties based on "hereditary hatreds" characterize both of Colombia's historic parties, what are the differences between them?

One view is that they have been little more than "rival bands of brigands fighting over literal loot," that party politics is little more than a contest of the "ins" versus the "outs," of rival patron-client networks competing for status and jobs—in short, for the spoils of office.[14] Nor can there be much doubt that over the years such motives have constituted much of the stuff of party competition in Colombia. On issue after issue and in case after case, it is clear that the strategic advantage of a particular party or faction has been the central concern, not program or ideology.[15] Indeed, "ideology" has often been little more than rhetoric, or mere posturing in an attempt to legitimize the struggle for power.

Yet there have been important shades of distinction between the ideologies of the parties, as well as in their policies when in power and in their social composition, that make them more than random collections of allies in the struggle for control of the government. Empirical research has shown that even today there are differences in the belief systems of Colombian party activists, somewhat less than those between Republicans and Democrats in the United States, perhaps, but not markedly so.[16] The most salient of those differences has a religious basis. Conservatives tend to be oriented toward the Roman Catholic Church and its proclaimed values and interests, while Liberals tend to have more of a secular and anti-clerical orientation. Conservative congressmen profess themselves to be high in religiosity by more than five to one over Liberals.[17] Such differences are reflected on issues like divorce and population policy, where Liberals have tended to favor, and Conservatives to oppose, government promotion of family planning.

Differences on matters of economic development and income distribution are not as pronounced, but are nonetheless noticeable. Liberals as a party, while hardly qualifying as radicals, have generally been somewhat more supportive of change in these areas than have Conservatives. Thus it was the Liberal Party that promoted the *revolución en marcha* and Liberals (in particular President Carlos Lleras Restrepo) who during the 1960s sought to make the state a more effective instrument of economic development and planning. Above all, it is Liberals, whether in the 1930s or the 1960s, who took the lead in agrarian reform and Conservatives who have most often led the resistance to the passage or implementation of the requisite legislation. A similar tendency can be perceived in the parties' approach to urban reform.[18] Such differences are reflected in the self-images of congressmen, with Conservatives several times more likely to consider themselves conservative in economic ideology than are Liberals.[19]

The ideological and programmatic differences between the parties should not be overstated. From the time of their founding in the 19th century, both parties have run a rather wide gamut of ideology and interest (as have the Republicans and Democrats in the United States). Moreover, as issues centered on church and religion have faded in importance (though they have not disappeared altogether), and as Colombian agriculture has become more "modern" and commercial, thus narrowing the differences between the "traditional" Conservatives and the industrializing and export-oriented Liberals, the ideological and programmatic differences between the two parties have diminished in importance. This tendency toward ideological convergence helped to make possible the National Front, following the divisions of the 1930s and 1940s, and the ensuing *violencia*. In fact, the allegedly wide ideological gulf between the parties did not prevent numerous (albeit briefer) temporary alliances between them throughout Colombian history.

Apart from ideology, there have been some meaningful, if not always great, contrasts between the parties in the composition of their leadership and their constituencies. These have been less of social class than between the more traditionalist, and generally more rural, parts of the country (Conservative) and the more commercialized, and generally more urban, areas (Liberal).

There are some discernible class differences between those who vote for the two principal parties, at least in urban Colombia, where data are available; but they are hardly great, and they tend to vary by the nature of a particular candidacy or election. Interestingly, there is not very much difference between the parties in the pattern of contact between interest groups (such as business or labor) and congressmen.[20] More important than the very modest shades of differences in class support is the centrality to the life of both major parties of relationships between patrons of high social status and national prominence, on the one hand, and clients of lower social status and more localized influence, on the other, signifying that they are multiclass in their social composition. Merchants and landowners, professional men, peasants, artisans, and workers belong to the Liberal as well as the Conservative Party.

Contrasts between the two major parties are sharper with respect to the urban-rural vote. The Liberal Party almost always carries all of the country's significant cities, with one or two exceptions, and in most cases by proportions greater than its overall edge over the Conservatives. However, the Conservative percentage of the urban vote has shown a tendency to increase in recent years, at least in presidential elections. In 1978, for the first time in memory, the Conservative candidate (Betancur) won a plurality in Bogotá. In 1982, Betancur again won a plurality in the capital, although the two

Liberal candidates combined exceeded his total by 55 to 43 percent.[21]

Regional contrasts between the parties are quite striking. With the notable exception of Antioquia, the historic seat of Colombian industrialization, Liberals tend to have their deepest roots in departments and towns, and even rural areas, where the Church has historically been weakest, commercial and industrial activities most developed, and institutions less well-established (as in areas of new settlement). Conservatives tend to be the opposite: strong in more traditional, pro-clerical regions of the country. Even Conservative Antioquia conforms substantially to the pattern. Although industrial at its core, it has historic ties to the Church and numerous small landholders.

The sociological differences in the parties are, then, not primarily those of social class. They are better characterized as cultural in the broad sense.[22] Beginning in the mid-19th century, those groups that identified with the Church, with traditional agricultural pursuits, and with inherited Hispanic values tended to align themselves with the array of patrons and clients that called itself Conservative. Those who sought to reduce the power and influence of the Church, those engaged in commerce and in export-import agricultural pursuits, and those who looked to secular and liberal values generally became Liberals. There is also some evidence that, at least in cities of intermediate size, Conservatives tend more often than Liberals to derive from old families of high social status, suggesting that the Liberals historically absorbed more upwardly mobile individuals.[23] Exceptions were of course numerous, and the real motive for partisan combat undoubtedly remained, for most, the competitive struggle for public office and its attendant rewards. Moreover, the parties, and particularly their elites, have over time grown more to resemble each other, the experience of the National Front, the increasing fusion of elite economic interests as a result of such factors as urbanization and the relative decline of traditional agriculture, and the fading of conflict over the role of the Church being among the contributing factors. There is a real sense in which they form a homogeneous elite. Still, there are, and have been, shades of difference in ideological and policy orientations, and in the kinds of people who lead and vote for the Conservative and Liberal parties—differences that, though not as great as in rhetoric and in folklore, do have at least some impact on both politics and public policy.

THE PARTY SYSTEM

If by "two-party system" we mean literally two, and only two, parties, then Colombia's party system does not meet the criterion. Few do, including the "classic" instances of the United States and Great Britain. For in Colombia, as in other so-called two-party systems, there have been other, minor parties. But if by a "two-party system" we mean that at any given time not more than two parties have a real chance to win power, and that over time those same parties alternate in power, then Colombia does fit the definition, though not wholly without qualification. Surely it is a strange two-party system in which, prior to 1974, only one 20th-century presidential election (that of 1922) was contested strictly along party lines, with both parties fielding a candidate and neither more than one. True, the National Popular Alliance (ANAPO), the movement—subsequently a party—founded by former president Rojas Pinilla, did almost win the presidency in 1970. Yet it did so by running under a Conservative factional label during the mandated two-party days of the National Front. And the Republican Party that held office in 1910–14, and earlier parties like it, proved essentially a temporary coalition of leaders of the two historic parties. Minor parties not attributable to major-party factionalism, such as the Communist Party of Colombia (PCC), have never won many votes or seats in Congress, and have never come anywhere close to winning the presidency.

To be sure, the major parties have often found themselves divided into nationally structured factions that have at times run competing candidates for president and for legislative bodies. But those factions have continued to carry the party label and to consider themselves, and to be considered by others, as part of the same "historic collectivity." To do otherwise—to adopt a new identity and a new name—would lose the electoral advantage that many years of political socialization have given the party labels Conservative and Liberal.

Yet if Colombia is definitionally a two-party system, that system frequently functions in ways most unusual for the two-party systems familiar in the Anglo-American world.

One such unusual attribute is the nature of its factionalism. Although Colombia's traditional parties may be elitist, with a tendency toward self-perpetuation among their leaderships, they are hardly monolithic and have been prone to division almost from their inception. At present the Liberals are divided (primarily) between the *oficialistas* and Nuevo Liberalismo, whose principal spokesman is Luis Carlos Galán; each ran a candidate in the 1982 presidential election, as well as separate legislative slates in 1982, in the 1984 midterm elections, and again in 1986. Conservatives are divided between Pastranistas (Ospinistas) and Alvaristas, factions that derive from the 1940s.

Factions, like the parties, have derived above all from personal and regional rivalries, as well as from competing claims on the status and benefits derived from public office, and are typically headed by a former president or a potential presidential candidate. But, also like the parties, there have often been shades of difference with regard to public policy and the base of their support. Nuevo Liberalismo tends to be more technocratically oriented, and more concerned with promoting the role of the state in economic development and social reform, than is the main body of the Liberal Party. It finds its principal support among the urban middle class, especially in Bogotá. The majority "official" wing of the party is more broadly based, and more reliant on traditional patron-client ties and partisan appeals to mobilize support. Among Conservatives the Alvaristas (named after Alvaro Gómez, a son of the late Conservative leader) have somewhat stronger ties to traditional-style agriculture and to areas such as the Atlantic coast departments; the Ospinistas or Pastranistas (named after former presidents Mariano Ospina Pérez and Misael Pastrana Borrero) are closer to Antioqueño industrialists and to the coffee trade. Again, these are tendencies only, and it is by no means unheard of for individuals to switch their allegiance from one to the other as political calculations dictate. Such switching almost never happens between parties, however, although it occasionally did in the 19th century (the cases of Tomás Cipriano Mosquera and Rafael Núñez come to mind).

Factions, or at least factional tendencies or "wings," of course appear in other two-party systems. However, their basis is usually more substantially that of policy or ideology than in Colombia. Perhaps more significant, factions in Colombia frequently operate with their own directorates and even conventions (although they may be represented as well at their regular party conventions). They are therefore much more structured than most factions elsewhere, and in some respects act as virtually independent parties. Additional, often ephemeral, dissident factions may occur at the local and departmental levels, usually for the purpose of furthering a political career or gaining greater representation for a particular regional interest by taking advantage of Colombia's list system of proportional representation (see below). Politicians unhappy with their placement on a list may seek to improve their chances of election by heading their own lists.

Factionalism obviously dilutes any president's ability to command the loyalty of his party while in office by making him more dependent for the enactment of policy on negotiations with factional leaders. It means, too, that the party directorates are not always able to direct; factional leaders (not necessarily members of national, or even factional, directorates) may be the more important party figures. In Colombia the faction is in a sense more critical for the functioning of the political system than is the party. Throughout Colombian history factions have often served as the functional equivalents of opposition parties, either during those long periods when one party held virtually hegemonic sway or when, as during the National Front, the two parties (or factions thereof) formed a coalition government.

Factionalism has played another critical role in the operation of the Colombian political system by providing the basis (and to date virtually the only basis) for a change of the party in power. Prior to the 1986 election when each party presented but a single candidate, on every occasion that power was alternated between the parties, with the exceptions of the accession of the Liberals in 1861 through successful armed revolt and the constitutionally mandated alternation of the National Front years, a change in the party in power has been substantially attributable to a split in the dominant party. This was true in 1982, and in 1946 and 1930. Whereas in the United States shifts in the lengthy predominance of one party to that of the other may depend on "critical" elections like those of 1896 and 1932, when categories of supporters (such as "labor" or "Catholics") moved semipermanently into the opposite camp, in Colombia the governing party, when unified, has virtually always been able to win the next election. Given the fixity of party loyalties, turnover has had to depend either on large-scale abstention by the supporters of the governing party[24] or on the dominant party's running two presidential candidates and thereby splitting its votes.

A further trait of Colombian factionalism is curious in comparative perspective. Party divisions, even when they have led to the temporary formation of third parties, as well as the case with the

19th-century Nationalists and the post-1910 Republicans, have not led to permanent disruption in the two-party order of things. Their members seem to have continued to consider themselves ultimately loyal to the body of tradition and sentiment that has grown up around each historic party. This was true, for example, of López Michelsen's Revolutionary Liberal Movement (MRL) during the 1960s and even of most followers of Rojas Pinilla's ANAPO, which, although formally constituted as a separate party in 1971, saw the bulk of its leaders and adherents shortly revert to their original partisan homes.

Splits in the major parties therefore have not led to the permanent creation of new parties, nor served as a transitional step whereby a dissident group gradually transferred its allegiance to the opposing party. In Colombia dissidents have invariably remained within, or returned to, their original party. The overall framework of the two-party system has thus been maintained, producing in that sense a kind of rigidity. In another sense, however, the workings of Colombian factionalism have allowed outlets for political ambitions, conflicting interests, and policy differences within each party that might otherwise have led to the destruction of the parties and the sundering of the two-party system. Not least, such flexibility has allowed the parties more readily to adapt to social and political circumstances, thus tending to preserve the political system as a whole.

Another unusual feature of the Colombian party system, again qualifying but not obviating its two-party nature, has been the frequency with which the parties, or factions of them, have joined in regimes of coalition or national unity, with the National Front but the latest example. At certain critical junctures the party elites seem to have viewed their common interests in the maintenance of the system as overriding the stakes of partisan strife. Coalition governments have at times provided a respite from civil strife, as after the War of the Thousand Days and in the wake of *la violencia.* On other occasions, as in 1930, they have served as transitional regimes for the transfer of power from one party to another, thus presumably allaying the fears of the losers that they will be abruptly or completely cut off from the public trough. Unity governments have also enabled Colombia's partisan elites to shore up their positions when interparty conflict, as it seemed it might during the 1950s, shows signs of becoming transformed into a challenge from below to the social order.

Colombia's partisan division along dualist lines has therefore at one and the same time masked a pluralist reality of several major (and many minor) factions, as well as a bedrock unity of the country's political elites. Paradoxically, while often seeming to disrupt the workings of straightforward two-party politics, both factionalism and the tendency to form coalitions at critical junctures have been highly useful to the survival of what otherwise might have become either an impossibly rigid system or a badly fragmented multiparty one.

Long periods of hegemony for one or the other party have been another feature of Colombia's party politics. The Liberals predominated for most of the period 1849-86, the Conservatives during the years 1886-1930, the Liberals again between 1930 and 1946, and so on. Having attained office, the government, or its partisans, was able to use the weapons of authority—control of the police, and the appointment of governors and mayors, for example—as well as the blandishments of public office—the letting of contracts, the distribution of regional largesse, and the like—to retain office for many years. Elections, while not as a rule fraudulently manipulated in any massive way from the center, could nevertheless be "biased" in a direction favorable to the governing party by the actions of local officials across the country.[25] The use of such devices by a party to perpetuate itself in power of course was a major contributor to armed revolt during the 19th century. Since the incumbents almost always were victorious in those civil wars, turnover in office invariably came when a split in the governing party deprived it of its firm control over these electoral assets.

Hegemony was not solely the result of actions by the governing party, however. The "out" party, in an effort to deny legitimacy to the incumbents, would often abstain from participation in elections, thus leaving the field to the opposition and biding its time until victory seemed a more realistic possibility (as with a split in the governing party).

At the same time, the deep attachment of Colombians to both parties, and the parties' hold on particular regions and localities, meant that the opposition always survived, ready for an opportunity for a comeback. The incumbents could harass the opposition party and discriminate against it, but they did not seek to destroy it (and could not have done so). Even during periods of Conservative or Liberal hegemony, the enduring strength of the other party was such that it was able to retain its hold in certain sections of the country or to make it costly for the government to ignore it completely. During the decades of Conservative hegemony following the War of the Thousand Days, Liberals were often included in cabinets, and the system of the "incomplete vote" adopted in 1910 mandated that a third of legislative seats go to the largest minority party in a given electoral jurisdiction (such as a department). Therefore, despite prolonged periods of party hegemony, full-blown civilian dictatorship has been almost as rare in Colombian history as has military dictatorship.

In summary, at times the Colombian party system has seemed to function as a one-party system. Most recently, there were those who referred to the National Front as such an arrangement. At still other times (or simultaneously) factionalism has appeared to make Colombia a de facto multiparty system, whatever the rhetoric about the two "historic collectivities." Yet the dualism of the Colombian party system retains a reality around which the other features of the system, such as factionalism, hegemony, and coalition formation, revolve and to which the system always tends to return. Thus today, and for the foreseeable future, only the Liberal and Conservative parties have realistic chances of capturing the presidency. The nature of Colombia's dualism suggests that two-party systems do not arise only in homogeneous, pragmatic political cultures like those of the United States and Great Britain.

THE OPPOSITION

Prospectively serious challenges to Colombia's social and political order have come almost exclusively from factions of the major parties or their derivatives, and have been essentially reformist rather than genuinely revolutionary in nature. They have included the Gaitanistas of the 1940s, the Revolutionary Liberal Movement (MRL) of the 1960s, and Rojas Pinilla's ANAPO.

During the 1930s Jorge Eliécer Gaitán and other dissident Liberals founded the Revolutionary Leftist National Union (UNIR) when the Liberal Party failed to make a "revolution" after its electoral victory in 1930. Interestingly, given the urban focus of Gaitán's subsequent political career, he and UNIR concentrated on mobilizing poor campesinos on coffee haciendas not far from Bogotá; workers were a lesser element in the movement. The UNIR faded away, however, when it failed to take hold, and Gaitán returned to the Liberal fold. The more serious, though short-lived, Gaitanista challenge to the "oligarchy" came in Gaitán's presidential campaign of 1946 and ended two years later with his assassination, although by then Gaitanismo had become the dominant party faction and perhaps less of a challenge than it had seemed during the 1946 election campaign.

The MRL attained its high point in 1962, when it won more than a third of the Liberal congressional vote. It adopted a platform centered on the provision of "health, education, and housing for all Colombians," pro-union legislation, and a foreign policy both mildly critical of the United States and mildly sympathetic to Fidel Castro. The MRL also showed some inclination for tactical alliance with the Communist Party, and challenged such features of the National Front as presidential alternation. Yet the MRL was essentially a political vehicle for López Michelsen, and it faded out of existence when he rejoined the "official" wing of the party in 1967, subsequently becoming a governor, foreign minister, and, in 1974, president of Colombia. Despite its name and its stated programmatic intentions, in the end the MRL bore considerable resemblance to the traditional personalistic party faction.

ANAPO has been the most effective opposition movement in recent Colombian political history, yet soon after almost winning the presidency in 1970, it went into a precipitous decline. Originally (1961) ANAPO was essentially a political vehicle for former president Rojas Pinilla to effect a political comeback by challenging the political arrangements of the National Front, perhaps by inciting a coup or an insurrection.[26] It soon began to run candidates as a Conservative faction under the mandatory (but permissive) two-party framework of the Front. Soon it added a Liberal faction as well, thus in a sense bridging Colombia's traditional partisan divide. Its leadership and its support continued to come primarily from Conservatives, however, and Rojas ran under the Conservative label when he sought the presidency in 1970. In 1971, with the National Front drawing to a close, ANAPO formally became a separate party, competing as such in subsequent elections. However, its vote declined from 39.1 percent in the 1970 presidential election (35.5 percent for its congressional candidates), to 18.8 percent in the 1972 elections for departmental assemblies and municipal councils, to 9.4 percent of the vote in the 1974 presidential race. Meanwhile Rojas, by now over 70 and with a heart condition (he died early in 1975), had yielded direction of the party (and the 1974 presidential candidacy) to his daughter, María Eugenia Rojas de Moreno. By the mid-1970s ANAPO had divided into several independent factions and had virtually faded away as a distinctive force in Colombian politics. Rojas's daughter did support the candidacy of Belisario Betancur in 1982, however, and was credited with some influence in helping him gain a plurality in Bogotá.

ANAPO's leadership was always highly centralized in the Rojas family, and the party was hierarchically organized in the extreme. In its heyday it had a very effective barrio-level organization in cities such as Bogotá; outside the large cities it was structured mostly along the patron-client lines of the traditional parties. Aside from Rojas and his close associates, ANAPO's leadership was largely composed of disgruntled Conservative (and a few Liberal) politicians seeking a way to challenge the dominant party factions of the National Front era. Particularly in its early years, it had the support of a number of retired military officers. Its followers, especially at its peak in 1970, derived disproportionately from the lower- and lower-middle classes in Colombia's largest cities, as well as from campesinos in some of the more traditionalist agricultural regions.

Although, exceptionally for Colombia, voting in the large cities in 1970 was largely along class lines, ANAPO's appeals were hardly those of revolutionary apocalypse. In fact, its program and ideology were rather vague, manifesting elements of nationalism, traditionalism, and socialism *a la colombiana.* Its rhetoric was largely negative in tone, stressing attacks on "oligarchs" and the nefarious political institutions of the National Front. Little concerned with structural change, its promises centered on jobs and material benefits for those (both politicians and followers) who felt left behind by the machinations or policies of the National Front coalition.

As a curious blend of traditional political styles and mass mobilization politics, ANAPO can fairly be dubbed "populist," one of the few such political movements to have had even partial success in Colombia. For a time it not only threatened the continuation of the National Front but, in 1970 at least, it seemed to presage a restructuring of the Colombian electorate along class lines. Its success in the cities encouraged the subsequent administration to pay more explicit attention to the problems of urban Colombia, albeit rather halfheartedly and not very successfully.

In the final analysis, though, the hold of traditional party attachments and their networks of patron-client ties proved too strong; and with the end of the National Front and of its status as a faction (or factions) of the established parties, ANAPO quickly declined. Rojas's distancing from the party for reasons of health, an attempt to re-direct it in a more radical direction, and doubts over whether it would be allowed to win power (given the experience of the alleged fraud of the 1970 election) probably also contributed to ANAPO's demise. In the end, it proved difficult for the party to survive with-out at least the prospect that it would soon share in the jobs and out-put of the public bureaucracy.

Wholly distinct third parties—that is, apart from those operating as temporarily dissident factions of the two major parties—have never had much importance in Colombia. Electorally, the oppositional Left has ranged from weak to virtually nonexistent, although it has occa-sionally elected members of Congress, departmental assemblies, and municipal councils. Until 1986 it had never won as much as 5 percent of the vote nationwise in either presidential or legislative elections.

The history of socialism in Colombia is a modest one. A party of reformist bent calling itself Socialist was founded in 1919 and won several seats in legislative bodies in the years immediately thereafter, but it failed to prosper. Several Marxist study groups subsequently coalesced in 1928 to found the Revolutionary Socialist Party (PSR), which was admitted to the Third International. Composed of dis-parate elements, including Liberals searching for an alternative vehicle with which to oppose the Conservatives, it effectively dissolved in the wake of the Liberal victory of 1930, some of its members return-ing to the Liberal Party and others joining that same year in consti-tuting the Communist Party of Colombia (PCC). Some small socialist groups persisted over the next two decades until, in the early 1950s, Antonio García, a leading leftist intellectual, undertook the organiza-tion of the "nationalist, popular, democratic, socialist, autonomous" Colombian Popular Socialist Party (PPSC). It was to be neither uto-pian, nor Marxist, nor European socialist, claiming to represent a third position between capitalism and communism. However, García allied himself with the regime of Rojas Pinilla, and the PPSC was dis-credited along with that regime. Although socialist groups continue to exist, they hardly constitute a major political force even within the Colombian Left.

The PCC likes to consider itself Colombia's third party, and in fact is the longest-surviving third party in Colombian history.[27] Its current secretary general. Gilberto Vieira White, is very much in the tradition of long-enduring Colombian political leaders, having assumed the leadership of the party in the late 1940s. The PCC aligned itself with López's *revolución en marcha* in the 1930s and joined in founding the Colombian Confederation of Workers (CTC) at that time. It elected four members to Congress in 1945 but subsequently declined as the result of internal divisions, tactical errors, and persecution by the post-1946 Conservative governments. Declared illegal by Rojas Pinilla in 1954, it recovered its legal status by the plebiscite of 1957 and has retained it since. Since the phasing out of the National Front, it has run candidates in various legislative elections, usually joining with other leftist groups in supporting a joint candidate for president. Following the 1986 elections the Unión Patriótica (UP), the electoral front of the PCC and its guerrilla allies, the Revolutionary Armed Forces of Colombia (FARC), could boast 1 senator and 10 members of the House.

The party's membership in 1982 was estimated at about 12,000, the fourth in size in Latin America after the parties of Cuba, Mexico, and Argentina.[28] It published a weekly newspaper and a variety of periodicals. Rather than in the numbers of its voters or militants, however, Communist strength—and it should not be overestimated—lies in its close ties to one of the country's principal labor confederations, the Labor Confederation of Colombian Workers (CSTC), and to one of the main peasant-based guerrilla organizations, the FARC. The PCC is not without influence among students and intellectuals as well, but the latter tend to find a more congenial home among less orthodox elements of the Colombian Left. For all their more than 50 years of existence, Colombia's Communists have so far played but a marginal role in the country's political life.

The years since 1960 have seen the birth of a variety of other parties and political movements, including some of Maoist, Castroite, and Trotskyist inclinations—all of them very small and many of them ephemeral. The most important is probably the Independent Workers' Revolutionary Movement (MOIR). Since 1959 Colombia has also had a Christian Social Democratic Party (PSDC). More reformist than revolutionary, the PSDC backed Father Camilo Torres's short-lived attempt to create a united leftist movement, the United Front, in 1966. More recently it ran its own candidate for president in 1974, but he received fewer than 6,000 votes. In 1982 it backed the "National Movement" candidacy of Belisario Betancur. Always a tiny party, the PSDC has so far played a negligible role in Colombian politics, despite what might seem its potential, given the historic role of religion in Colombian public life.

The failure of political parties and movements opposed to the existing pattern of elitist, two-party rule, whether they be reformist, populist, or revolutionary, is in large measure the counterpart of the hold on Colombians of the sentiments, political ambitions, and networks of patron-client ties attaching to the traditional parties. Yet up to a point such an argument is circular; the inability of any party to mobilize a permanent mass base outside the framework of the Liberal and Conservative parties needs further explanation. The weakness and generally nonradical inclinations (at least until recently) of Colombian labor, and the fairly widespread landownership among Colombian peasants, may well be an important part of the explanation (see chapter 6 for further elaboration). The relative weakness of Colombian nationalism as a potentially cohering factor is probably another. Nor have the errors and fragmentation of the opposition forces helped their cause. Finally, one must consider the fact that at key junctures, such as the early 1930s and during the National Front years, the party elites were both willing and able substantially to co-opt the personnel and policy proposals of those who sought change; prospective counterelites seemed always to be absorbed, or reabsorbed, into the major parties. To some extent, at least, it is just such failures, and just such co-optation, that have, in recent years especially, moved elements of the opposition in their frustration to take up guerrilla warfare, as well as other less violent forms of direct action, both rural and urban.

Finally, the electoral and organizational weakness of the opposition is somewhat deceptive. The stirrings of the Left during the 1920s quite possibly had the effect of moving the Liberal Party in a reformist direction once it had assumed power in the following decade, much after the pattern of third parties in the United States in the early decades of the 20th century. Moreover, such weaknesses are to a certain extent compensated for by a measure of strength in other areas. It is here—in the labor movement and among peasants and intellectuals—that one should look for the Left's potential impact, rather than in the electoral arena.

ELECTIONS AND POLITICAL PARTICIPATION

Presidential elections take place every four years in Colombia. Congressional elections occur every four years as well; beginning in 1978 they have been held two or three months prior to the presidential elections and have sometimes been used as a kind of de facto primary (especially by the Liberal Party), whereby the candidate whose supporters win the largest number of seats becomes the party's presidential nominee. Elections for departmental assemblymen and municipal councilors are held every two years; when they take place in nonpresidential years, they constitute Colombia's only real midterm (*mitaca*) elections.[29] Presidential elections are by direct popular vote, with a plurality sufficient to elect. Elections for the various legislative bodies are conducted according to a system of proportional representation known as the electoral quotient. Each party (or faction) presents a list for the given electoral jurisdiction (which is the department in the case of Congress). The total votes for a given office are divided by the number of seats at stake in order to determine the electoral quotient. The quotient is then divided into the various parties and/or factions. Any seat remaining after such a division goes to the party (or faction) with the largest residual.

Individual candidates win elections according to their rank order on their respective party or factional list. A voter may choose only a list in legislative elections, not particular candidates, although he may choose different party lists for different offices. Needless to say, such a system gives party leaders considerable leverage, since it is the candidates ranked near the top of a party's list who are most likely to be elected. The list system and the electoral quotient help to promote intraparty factionalism, since any individual who finds himself not placed high enough on his party's list to obtain a seat on the basis of the quotient can still hope to marshal enough votes for his independent list to beat the residual.[30]

Legislators do not have to be residents of the department or *municipio* for which they are elected, although they often are. Further, multiple officeholding (at different levels) is permissible and not infrequent, with prominent individuals heading lists in more than one locality in order to attract votes. This is facilitated by listing alternates (*suplentes*) on the ballot, so that if a principal does not actually occupy the office for which he is elected, a *suplente* may. The lack of a residency requirement and the use of *suplentes*, and of course the list system itself, not only enhance the manipulative power of the party leadership but also help to dilute the accountability of representatives to their constituencies.

Since the 1930s most restrictions on the right to vote have been eliminated. Both literacy and property qualifications for voting were struck from the constitution in 1936 (as they had been during 1853–61), as part of President Alfonso López Pumarejo's *revolución en marcha.* Women were accorded the vote (by Rojas Pinilla) in 1954, as confirmed by the plebiscite of 1957 that instituted the National Front. The voting age was lowered from 21 years of age to 18 in 1975. To be eligible to vote, one must in addition be a citizen and hold a *cédula* (identity card).

In the past, fraud and voter intimidation were quite prevalent at the local level, and together constituted a limitation on the democratic process probably as great as any legal restrictions. Since the onset of the National Front, the use of such devices has diminished considerably, although it occasionally recurs, with some areas of the Atlantic coast departments having a particular reputation for vote-buying, for example. There are also charges of inefficiencies in the Registraduría Nacional del Estado Civil (the Electoral Registry) along the following lines:

> If one were to make a sustained analysis on the basis of the Registry's figures, one would find that the average life span of Colombians is the longest in the world, owing to the fact that *cédulas* are never retired; and curiously one would find, as well, that in some regions . . . people never die . . . the truth is that in Colombia people die everywhere except in the Registry.[31]

Still, today Colombian elections must be accounted as substantially fair and competitive in the formal sense. The remaining limitations on the democratic nature of the electoral process in Colombia reside, in the main, neither in legal restrictions nor in electoral manipulation, but in characteristics of Colombian society, in particular the very wide disparities in educational attainment and material resources, as well as conditions of employment or rural isolation that in some areas of the country still make the many dependent on the few for their political direction.

Voting is not compulsory in Colombia. Rates of voter participation are therefore not strictly comparable with those in nations (such as Venezuela) where there are legal penalties for not voting and electoral participation ranges above 80 percent of those eligible. Even so, Colombia's level of voter participation must be considered low, and there has been constant hand wringing among political pundits to the effect that Colombian democracy is at risk as a result. Well over half the eligible electorate typically abstains in a Colombian election.[32] (See Table 5.1.)

Electoral abstention takes two forms. One is group or "directed" abstention, in which a party directs its followers to abstain as a gesture designed to undermine the legitimacy of the results of an election or of an incumbent government. Prior to 1974 there were only three presidential elections in the 20th century in which both parties contested the presidency (1922, 1930, and 1946), although there were other occasions (as in 1942) when the party out of power supported a dissident candidate of the incumbent party.[33]

Individual abstention is another matter and has been the more prevalent form, at least since the inception of the National Front. Voter participation reached a peak in 1958, at the very outset of the Front, then declined (albeit with some fluctuation), only to surge modestly again in 1970. The surge resumed when competitive elections for the presidency and Congress were renewed in 1974, only to decline in subsequent elections (of all types), with the exception of the 1982 presidential election.

Some have argued that the high rates of abstention beginning in the 1960s are principally rooted in disaffection from the political system generally and its failure to produce results for the disadvantaged. Such arguments gained particular strength during the National Front years, when parties reflecting alternatives to the traditional parties were barred from presenting candidates in their own names. Post-National Front elections have failed to produce more than a minuscule vote for anti-system parties, however, thus somewhat detracting from the argument that abstention reflected opposition to the system (as distinct from opposition to the government of the day). Moreover, the fact that most elections since 1974 have witnessed turnouts about as low as the lowest levels of the National Front years argues that low voter turnout was not simply due to the absence of interparty competition in the years after 1958. In fact, evidence from opinion polls shows that abstention in Colombia is often the

TABLE 5.1. Electoral Returns by Party and Rates of
Participation, House Elections, 1947-86 (percent)

	Liberals	Conservatives	ANAPO[b]	Other[c]	Percent Voting[d]
1947	54.7	44.4	—	.9	56
1949	53.5	46.1	—	.4	63
1951[a]	.6	98.6	—	.5	n.a.
1953[a]	—	99.7	—	—	n.a.
1958	57.7	42.2	—	—	69
1960	58.1	41.7	—	—	58
1962	54.5	45.4	(3.7)	—	58
1964	51.2	48.5	(13.7)	—	37
1966	55.4	44.2	(17.8)	—	44
1968	53.2	46.5	(16.1)	—	37
1970	51.1	48.6	(35.5)	—	52
1974	55.6	32.0	9.5	3.1	57
1978	55.1	39.4	—	4.3	33[e]
1982	56.3	40.3	—	2.5	41
1986	56.2	37.0	—	6.8	n.a.

[a]The Liberals did not present candidates in 1951 or 1953, during the peak of *la violencia* and government repression.

[b]For the years 1962-70 ANAPO's candidates ran as Conservatives or Liberals, as required by the constitutional dispensations of the National Front; its vote is included in the respective party totals for those years.

[c]"Other" includes, primarily, the Communist Party and other leftist groups.

[d]Represents the percentage of those registered (that is, having a *cédula*) who voted.

[e]1978 was the first House election following the lowering of the voting age to 18.

Sources: Departamento Administrativo Nacional de Estadística (DANE), *Colombia Política* (Bogotá: DANE, 1972), pp. 154, 228; Registraduría Nacional del Estado Civil, *Estadísticas Electorales. Corporaciones Públicas. Marzo 14 de 1982* (Bogotá: RNEC, 1983), p. 513; and Latin American Weekly Report (London), March 21, 1986, p. 3.

result of "lack of interest" or "inconvenience" in going to the polls.[34] Such aversion to voting on the part of a sizable proportion of the population is not necessarily healthy for Colombian politics or for the legitimacy of the system. At the same time, abstention may support system stability in the sense that it appears to indicate that voters are at least satisfied enough with the system not to translate any disaffection into votes for the opposition.

The fact that women have voted in elections beginning with the plebiscite of December 1957 may account in part for generally lower levels of participation compared with the last competitive elections of the pre-National Front period (those of 1947 and 1949). Presumably women—new to the political process and more "traditional" in their attitudes—could be expected to have lower levels of participation than men. However, if levels of education—distinctly higher for men than for women—are held constant, levels of female voting approximate those for males.

Generally, though, women have played a minimal role in Colombian politics. In the years since 1958 women have held only 3 or 4 percent of the seats in Congress, and only a little more than that in the (less powerful) municipal councils and departmental assemblies.[35] There have been several women cabinet members, and President López Michelsen (1974–78) named six women governors. Both parties have had women's affiliates, which seem to play a significant role mainly at election time. Yet most women's political involvement has heretofore taken the form of roles supportive of men. The few women who have come to play important political roles have usually been wives or daughters of prominent political figures—for example, Berta Hernández de Ospina, wife of former president Mariano Ospina and a leader of the Pastranista faction of the Conservatives, and María Eugenia Rojas de Moreno, daughter of former president Gustavo Rojas Pinilla, and his heir as leader of ANAPO.

The lowering of the voting age from 21 to 18, beginning with the midterm elections of 1976, undoubtedly has helped to raise abstention levels in recent years, since in Colombia, as in most other countries, the young tend to vote in smaller proportions than do other age cohorts of the population.[36]

The significant fluctuations in voter turnout remain largely unaccounted for. The fact is that when Colombians perceive their votes to entail some real choice, they tend to turn out in much larger numbers than otherwise. Thus the 1958 turnout could be interpreted as a reaffirmation of the country's desire for political peace and the end of dictatorship. The 1970 election brought the candidacy of the populist former president, Gustavo Rojas Pinilla, and an opportunity for those disaffected from the National Front to express their opposition. The election of 1974, the first interparty competition for the presidency since 1946, again brought forth an outpouring of votes. On the other hand, elections that fail to evoke the mobilization of old party loyalties, as was the case with most elections during the National Front, or seem unlikely to bring much change in policy orientations or the conditions of life, tend to produce apathy.[37] Similarly, midterm elections for such relatively powerless offices as departmental assemblyman and municipal councilor lead to low voter turnout, whereas presidential elections are likely to increase voter participation, even compared with congressional elections held only a few months before.[38]

Rates of abstention vary considerably among elements of the population. Urban voters are less likely to vote than the rural electorate, probably indicating the diminished ability of party caciques to mobilize the city vote and the diminished salience of patron-client ties in larger communities, as well as a kind of disaffection that does not translate into an anti-system vote for the Left. In the eight elections for the House between 1958 and 1974, the average abstention rate for departmental capitals was 63.7 percent, while for the nation as a whole it was 48.5 percent. Moreover, the larger and more "developed" the city, the higher the rate of abstention.[39] Although the poor (at least in urban areas) are less inclined to vote than the members of other social classes,[40] the disparities between urban and rural voting patterns means that the less-educated members of the electorate (the campesinos) have a disproportionate effect on electoral outcomes. It is this *voto cautivo* (captive vote), more readily mobilized and controlled by regional caciques and *gamonales*, that sustains Colombian democracy by turning out to vote.

SUMMARY AND TRENDS

Much of what is true of the Colombian party system today might also have been said of it in the 1960s, in the 1930s, or even earlier. It may fairly be called a two-party system, yet its highly articulated factionalism and its recurrent tendency to share power between the parties often cause it to function almost as a multiparty or a one-party system, respectively. While under certain circumstances able to mobilize the political loyalties of many Colombians, and despite operating in an increasingly urban and literate society, Colombia's two historic parties remain at their core parties of notables with their attendant patron-client networks. Although there are differences among the parties in their historical traditions, their sociological bases, and their ideological "temperaments," in most crucial respects they are more alike than not and their behavior in office is quite pragmatic. They are not primarily parties of ideology or of class conflict.

Opponents of the two parties, while at times quite vocal and at times even forming guerrilla bands, have so far posed little direct threat to the survival of the political system. High rates of voter abstention, while seeming to pose questions concerning the legitimacy of the system, have shown a tendency to diminish at moments of crisis, or when the electorate has perceived a genuine choice to be involved. A distinct mark of the stability of the party system is the fact that the electoral margin between Liberals and Conservatives remained in 1986 about what it was in 1958 (or 1947, for that matter), with the Liberals generally having an advantage of roughly 55 percent to 40 percent in post-National Front elections. (See Table 5.1.)

There is little sign of the permanent emergence of patterns of class voting in Colombia. The 1970 election, with ANAPO in its heyday, witnessed by far the most clear-cut class alignment of any Colombian election—one of the most clear-cut in Latin America, for that matter.[41] Subsequent elections have generally seen Liberal presidential candidates draw better than Conservatives among lower-to-middle-class voters, at least in urban areas. At the same time, the Conservative Betancur drew well among these groups, too, and there is some modest indication that the Conservatives have done better than in the past among urban lower-status voters. In all, while class is not an irrelevant factor in Colombian electoral politics, there is little real evidence that a class-aligned politics is emerging; 1970 was a marked exception, caused by very particular circumstances.[42]

Finally, despite operating under the rules of formal democracy, and an electoral system that has for the most part functioned free of governmental manipulation, the nature of the Colombian party system continues to have the effect of excluding the majority of Colombians from an effective voice in government. The very wide disparity among Colombians in the skills and resources necessary for such participation, the internal structures of the parties and the importance in Colombian politics of negotiations among elites, the list system of elections, and a legacy of "hereditary hatreds" that has tended to blur other lines of conflict have all contributed to that end. Traditional party loyalties have heretofore been a major factor in explaining the ability of the elites to co-opt potential challengers. Populist movements, when they have emerged, have largely done so under the rubric of one of the major parties and have eventually been reabsorbed by that party. Even the middle class, in contrast with most other Latin American countries, has never been able to forge a permanent vehicle of autonomous political expression. Many in the urban middle class find themselves increasingly among the abstainers on election day, seemingly discontent with the elite-dominated traditional parties and suspicious of the options put forward by the opposition, yet unable or unwilling to construct their own alternative.

There are only a very few other Latin American party systems (Mexico and Costa Rica come to mind, and perhaps Venezuela) where so little of a fundamental nature has changed since 1958. Yet changes there have been, changes that, if they accelerate their tempo over the next few years, could have deep-seated implications for Colombian politics.

In the first place, there are signs that although the two-party share of the vote continues at its usual level of 95 percent or more, Colombians' traditionally intense identification with one or the other of the parties is beginning to diminish. While levels of party identification are still high by cross-national standards, opinion polls indicate an erosion in party identification in the large cities; a number of urban Liberals either were willing to vote for the Conservative presidential candidate in 1978 and again in 1982, or at least were unwilling to rally behind party banners even in a close contest with the formerly hated partisan enemy.[43] Though party ties still bind, those ties appear to be loosening.

Second, Liberal electoral predominance, while it persists nationwide, has been somewhat shaken recently, not only by the election of a Conservative president in 1982 but also by long-term Conservative gains in the cities. The Conservative vote in the capital cities of the departments increased from 16.8 percent in 1958 to 30.4 percent 20 years later.[44] Since urban areas are gaining in their relative electoral weight, the presumption, under normal conditions, of national Liberal predominance could be called into question in the not too distant future.

Third, there are indications that party has been giving way to the institutions of government, and to interest groups, in terms of its centrality for Colombian politics. The fact that President Betancur ran his 1982 campaign as removed as possible from the Conservative Party label is one such indication; another has been the increasing proliferation of legislative lists (most of them unsuccessful) in the name of nonparty groups. More important has been an apparently increasing separation between the world of patron-client politics (the *país político*) still prevalent at the provincial level and in the halls of Congress, and the world of public policy making at the national level (the *país nacional*).[45] In any case, parties in Colombia largely fail to perform the critical function of aggregating the economic interests of diverse groups and proposing broad policy alternatives. In a manner comparable with much of the rest of Latin America, that function has fallen increasingly to the president, government technocrats, and interest groups.

NOTES

1. For the distinction between cadre and mass parties, see Maurice Duverger, *Political Parties*, trans. Barbara North and Robert North (New York: Wiley, 1964), esp. chap. 2. A cadre party is essentially a loosely knit party of notables with little, or only nominal, mass membership; mass parties, on the other hand, tend to be centralized, tightly organized parties with elaborate means of mass recruitment, dues paying, and the like.

2. Gabriel Murillo Castaño and Ismael Rivera Ortiz, *Actividades y Estructura de Poder en los Partidos Políticos Colombianos* (Bogotá: Universidad de los Andes, Departamento de Ciencia Política, 1973), pp. 57–60; see chap. 4, above, for data on the level of university education. Interestingly, political leaders responded to a survey question by affirming that "the rich" governed in Colombia (Murillo and Rivera, p. 114n).

3. Such urban-provincial contrasts date from at least the turn of the century; see Charles W. Berquist, *Coffee and Conflict in Colombia, 1886–1910* (Durham, N.C.: Duke University Press, 1978), pp. 95–99. The difference of course is that today's cities are much larger, and contain a proportionately larger share of the population. In reference to today's politics, Enrique Ogliastri notes the difference between intermediate-size cities, where politicians are known personally and a personal touch is still essential for political success, and larger cities such as Bogotá, where one's public image, especially in the press, has greater relative importance; see Enrique Ogliastri Uribe, "Liberales Conservadores versus Conservadores Liberales: Faccionalismos Trenzados en la Estructura de Poder en Colombia" (paper prepared for the annual meeting of the Latin American Studies Association, Mexico City, October 1983), p. 11.

4. For the view of Colombian parties as in large measure electoral parties, see Mario Latorre Rueda, *Elecciones y Partidos Políticos en Colombia* (Bogotá:

Universidad de los Andes, Departamento de Ciencia Política, 1974), esp. p. 261. Presidential election campaigns are lively affairs in Colombia, featuring numerous *giras* (speaking tours), *manifestaciones* (rallies), *homenajes* (testimonials to the candidates), lively exchanges in the press, and the like. Candidates have also begun to use polling and media advisers imported from the United States.

5. See Murillo and Rivera, *Actividades y Estructura de Poder*, pp. 115-16, 129. A bipartisan commission reported in late 1983 that there was no evidence of presidential campaign funding with drug money. At the same time, the commission noted that many campaign contributions were difficult to trace; *Latin American Weekly Report* (London), January 6, 1984, p. 8.

6. Concerning the Colombian press and its connections to other elements of the Colombian power structure, see *Latin America Weekly Report*, July 15, 1977, p. 211; for a similar analysis of radio and television, which has generally played a less prominent political role, see *Latin America Weekly Report*, July 29, 1977, p. 227.

7. Guillermo Hernández Rodríguez, *La Alternación ante el Pueblo* (Bogotá: Ediciones América Libre, 1962), p. 168.

8. For a comparison of Colombia in this respect with Ecuador and Peru, see James L. Payne, *Patterns of Conflict in Colombia* (New Haven: Yale University Press, 1968), pp. 128-29.

9. Orlando Fals Borda, *Peasant Society in the Colombian Andes: A Sociological Study of Saucío* (Gainesville: University of Florida Press, 1955), pp. 241-42, 210. Payne, in *Patterns of Conflict*, refers to it as a "defensive feud."

10. For the view that this aspect of late-19th-century party conflict amounted to a virtual holy war, see Orlando Fals Borda, *Subversion and Social Change in Colombia*, trans. Jacqueline D. Skiles (New York: Columbia University Press, 1969), pp. 104-10.

11. Cited in Malcolm Deas, "Algunas Notas Sobre la Historia del Caciquismo en Colombia," *Revista de Occidente* (Madrid) 43, no. 127 (October 1973): 135.

12. Manuel Serrano Blanco, quoted in ibid.

13. Departamento Administrativo Nacional de Estadística, *Boletín Mensual de Estadística* (Bogotá) nos. 268-69 (November–December 1973): 68, 307-18; and Jonathan Hartlyn, "Consociational Politics in Colombia: Confrontation and Accommodation in Comparative Perspective" (Ph.D. diss., Yale University, 1981), pp. 292-94. There is evidence that in some parts of the country, such as the department of Tolima, *la violencia* might well have accentuated such political homogenization; see Latorre, *Elecciones y Partidos*, pp. 131-32.

14. For this view, see Fernando Guillén Martínez, *Raíz y Futuro de la Revolución* (Bogotá: Edicones Tercer Mundo, 1963); and Vernon Lee Fluharty, *Dance of the Millions: Military Rule and the Social Revolution in Colombia 1930-1956* (Pittsburgh: University of Pittsburgh Press, 1957), pp. 23, 227-33. For the thesis that Colombian party conflict is little more than a clash over status (for elites) and jobs (for followers), see Payne, *Patterns of Conflict*.

15. The fact that about a third of the clauses of the inter-party agreement (the Pact of Sitges, 1957) that formed the basis for the National Front concerned the depoliticization of the bureaucracy is one such indication.

16. See on this point Harvey F. Kline, "Las Ideologías en la Política Colombiana," *Razón y Fábula* (Bogotá) no. 31 (January–March 1973): 45–58; and Gary Hoskin, "Belief Systems of Colombian Political Party Activists," *Journal of Interamerican Studies and World Affairs* 21, no. 4 (November 1979): 481–504.

17. Gary Hoskin, "The Impact of the National Front on Congressional Behavior: The Attempted Restoration of El País Político," in R. Albert Berry, Ronald G. Hellman, and Mauricio Solaún, eds., *Politics of Compromise* (New Brunswick, N.J.: Transaction Books, 1980), p. 118. Behavior (e.g., attendance at Mass) also differs substantially; see Ogliastri, "Liberales Conservadores," pp. 12–13.

18. For a thorough study of both agrarian and urban policy making during the National Front years that reflects these differences, see Bruce Bagley, "Political Power, Public Policy and the State in Colombia: Case Studies of the Urban and Agrarian Reforms During the National Front, 1958–1974" (Ph.D. diss., University of California, Los Angeles, 1979).

19. Hoskin, "Impact of the National Front," p. 116. Another, more recent, survey of Colombian politicians found 39 percent of the Liberals (in contrast with 4 percent of the Conservatives) in agreement with the statement "A socialist solution would contribute greatly to the development of the country"; Ogliastri, "Liberales Conservadores," Table 4. The meaning of socialism to the respondents in this context is unclear, but the contrast between the parties is nonetheless sharp.

20. Harvey F. Kline, "Interest Groups in the Colombian Congress," *Journal of Interamerican Studies and World Affairs* 16, no. 3 (August 1974): 281.

21. For data, see Gary Hoskin, "The Colombian Political Party System: The 1982 Reaffirmation and Reorientation" (paper delivered at the annual meeting of the Latin American Studies Association, Mexico City, 1983). The Liberals continued to outdistance the Conservatives by a wide margin in legislative elections in Bogotá, however; ibid., p. 35.

22. For a more extended interpetation along these broadly "cultural" lines, see Robert H. Dix, *Colombia: The Political Dimensions of Change* (New Haven: Yale University Press, 1967), chap. 9; see also Frank Stafford, "Social Aspects of Politics in Nineteenth-Century Spanish America: New Granada, 1825–1850," *Journal of Social History* 5, no. 3 (Spring 1972): 344–70.

23. Ogliastri, "Liberales Conservadores," p. 7.

24. The failure of the Liberal political machine to mobilize Liberal voters in the Atlantic coast departments in the presidential election of 1982—votes that had been mobilized for Liberal legislative candidates only a few months previously—probably contributed to the defeat of former president López Michelsen in that contest. Interestingly, though, some preelection polls suggested that without a second Liberal candidate in 1982, Belisario Betancur might have won the election even more handily, presumably because most of the dissidents would have voted for him instead of the official candidate of their own party. This kind of "swing" vote is highly unusual for Colombia; see Jonathan Hartlyn, "Colombia: Old Problems, New Opportunities," *Current History* 82, no. 481 (February 1983): 63.

25. See Payne, *Patterns of Conflict*, concerning such "creeping" fraud.

26. For more extended treatment of ANAPO see, in particular, Daniel Premo, "Alianza Nacional Popular: Populism and the Politics of Social Class in Colombia, 1961–1970" (Ph.D. diss., University of Texas at Austin, 1972); Robert H. Dix, "Political Oppositions Under the National Front," in Berry et al., *Politics of Compromise*, chap. 5; and Judith Talbot Campos and John F. McCamant, *Cleavage Shift in Colombia: Analysis of the 1970 Election* (Beverly Hills, Calif.: Sage, 1972).

27. The best sources concerning the early development of the PCC are Comité Central del Partido Comunista de Colombia, *Treinta Años del Partido Comunista de Colombia* (Bogotá: Ediciones Paz y Socialismo, 1960); and Robert J. Alexander, *Communism in Latin America* (New Brunswick, N.J.: Rutgers University Press, 1957), pp. 243–53.

28. Cole Blasier, *The Giant's Rival: The USSR and Latin America* (Pittsburgh: University of Pittsburgh Press, 1983), p. 76.

29. Congressional elections had also taken place every two years until 1970.

30. By retaining the label of one of the traditional parties, rather than forming a separate party, the candidate retains the advantage of voter loyalty to the party label, as well as the prospect of rejoining official party ranks when the situation dictates.

31. Fernando Cepeda Ulloa, "Qué Pasó en las Mitacas?" *Boletín de Sociedad Económica de Amigos del País*, April 1984, p. 7. Latc in 1983 a bipartisan commission recommended that the Registraduría be "revitalized."

32. However, it should be noted that official data may overestimate the potential electorate by some 10 percent, for they include the *cédulas* of a number of persons ineligible to vote: members of the armed forces, many Colombians living abroad, and the dead who have not been purged from the rolls, among others; see *La Abstención* (Bogotá: ANIF, 1980), pp. 11–12. The latter volume is a symposium on abstention that included both politicians and scholars. For an analysis of abstention under the National Front, see Rodrigo Losada, "Electoral Participation," in Berry et al., *Politics of Compromise*, pp. 87–103.

33. Congressional (and other legislative) elections were nonetheless sometimes genuinely competitive during this period, as they were between parties from 1939 to 1949, or among factions, as they were during the National Front. At the same time, it has only been since 1974 that modern Colombian politics has been consistently competitive between (as well as within) the parties.

34. Cf. Fernando Cepeda Ulloa and Claudia González de Lecaros, *Comportamiento del Voto Urbano en Colombia: Una Aproximación* (Bogotá: Universidad de los Andes, Departamento de Ciencia Política, 1976), p. 59.

35. Shirley Harkness and Patricia Pinzón de Levin, "Women, the Vote, and the Party in the Politics of the Colombian National Front," *Journal of Interamerican Studies and World Affairs* 17, no. 4 (November 1975): 443.

36. Gary Hoskin, "Post-National Front Trends in the Colombian Political Party System: More of the Same?" (paper prepared for the annual meeting of the Latin American Studies Association, Pittsburgh, April 1979), pp. 34–35.

37. For an analysis of such contextual factors in influencing voter turnout, see ibid., pp. 11–15.

38. Conversely, during the National Front years, when as a rule congressional elections were competitive (among factions) and presidential elections were not, turnout was higher for the former.

39. Hoskin, "Post-National Front Trends," p. 15; and Cepeda and González, *Comportamiento del Voto Urbano*, p. 26.

40. Hoskin, "Post-National Front Trends," pp. 31, 33.

41. See Campos and McCamant, *Cleavage Shift*.

42. See Hoskin, "The Colombian Political Party System," pp. 21–26, for a discussion of this point. For a trenchant argument that little has changed in this and other respects in the Colombian party system, despite repeated prognostications of change, see John Peeler, "Colombian Parties and Political Development," *Journal of Interamerican Studies and World Affairs* 18, no. 2 (May 1976): 203–24.

43. The number of people who refused to identify with a political party in a Bogotá survey increased from 5.3 percent in 1970 to 38.2 percent in 1982, although the particular circumstances of those elections naturally cannot be discounted as conditioning factors. According to the 1982 survey, these independents were concentrated among the young (those under 25 years old), the middle class, the better-educated, and erstwhile Liberals; Hoskin, "The Colombian Political Party System," pp. 26–27. The experiences of the National Front and of the bipartisan structure of ANAPO may have helped to accelerate the process.

44. Ibid., p. 4.

45. Hoskin points up the difference between legislative elections, where mobilization along traditional lines of the *voto cautivo* is particularly effective, and presidential elections, where other kinds of criteria come to the fore, especially among urban voters, and mobilization of the party faithful is less central to victory; see ibid., pp. 6–7.

6

INTEREST GROUPS

Organized interest associations have both proliferated in number and increased in visibility in Colombia since the 1960s. The identities of some, such as the National Association of Industrialists (ANDI), and some of their political actions, such as lobbying in Congress or use of the media to influence public opinion, would seem natural to any observer of politics in the United States. Other features of interest group structure and behavior contrast rather markedly, however, with those of North America. Such differences include a generally closer, often institutionalized, relationship to government, at times suggesting certain attributes of a corporate state; paradoxically, given the previous point, the much more frequent use by a broad range of groups of tactics, like protest demonstrations, that fall outside regular institutional channels; the prominence of certain institutional groups (such as the military, the Roman Catholic Church, and foreign governments and organizations) only marginally relevant to the politics of most Western democracies; and the involvement of many interest groups—most notably, but certainly not only, the military—not merely in issues affecting their policy demands but in the determination of the survival of governments and regimes.

PRODUCERS' ASSOCIATIONS

The Colombian Agricultural Society (SAC) was founded in 1871, and the National Federation of Coffee Growers (FEDECAFE) in

1927, but it was only after the mid-1940s that producers' associations began to proliferate in response to the increasing size and diversity of the Colombian economy, as well as to the growth of state intervention in the economic life of the country. Four decades later there was a wide variety of organized interest groups in such areas as agriculture, industry, commerce, construction, banking, and insurance. Some were quite specialized (for instance, the Association of Exporters of Frozen Beef, ASOFRIGO); others, like ANDI, encompassed a broad range of industrial, commercial, and financial firms. Many of these organizations have departmental and local affiliates; some have specialty subgroups as well. A few, particularly the larger ones such as ANDI and FEDECAFE, have quite elaborate organizations that serve their member firms or growers in a variety of ways. In addition to periodic conventions, they have professional staffs that conduct research, compile statistics, disseminate information through regular publications, and carry out public relations campaigns. Most producers' associations, however, lack such paraphernalia and remain poorly financed.

For the most part these *gremios* (guilds or associations) have been careful to avoid strictly partisan issues and affiliations, and sometimes go out of their way to ensure bipartisan representation on their boards of directors. For instance, with the onset of the National Front in 1958, FEDECAFE increased the elected (nongovernmental) members of its board from five to six in order to allow for an equal number of Conservatives and Liberals. The partisan affiliations of the country's business executives are in fact fairly evenly distributed between the two major parties, although Liberals are in a clear majority.[1]

The routes of political access for such groups are various. They include media campaigns, contributions to political parties and candidates, and congressional lobbying. Yet on the whole, compared with the United States, the relationship of producers' groups to government tends to be more structured, more exclusively concentrated on the executive branch, and more reactive than initiative.

In the first place, most government corporations and agencies have boards of directors composed of representatives of those groups most directly affected. For example, the Colombian Institute of Agrarian Reform (INCORA) has by law regularly included representatives of the Cattlemen's Association (FEDEGAN) and SAC, even though both have long been opposed to many aspects of the agrarian reform. ANDI at one point was said to have representatives on more than a dozen government committees and boards of decentralized agencies at the national level alone.[2] Conversely, government officials are occasionally on the boards of interest associations. Notable is FEDECAFE: by law representatives of eight government ministries and entities (such as the Agrarian Credit Bank) are board members ex officio.

As a rule there is also considerable overlap between the leadership of interest associations and the top officeholders of the executive branch (the president and his ministers). This seems to have been particularly true of the Ministry of Agriculture, where the minister has quite regularly been a former manager, or a member of the board, of one of the major agricultural associations.[3] The overlap between interest group leaders, on the one hand, and political party directorates and legislative posts at the national, departmental, and local levels, on the other, is likewise substantial. A study done in the 1960s found that 56.4 percent of former ministers and high officials, 41.9 percent of congressmen, and 42.9 percent of high-level bureaucrats had held a position in a producers' association.[4] The two-way flow between interest associations and positions in government is therefore significant. On the whole, though, representatives of such associations are less likely to contact members of Congress than are representatives of other sectors.[5] Their focus tends to be the executive, which in Colombia is almost exclusively the center of policy making. It is also probable that informal contacts with social peers minimize the necessity for more formalized relationships.

Finally, the government occasionally subsidizes producer groups or certain aspects of their activities, or relies upon them to carry out quasi-governmental functions such as setting and enforcing price levels for a given commodity. Indeed, it is not unknown for governments to instigate the formation of an interest association in order to cohere into a single voice the many and time-consuming claims of a particular sector, as President Alfonso López did in 1944 with ANDI. Conversely, producers' associations may on occasion choose a leader because of his known connections with the president or other high officials.

The most elaborate and significant instance of the use of a private entity in a public capacity is FEDECAFE, which concerns itself with such tasks as the stabilization of coffee prices and the collection of an export tax on coffee, in effect acting as an agent of the state.

FEDECAFE also carries on a massive program of agricultural "extension" involving production and marketing techniques, and assistance for a variety of farmers. It has been defined by the Colombian Supreme Court as "a private company carrying out essential public functions for the national interest." Its manager, named by the president from a panel of three submitted by FEDECAFE, negotiates with the representatives of other coffee-producing countries.

Access of producers' associations to government therefore has considerable, often structured, potential. Yet potential does not always translate into effective influence. Group representatives on boards of directors of the numerous decentralized institutes and agencies may disagree among themselves, and may find it difficult to monitor the day-to-day performance of government-appointed managers or directors. Nor does the fact that a cabinet minister has previously been an officer of an interest association necessarily translate into a preference for its interests over those of the incumbent president.[6] Changed roles may, after all, entail altered policy preferences.

Not least, a president can, and often does, ignore the demands of producers' associations if he is determined on his own policy course.[7] In the end the reputed political power of these groups comes not only from their economic power or their political connections, but also from the force of their arguments, backed by their representatives' technical information, scholarly credentials, and force of personality, and by their ability to stir public opinion through statements and criticisms in the press.

Most producers' associations oppose any significant change in social and economic structures, and tend to be content with the status quo. Although they may look to government assistance (as the cotton growers did in the late 1970s) or policy changes (such as greater tariff protection for Medellín's depressed textile industry) when faced with serious economic difficulties, generally they prefer less state intervention than more. When added to the executive-centered nature of Colombian government (see chapter 7) and the paternalistic style of the political culture, this leads to a much greater emphasis on trying to block policy changes or thwart their effective implementation (as with agrarian reform) than on proposals for new legislation. Such a reactive posture with regard to government policy initiatives almost by definition gives interest groups an oppositional role. In fact, the executive and one or more interest associations have often proved to be antagonists on specific policy issues, among them taxation, agrarian reform, and urban reform.

It nonetheless goes too far to suggest that producers' associations are political "paper tigers." For they—or at any rate their individual members, or politicians articulating their interests—have frequently been able to emasculate, or at least to modify, the proposals of the president and his ministers. For instance, in the early 1970s several agricultural associations succeeded in eviscerating an attempt by the president to revive an almost moribund agrarian reform enacted in the early 1960s.[8]

None of this opposition to specific government policies should be seen as opposition to the regime itself, or to the quasi democracy that currently reigns in Colombia. A number of major producers' associations, led by ANDI, the National Federation of Merchants (FENALCO), and the Bankers' Association (ASOBANCARIA), helped to bring down the regime of General Rojas Pinilla through their support of lockouts and a civic strike in May 1957. And they supported the National Front—in fact, some business leaders were instrumental in its creation. Whatever their other differences with politicians, they have in moments of crisis generally thrown their weight behind governments led by those same politicians. For instance, in 1970, in an atmosphere of tension that surrounded charges of fraud in the presidential election of that year by the followers of Rojas Pinilla, a number of the associations made explicit their backing of the government and for the time being muted their criticisms of government policy. And in 1981, in the wake of another threatened general strike, leaders of the main producers' associations helped to head off a serious situation.

In short, their posture seems to be that, whatever their particular differences with the post-1958 governments, any foreseeable alternative regime would lead to even greater dangers and uncertainties. It is ultimately their access to the press and to Congress, and an elected president's need to mobilize support from a variety of sectors if his policies are to prevail, that give Colombia's interest associations the ability to block at least some of the proposed laws and other actions of government that might adversely affect them. Indeed, the fact that many of those groups are federally organized contributes to the pluralism of the Colombian political process.

The producers' associations, and the firms and individuals they represent, do in various ways have privileged access to the policy-making and policy-implementation machinery of the executive branch. Since the 1960s they have increased in numbers and influence in the wake of a corresponding relative decline in the influence of the parties under the conditions of bipartisan government (much of the essence of which has continued to prevail even after the formal end of the National Front in 1974). Yet personal, regional, and policy differences, occasionally leading to formal splits within them and among them, tend at times to mitigate their influence.[9] And when all is said and done, the state retains an important measure of autonomy and self-directedness that cannot be subsumed by any set of interests—beyond the survival of the essentially elite-directed, yet pluralistic, system itself.

ORGANIZED LABOR

A few scattered labor unions formed in the early years of this century, and there was an occasional strike. A short-lived labor confederation was organized as early as 1918 and some major strikes occurred during the 1920s, notably among transport, petroleum, and banana workers. The latter led to a declaration of a state of siege in the Atlantic coast region and deaths of numerous strikers in a confrontation with the army.[10]

During this period socialist and anarcho-syndicalist influences were important in the Colombian labor movement. The modern history of that movement begins, however, in 1935 with the establishment of the first permanent national labor organization, the Confederation of Colombian Workers (CTC), under the benevolent auspices of Alfonso López's *revolución en marcha.* The CTC flourished during the following years, but by the late 1940s internal divisions between Liberals and Communists, and the leadership's decision to back the official Liberal candidate instead of the populist Jorge Eliécer Gaitán in the 1946 election (thus losing its credibility with its membership) had weakened it internally. Following López's resignation in 1945, antilabor attitudes on the part of government added to its difficulties. A labor movement that had relied on an alliance with government to achieve its gains was bereft of support when government's attitude changed.

In 1946 the Jesuits, under the benign eye of the new Conservative administration, founded the Union of Colombian Workers (UTC) as a means of combating the perceived leftist domination of Colombian labor. As of 1981 the UTC could claim the affiliation of about 40 percent of organized labor and the CTC 20 percent. Another 12 percent were counted as members of the Communist-linked Labor Confederation of Colombian Workers (CSTC), founded in 1964. A fourth confederation, the General Labor Confederation (CGT), founded in 1971 and having Christian Democratic origins and affiliations, comprised some 9 percent of the unionized. The remaining 19–20 percent of organized labor was affiliated with independent unions, often of varying Marxist orientations (Maoist, Trotskyist, or other).[11] Tentative attempts at unity among two or more of the several confederations have so far foundered, despite occasional joint strikes or policy actions.

The union movement has never been very strong in Colombia—certainly nothing approaching the strength of labor in Argentina, in pre-1973 Chile, or in post-1958 Venezuela. Not only has it been organizationally and politically fragmented, but it has apparently never been able to organize as much as 20 percent of the work force.[12] The fact that the stronger unions have often been reluctant to forgo gains for themselves has additionally helped to keep levels of class mobilization low. The existence of a large pool of the unemployed and underemployed (accentuated by Colombia's relatively late, capital-intensive industrialization), plus low levels of dues collection (substantially due to low incomes), has made it difficult to sustain strikes. The relatively low number of workers employed in mining and manufacturing has also militated against union strength. In fact, a great many members of the urban lower classes—residents of shantytowns employed (when they are employed) in temporary jobs or petty entrepreneurship—are not readily organizable, although a few tenants' organizations do exist among them.

Last, though hardly least, legal strictures and government repression have hampered the growth and activity of the Colombian labor movement. The requirement (as in most Latin American polities) that all organizations obtain their *personería jurídica* (legal personality) from an agency of the state, though seldom an obstacle to producers' associations, has sometimes been used to deny legal status to unions.[13] Other legal restrictions include a requirement that union officers be full-time workers in their industries and a ban on strikes in public services (broadly defined to include transportation, communication, the entire public sector, and banking).[14] Legislation making it difficult to organize industrywide unions (as distinct from those confined to a single firm) further tends to promote smaller unions that are financially weak. In addition, the government has rather often used its powers under the state of siege to repress or contain strikes. In fact, it has been argued that the real reason for prolongation of the state of siege during much of the 1960s and 1970s was not to combat guerrillas in the countryside, but to suppress strikes and other forms of urban unrest that were a greater immediate threat to elite interests.[15]

In some respects labor's links to government resemble those of the producers' associations. Either or both the UTC and the CTC are represented on the boards of a number of the decentralized agencies and, typically, on the special boards or commissions that are from time to time formed to propose policy or resolve crisis situations created by threatened general strikes, even though labor's representatives are usually far outnumbered by those of producers' and professional associations.[16] Both the UTC and the CTC, as well as other unions (though not the CSTC or the CGT), receive sizable government subsidies for such purposes as the holding of conventions or the construction of new headquarters;[17] overall there is greater dependence on government in this respect than is the case with producers' associations, many of which, like ANDI, receive no government financial support. Another major difference between labor and the producers' groups is that there is almost no overlap between labor officials and government positions, apart from an occasional legislative office.

While the access of labor to government is therefore considerably less than that of owners, and while labor's dependence and vulnerability vis-à-vis government is obviously much greater, there have also over the years been persistent efforts by both government and the parties to co-opt labor by assuaging its demands or encouraging its organization. The *revolución en marcha* was notable in this respect, and the CTC has maintained close, albeit sometimes frayed, ties to the Liberal Party ever since. The UTC was initially sponsored by the Church and favored by the Conservative governments of the 1946–53 period, although it has never really been tied to the Conservative Party and has manifested considerable independence from both parties and from the Church in recent decades. Some of its leaders have in fact been Liberals. For the most part its stress has been on collective bargaining with the individual enterprise, rather than on obtaining its ends through political means or political threats (political bargaining, as it is sometimes called), as is more common in other parts of Latin America, and as has more often been the case with the CTC, and certainly the CSTC.[18]

Nonetheless, given government's central role in economic and social policy, and even in the setting of wages and prices, and given labor's relative lack of access compared with employers, unions have increasingly resorted to demonstrations or strikes, including on occasion general strikes and threats or acts of violence designed to put pressure on the government. This has been most common in the case of government employees—including teachers, judicial employees, and the staff of the social security system—who (for the most part illegally) have gone on strike to accomplish such ends as the payment of back salaries. Like employers' groups, unions have sometimes been able to block (although seldom to initiate) a proposed action of the government, such as an increase in gasoline taxes or a reorganization of the social security system,[19] although the methods employed (threatened or actual strikes in the case of labor) have not usually been the same. Labor's policy successes have usually been either the result of government preemption or co-optation, or of labor's threatened disruption of public order and the paralysis of economic activity.

As with employers, differences with government over particular policies should not necessarily be read as challenges to the political regime, although in labor's case antiregime connotations have been increasingly present in recent years. At election time or at moments of crisis, the UTC and the CTC have usually supported the government, or at any rate have backed away from confrontation.[20] General strikes have usually either been averted or aborted because of concessions made on both sides.

Indeed, in comparative terms the Colombian labor movement has historically been quite moderate and strike levels low.[21] That a reformist government (the *revolución en marcha*) intent on mobilizing labor as a political base was in power during the critical early stages of industrial expansion and growth of the labor movement undoubtedly has been partly responsible. Closely allied with the established parties or the Church, the Colombian labor movement as a whole never became truly oppositional. Moreover, although workers by no means share equally in the economic and political resources of Colombian society, they, and especially their leaders, have often experienced improvement in their living conditions, as well as a degree of upward social mobility, over the years. Workers rather than intellectuals, Colombia's labor leaders have generally tended to be more pragmatic than ideological. Labor has had a measure of structured access to the decision-making process as well. Even Colombia's more authoritarian regimes have not closed those avenues altogether. Thus the UTC flourished under the Gómez regime of the early 1950s and under Rojas Pinilla (who sought to foster his own, captive, labor movement as well). Finally, the historically modest importance of foreign capital in Colombia must be kept in mind in any discussion of trade union radicalism. The most violent early strikes were against U.S. firms, and Communist unions were most effective in those companies. Had foreign enterprises been more common, labor-management relations might well have developed along more radical lines.

Nevertheless, there is considerable evidence that Colombian labor has become more militant in recent years, and that an increasing proportion of workers may be looking to radical solutions of society's perceived inequities. Both the UTC and the CTC show evidence of a weakening of past ties with established parties and institutions. The Communist CSTC and independent radical unions have grown in strength since 1975. The propensity to strike seems greater as well. In September 1977 all of the labor confederations joined in a general strike that paralyzed the country and led to dozens of casualties. Another general strike, this time with less cohesion and less success, occurred four years later. Most recently, in May 1984 the four confederations together presented President Bentancur with a list of demands including revision of the labor code and agrarian reform. The middle-class (white-collar) elements of unionism, which have become increasingly important numerically and in their rates of unionization in recent years, and are particularly vulnerable to government policies and actions, may well hold the key to Colombian labor's future attachment to the country's quasi democracy.

PEASANTS

Colombia's peasants historically have been even less effective and less militant as political actors than has urban labor. By about 1918 the first (ephemeral) peasant organizations had appeared, and the first peasant demonstrations and strikes had taken place. The decade

1925–35 saw mounting unrest both in the banana-growing areas of the Atlantic coast region, where plantations owned by the United Fruit Company dominated production, and in coffee-growing areas of the Andean region. Some conflicts in the coffee areas concerned working conditions on haciendas; others had to do with the validity of land titles and the attempt by some campesinos to grow coffee on land they farmed but did not own, thus raising the specter for landowners (given the long-growing coffee plants) of a permanent claim to the land. Eviction of peasants by local police, land invasions, and strikes occurred in scattered parts of the countryside. Some of the peasant actions were spontaneous; others were led or encouraged by urban politicians (for instance, the Communist Party and Jorge Gaitán's Revolutionary Leftist National Union [UNIR]). Yet by the mid-1930s the actions of López's *revolución en marcha*, the Communists' "Popular Front" stance of support for the López regime, and a relative increase in wages in the countryside brought a diminution in agrarian conflict.

A second, quite different era of peasant political action, *la violencia*, began in 1946 and continued into the early years of the National Front. Pitting peasant against peasant, initially it had little to do directly with the land or work situation of the campesino (although it was obviously rooted in the context of rural Colombia). As time passed, however, there erupted in some localties economic and social conflicts of a kind that had been evident earlier, and several explicitly revolutionary guerrilla organizations emerged that sought or claimed the peasants as their mass base, generally with only marginal success.

In fact, for most peasants most of the time, such little access as they had to government largely depended on individualized patron-client linkages. A partial exception was the small coffee grower, whose interests as a coffee producer (if not as a smallholder) were to some extent represented by FEDECAFE. Then, beginning in the late 1940s, the UTC and its Jesuit advisers constituted the National Agrarian Federation (FANAL), which by the 1970s totaled an estimated 20,000 members. Through the invasion of "uncultivated" and public lands, and with the approval of Church advisers and sometimes led by priests, unions affiliated with FANAL made de facto property owners of a number of peasants.[22] FANAL's leader, himself a small farmer, was for a time a representative in Congress.

The National Front brought some new departures in peasant organization, departures that pointed up the co-optative nature of Colombia's political system and left peasant influence at the centers of power not too different from what it had been before.

One of those innovations was Community Action (Acción Communal, AC), a program designed both to improve the material well-being of Colombians at the local level and to generate a spirit of self-help among the campesinos (and to a lesser extent among the urban poor). The underlying objectives seem to have been to further the country's development by mobilizing untapped local resources and to combat the lingering effects of *la violencia.*[23] In effect, the 1958 law that launched AC provided that if a community would organize a junta of its residents, and contribute volunteer labor and perhaps some funds for such projects as schools, clinics, roads, and water systems, the central government would contribute funds or materials and ideally a promoter (perhaps also a team including technical and medical personnel) to help organize the community and educate it both in the ways of self-help and in the means of obtaining government assistance.

This community development program was in some ways resoundingly successful. By 1974, 18,000 juntas had been created and thousands of schools, roads, community centers, and the like had been built. Socially and politically, the juntas in many cases became the focus of community life and helped to reestablish local leadership and the visibility of the government in the wake of *la violencia.* At the same time, the juntas became primary channels for dispensing governmental aid and patronage at the local level. Many became the electoral vehicles of local politicians and were used to dispense governmental largesse to communities that favored pro-National Front political factions. Some juntas, however, began to extend their activities to petitioning and land reform and otherwise expressing their grievances to government. Some formed regional federations to press their claims. In the face of this incipient attempt at independent mass mobilization, the last two governments of the National Front reorganized the AC program to bring it under tighter control by the central government. As a result of these and related actions, by the early 1970s the regional federations were neutralized as a potential political force, and the juntas "essentially reverted to their previous roles as vehicles of patronage distribution and vote mobilization with no significant role in either local or national level policy-making."[24]

Acción Comunal was of course organized along community, rather than occupational, lines and was not composed solely of peasants. The National Association of Peasant Users (ANUC), on the other hand, was an explicit attempt by the administration of President Carlos Lleras Restrepo (1966–70) to mobilize peasants. The objective was to create a peasant clinetele group for Lleras's proposed reinvigoration of the agrarian reform program (and possibly to serve as an electoral base for Lleras in future runs for the presidency), while separating peasants from the potentially radicalizing contacts with the urban elements of the AC program and keeping them under closer government control.[25]

The program was placed under the minister of agriculture and a nationwide hierarchical structure was created, headed by a national assembly and an executive committee. Its representatives were to sit on the boards of the Agrarian Bank, INCORA, and other institutions. However, ANUC soon became radicalized and showed a tendency to escape government direction. The result was land invasions, protest marches, civic strikes, and the occupation of INCORA offices. Demanded, among other things, was an accelerated land distribution program.

The organization soon split between pro-government and radical factions, and eventually into several other splinter groups. Arrests of ANUC leaders, accused under the National Security Statute of 1978 of linkages with guerrillas, and the assassination of a number of others further hampered the organization. The CTC, the UTC, and FANAL opposed ANUC, and even organized a march to oppose it. The Communist Party also came to oppose ANUC, at least partly because opposing radical groups gained control of its principal wing (the Linea Sincelejo), and joined in support of the government's efforts to weaken it.

Internal dissension and the opposition of some of ANUC's most obvious allies, plus government repression and co-optation, had by the early 1980s considerably reduced ANUC's cohesion and effectiveness, although it continued to receive government subsidies and to be represented on various government boards. In its time it had served both to mobilize and to radicalize peasants to a degree unheard of before in Colombia. Yet, without external support from parties, unions, or government, the high levels of organization and militancy of ANUC's early years seem unlikely to recur in the near future.

THE MILITARY

Among the political actors common to Colombia, as to much of Latin America, are the armed forces. The political significance of the Colombian military has, however, been considerably less than in any other Latin American country except Costa Rica. Many of the stereotypes, and many of the explanations, concerning the military's prominent political role in Latin America therefore do not apply in Colombia. To be sure, men with military titles were prominent in Colombia's 19th-century political life, but they were essentially civilians who took up arms in the country's numerous civil wars rather than professional soldiers or members of a military institution. Professional soldiers have held office only occasionally and for brief periods throughout Colombian history (see chapter 2). Nor have they often played a notable role in determining which civilians should hold the presidency, although it was not unheard of before 1930 for soldiers to be marched to the polls at the behest of a civilian government, to help swing the outcome of an election.

Once independence had been consolidated, Colombia's army was reduced to fewer than 2,500 men and placed constitutionally under the ultimate control of Congress (instead of, as is usual, that of the president). Its military *fuero* (including special military courts and similar corporate privileges) was abolished, not to be restored until 1886. By midcentury, following the defeat of the short-lived military dictatorship of General Melo (1854) by civilian armies of the two political parties, the army was reduced still further to a virtual corporal's guard (some 500 men) and relegated to such tasks as mail delivery and guarding prisoners. The military was still further weakened by loyalties among its officers to one or the other traditional party, though as an institution it played little role in the civil wars of the 19th century.[26]

There were several abortive attempts during the 19th century to create a more professional military, but not until 1907, in the wake of the War of the Thousand Days, was a Prussian-trained Chilean military mission brought in to launch a genuine career service and a military academy. Even then, the armed forces remained small and their budget low, despite some modest expansion at the time of a brief conflict with Peru over the area of Leticia in extreme southeastern Colombia (1932–33), and during World War II.[27] Nonetheless, although there was apparently a failed military conspiracy in

1936, only the heightening of political tensions in the mid-1940s led to the expansion of the military's role that was to result eventually (inexorably?) in the coup of June 13, 1953.

How does one explain such a divergent approach to the political role of the armed forces in comparison with most other Latin American countries? One thing is quite clear: almost from the beginning the military has been held in unusually low regard by the country's elites and has had low self-esteem as well. Even as late as 1959, when ex-president General Rojas Pinilla, a graduate civil engineer, was on trial before the Senate, he felt compelled time and again to defend the military against charges in the press that all military men were "crude sergeants [*sargentones chafarotes*] who barely know how to read and write."[28] In social origin mainly middle-class, military officers were not welcome or comfortable in the clubs and social circles of a highly status-conscious civilian elite.

Such attitudes toward the military seem to have taken root during the wars of independence. At the very outset (1810) the sons of some of Colombia's social elite joined the rebellion but were decimated in the early fighting. Thereafter the troops (and officers) that liberated Colombia tended to be (a) largely from the Venezuelan part of Gran Colombia, and (b) comprised substantially of crude plainsmen (*llaneros*) of racially mixed backgrounds. Thus social and regional antipathies led to an early, profound condescension on the part of Colombia's civilian elites toward the military that caused even military officers to doubt their own worth. To this set of attitudes must be added the depth of Colombians' attachments to civilian parties. Thus it has been argued that military coups take place especially when public support for a civilian president is inordinately low. Yet in Colombia, given the historic intensity of party identification and the relatively even balance in support for the two parties, support for the president has seldom dropped below an irreducible (yet rather substantial) minimum, thereby diminishing the incentives for a military coup.[29]

The increasing intensity of political conflict, leading to a virtual "collapse of the state," brought a gradual enhancement of the military's role in the 1940s. Resentment over Liberal President Alfonso López's attempts to interfere with promotions in the largely Conservative army, his building up of the national police as a counterforce to the army, and his generally condescending attitude toward the military led in 1944, in an atmosphere of increasing political tension, to an abortive coup. More significant for the long run, the government of President Mariano Ospina Pérez (1946–50) began to rely more and more on the army as *la violencia* heated up. In a number of localities military officers were appointed as mayors and governors. Troops were called in to restore order following the *bogotazo* in April 1948, and in an unusual move a military man was named minister of defense.[30] The military was gradually drawn deeper into the political arena in the wake of the failure of civilian politicians, largely on the initiative of those same politicians.

When the military under General Rojas Pinilla seized power in June 1953, it did so reluctantly, and under the benign eye of politicians of both parties. Moreover, while the military was clearly the center of power during the four years following, the majority of cabinet ministers continued to be civilians; in fact, during most of Rojas's tenure he governed with the close collaboration of the Ospinista wing of the Conservative Party. Although during the year of junta rule that followed Rojas's overthrow in May 1957, and in the first years of the National Front, there were several attempted coups or rumored coups by military dissidents seeking to restore Rojas to power, the military as a whole did not support them and they had little civilian backing. In sum, even as the military saw itself drawn more directly into politics beginning in the 1940s, generally it was hesitant, even halfhearted, and had only modest success.

Nonetheless, the Colombian military did not recede wholly into the background during the years of coalition government that followed. It necessarily played a central role in an effort to restore public order, particularly in the countryside. Under the leadership of General Alberto Ruiz Novoa, who had commanded the Colombian battalion that took part in the Korean War, and with the encouragement of the United States, the army engaged in programs of civic-military action in rural areas as a means of winning the support and cooperation of the guerrillas' potential peasant base. It launched a series of campaigns to simultaneously eradicate the so-called independent republics and to involve itself in the building of clinics, schools, and roads in the violence-prone areas.

While the civic-action program was a substantial success in restoring order to rural areas, General Ruiz's attendant calls for deep-seated socioeconomic change and his apparent political ambitions caused President Guillermo León Valencia (1962–66) to dismiss him as minister of war in January 1965. During the late 1960s and early

1970s civic action took a back seat to armed repression of the guerillas, a campaign that was for a time quite successful. The army was also increasingly called upon to suppress illegal strikes and other urban "disorders," including student protests. General Alvaro Valencia Tovar, army commander in the mid-1970s, argued, like Ruiz Novoa a decade earlier, that the guerrillas could be defeated in the long run only by social and political reforms. When his criticisms became more open, he, too, was removed by the president.[31]

The expansion of the military role into arenas of domestic strife continued in the years following the end of the National Front, and led many to fear that Colombia was coming to resemble the repressive military regimes of the southern cone of South America, albeit without the armed forces formally taking power as in Argentina, Brazil, Chile, and Uruguay. In fact, in certain militarized zones of the country the army virtually became the law. Meanwhile, President Betancur's efforts to seek a truce with the guerrillas aroused the ire of some in the army. When in early 1984 General Fernando Landazábal Reyes criticized President Betancur's policies toward the guerrillas and toward Nicaragua, he was replaced by the president.[32]

In all, Colombia's military is as large, as well-trained, and as professional as it has ever been, especially in counterinsurgency tactics.[33] While its morale and prestige are undoubtedly higher than in the past, the military as a career nonetheless still suffers in comparison with civilian professions. Accusations of human rights abuses and charges of corruption among officers have damaged the reputation for nonpartisan professional competence the military had begun to build on the basis of its successful antiguerrilla campaigns. The armed forces today clearly have a major voice and play an important role in matters of internal security and foreign policy. They are an important prop of a regime that in recent decades has faced considerable internal disorder, both rural and urban, and that has frequently governed under a state of siege. At the same time, they are not mere instruments of civilian elites; rather, their interests often tend to coincide on key matters of public order, even while they sometimes differ on the precise means.

It would be a considerable exaggeration to say that Colombia has become a militarized society, or the virtual equivalent of recent repressive military regimes in other parts of the continent. On every occasion since the end of military rule in 1958 when a military commander has appeared to challenge the civilian president, or has been accused in a scandal, he has been removed by the president with little overt negative reaction on the part of his fellow officers. The cases of General Ruiz, General Valencia, and General Landazábal are but three of the more prominent such cases since the 1960s. At the same time, by the mid-1980s there was mounting evidence that members of the army and national police were responsible for numerous acts of violence and "disappearances" under the guise of combatting the guerrillas, with the government increasingly ineffective in calling to account those responsible.

Given the right conditions (such as a genuinely mass-based revolutionary movement or the patent failure of civilian leadership), a coup certainly could not be ruled out. A pronounced decline in support for the traditional parties (and, potentially, for the presidency) also could minimize inhibitions against a coup. Yet there are few countries in Latin America where civilian authority has remained as consistently predominant over the military. There is probably no other where similar challenges to internal security would not have led much sooner to an outright assumption of power by the military; even should military rule return tomorrow, the long delay would in itself be a notable circumstance. The historic weakness of the military's self-esteem and corporate identity, plus the depth of attachment to the traditional parties on the part of both elites and masses, seem to have been primarily responsible for this relatively diminished role.

THE ROMAN CATHOLIC CHURCH

Colombia is one of the most Catholic nations in the world, with some 95 percent of the population baptized in the faith and a per capita ratio of priests exceeded in Latin America only in Chile and Ecuador. Priestly vocations are higher than elsewhere in the region, thus making the Colombian Church less dependent on foreign priests.[34] Whereas the political role of Colombia's armed forces has been less important than that of most Latin American military establishments, it seems fair to say, along with one of the leading scholars of the history of the Church in Latin America, that "the Catholic Church has been more tenacious in its hold upon national and civil life in Colombia than in any other Latin-American country."[35] As a comparative assessment, the statement remains valid in the 1980s, yet it should not be taken to mean that the Colombian Church lacks weaknesses and vulnerabilities, or that it somehow dominates the entire political process.[36]

Although with independence the Church lost the protection of the Spanish Crown and was thereby exposed to the new winds of liberalism and republicanism abroad in the land, it retained the ownership of large tracts of land and a virtual monopoly over such social functions as education, social welfare, the sanctioning of marriages, and the registration of births and deaths. In fact, many priests were members of the early republican congresses. Beginning in 1849, however, Colombia experienced several decades of extreme anticlericalism under the rule of the Liberal Party. Most Church property was expropriated, the Jesuits were expelled from the country, divorce was legalized, and Colombia became the first Latin American country to separate Church and state.

Much of this was reversed by the Constitution of 1886 and the ensuing (1887) concordat with the Vatican, a situation that has largely prevailed up to the present, albeit with some modifications, including a new concordat in 1973. While the Church did not regain its former lands in the 1880s, it was partially reimbursed and was granted a small state subsidy in lieu of their recovery. Except for the exclusion of priests from public office (other than education), the Church in most other respects regained its former role (including the reentry of the Jesuits). While the Catholic Church was nominally disestablished and other religions were to be tolerated, it was assured the special protection of the state. Regarded as an essential element of the social order throughout most of Colombian history, the Church has been accorded explicit corporate powers over important social functions while in other ways remaining dependent on, or limited by, government.

Why the Church should have been able to retain such a strong hold in Colombia compared with most of the rest of Latin America (despite the lapse of the post-1849 period) is a question difficult to answer. The fact that the proclerical Conservative Party dominated Colombian politics between 1886 and 1930—precisely the years in which most Latin American countries were disestablishing the Church—may have been partly responsible. So, too, may be the fact that the leaders of modern Colombian economic expansion were simultaneously assertively Catholic and Conservative, and thus were not required to challenge the Church in the interests (or the name) of economic progress, at least once Church lands had entered the economic mainstream following the disentailment of Church estates in 1863.

In any case, the Colombian Church continues to play a major role in the social and political life of the country. Its representatives have sat on the boards of directors of INCORA, the National Apprenticeship Service (SENA), and the National Population Council, and on government-appointed commissions to seek an end to *la violencia* and amnesty for the guerrillas, thus institutionalizing yet another form of Church-state linkage. Through the UTC and FANAL, and even some local affiliates of ANUC, priests have played an important role in the organization of urban labor and of peasants. Church personnel have also been active in Acción Comunal and other programs of community development. The Church has its own press (in particular, the weekly *El Catolicismo*) and its own research training institutes. Its Acción Cultural Popular (Radio Sutatenza) has advanced literacy by conducting educational programs (via radio) in rural Colombia. And the Church has carried a major charitable burden through Caritas Colombiana, and the ownership and management of hospitals in a society where government welfare and relief programs are generally inadequate and other forms of private philanthropy are few. Nor is it by any means unknown for one or another of the affiliates of the Church to encourage land invasions by peasants or to become involved in other efforts at "social revindication." Much of the Church hierarchy vocally supported the movement to bring down the regime of General Rojas Pinilla and actively backed the successor National Front.

Yet two other Church roles are probably most important. One encompasses the field of education and all that implies in the socialization of young Colombians. As of the mid-1970s, the Church controlled 3,500 schools and universities enrolling nearly 300,000 students. Those schools included an estimated 85 percent of those in preschool, 20 percent of those in primary grades, more than 50 percent of those in secondary school, and almost 40 percent of those enrolled in universities.[37] Since the late 19th century, the Church has had a voice in public education as well, including the selection of textbooks and the mandatory teaching of religion.

A second area of continuing great Church impact, although it is diminishing with urbanization, is the role of the priest in rural and small-town Colombia, at least in the more devout areas of the country. There the priest may serve as adviser, counselor, and intermediary in ways that go beyond the strictly religious, while the regular presence of religious symbols and rituals make being Catholic part of being Colombian, regardless of whether one regularly attends Mass. Even in urban areas, representatives of the Church are present at most official (and many private) functions, such as the dedication of a dam or a school.

Throughout most of its history, there have been differences within the Church between those who sought to align it with the Conservative Party in the defense of Catholic interests and values, and those who viewed the Church as above or apart from such conflict, for reasons either of theology or of long-run institutional survival. The experience of *la violencia*, when, because of the partisan attachments of many of its priests and bishops, the Church proved unable to play a mediating role, plus rapid social change, including industrialization and the growth of the labor movement, led to a transformation in the Colombian Church that was fully manifest by the late 1950s. First, the Church set out to strengthen its central bureaucratic structures and coordinating mechanisms in order to make a previously rather decentralized organization more coherent. Second, it eschewed its historic partisanship and instead reached a de facto accommodation with the Liberals that made the Church a major prop of the new bipartisan National Front. Third, beginning in the 1940s, but taking on much greater force after Vatican II two decades later, the Church injected itself into the arena of social action.

The latter stance in particular was not without its divisive implications. A traditionalist minority among the clergy continued to be suspicious of such involvement. A radical minority, centered initially in the so-called Golconda Group (1968–70), apparently the first such group of clergy in Latin America, spoke out for direct priestly involvement in social change, and even for the justice and utility of violence as the only means to achieve "liberation" from social and political structures they regarded as unjust and outmoded.[38] A very few, notably Father Camilo Torres, engaged in political violence. Father Torres, who in mid-1965 was reduced to the lay state by the archbishop of Bogotá for his outspokenness on political and social issues, founded a political movement, the United Front; shortly thereafter he joined a guerrilla band, and was killed in a skirmish with the army early the following year. Father Torres subsequently became the leading martyr of the Christian Left, not only in Colombia but throughout Latin America.

However, while the majority of Colombia's clergy (or at least of its bishops) saw clerical encouragement of social action on the part of the laity as a requisite of Church survival in the new age, they looked askance at direct clerical involvement, let alone violence or alliance with Marxists to achieve structural change. Speaking out against the inequities of Colombian society, and to that degree a critic of the established order, the Colombian Church has at the same time rejected liberation theology and the idea that sin resides above all in a set of malformed economic and social structures.[39] There has been some movement toward the establishment of "base communities" in Colombia, that is, the formation of small groups of lay persons designed to raise the consciousness of parishioners and thereby to renovate Church life; but the movement has not gone nearly so far as in Brazil, where it has played a significant role in stirring mass consciousness and participation in both religious and secular affairs.

The political role of the Colombian Church is therefore quite different from what it was in the late 1950s or early 1960s, while in relative terms it nonetheless remains one of the more conservative in Latin America. Its traditional influence in areas such as education and welfare and at the village level remains strong. Its influence in certain areas of social action (the labor movement, for example) has considerably diminished compared with the early years of the UTC but is not insignificant, especially in parts of the countryside. It retains an important voice as well (though hardly a controlling one) in such domains as divorce and birth control. From a political point of view, and despite dissenting voices, the Church has served as one more support for Colombia's elite-dominated version of quasi democracy and (modest) reform from above.

STUDENTS

University students, and to some extent secondary school students as well, are yet another of the actors whose political relevance is quite different from their role in the United States (except for a brief period during the 1960s).

University students participated in the overthrow of General Reyes in 1909 and made efforts to found a national student federation as early as 1911. Influenced, as were students throughout Latin America, by the University Reform Movement that began in 1918 at Córdoba, Argentina, Colombian students held several national congresses during the 1920s. Yet students' importance in Colombian politics remained at best marginal and their national organization weak to nonexistent, although the latter did serve to some extent as a testing ground for future political leaders.

It remained for the conjunction of the rapid expansion of the university population, in keeping with changes in Colombian society at large, and the political circumstances posed by military dictatorship followed by the bipartisan National Front, to make Colombian students significant and radical—though still secondary—actors on the political scene. Students were among the first opponents (and martyrs) of the Rojas regime, several being killed in a clash with police in a protest demonstration in June 1954. Students subsequently played a notable role in the overthrow of that regime—marching in the streets, taunting soldiers and police, and helping to enforce the "civic strike" that precipitated Rojas's fall.

In the ensuing years the strike, the protest demonstration, the occupation of university buildings, and the holding of hostages have been among the tactics employed by student groups. Often centered, at least initially, on university issues—the removal of an unpopular rector or protest against changes in graduation requirements, for example—they readily take on broader implications. In the first place, policies, personnel, and the allocation of resources for public universities are largely controlled by the national or provincial governments, so that disaffection on such grounds almost automatically becomes a political—even a presidential—concern. Second, the politicization of the students, and especially of their leadership, frequently leads them to take up issues beyond university life, or to interpret university issues in such terms. Anti-imperialism and the purported foreign influence in Colombian universities are frequent themes, as are increases in bus fares (which directly affect the mostly commuter students).

The causes of "direct action politics" and political radicalism among Colombian students, as among Latin American students generally, seem to be several: the image of the student in the society, that is, the expectations held both by students and by the public regarding their special status; their role as future leaders; the character of the university experience, which in many respects (part-time professors, inadequate facilities, outmoded curricula, and the like) frustrates the students' desire for an effective education; and the gap between students' ideals and expectations and the career opportunities open to them (especially those from the lower middle class) in a highly stratified society.[40] The rigidities and nonprogrammatic nature of Colombia's two established parties, accentuated by the institutionalized bipartisanship of the National Front and its aftermath, have undoubtedly added to the feelings of frustration.[41]

For all the militance of Colombian students (or at least the activists among them) since the 1960s, they have been notably unsuccessful in creating a powerful national organization. A number of efforts have been made and some, such as the National Federation of University Students (FUN), founded in 1963, have had some sporadic successes. Regional and political divisions have always plagued them, however. Student organization has tended to center on the individual universities (or faculties thereof). Often the de facto leadership of Colombian students as a whole has devolved on the Superior Student Council at the National University in Bogotá.

Government repression has also helped to damage the viability of Colombian student organizations. Several times since the 1960s the army or the police have invaded university campuses to arrest student leaders or to close down a university in response to student actions. Attendant clashes, as at the University del Valle in 1971, have resulted in a number of casualties. Student leaders are frequently expelled for their disruptive actions.[42]

More than any other group in recent Colombian politics, with the possible exception of teachers and of course the guerrillas (many of whom are former students), university students have been the most militant in their opposition to government and its policies. They have been the most prone to strikes and protest demonstrations, the most inclined toward radical ideologies, and the least co-optable by government or the traditional parties.[43] The government can never wholly ignore their potential for mobilization and "direct action" politics in key urban centers, including the capital. Student political behavior readily lends support to the dictum that in developing societies "the city is the center of opposition within the country; the middle class is the focus of opposition within the city; the intelligentsia is the most active oppositional group within the middle class; and the students (or at least the activists among them) are the most coherent and effective revolutionaries within the intelligentsia."[44]

Yet, except for the "days of May" of 1957, when students found common cause with the civilian elites seeking to overthrow the regime of General Rojas Pinilla, their attempts to join (or lead) others in opposition have proved sporadic and impermanent. Their actions have at times added to an air of political tension, or momentarily added weight to a strike of teachers or workers. But lacking any broad-based movement generated elsewhere to which they could attach themselves, they have remained gadflies—and perhaps reflective of a certain discontent among the urban middle class from which most of them derive—rather than central actors in the political system. Their principal social function may be to serve as critics of the status quo in a society where such opposition is frequently co-opted by government or the traditional parties, and where parties critical of the established order have been uncommonly weak.

INTERNATIONAL ACTORS

All political systems, of whatever description or location, are to some degree penetrated by actors from beyond their borders, whether those actors be multinational corporations; foreign governments and their agents, emissaries, and resources; international agencies and their advisers or representatives; or political parties, labor unions, churches, or guerrilla organizations with supranational linkages. The difference between the countries of Latin America and others of the Third World, on the one hand, and nations like the United States and the Soviet Union, on the other, is that a number of factors, including a relative dearth of resources, relatively lower levels of institutional development, and even the circumstances and timing of historical processes such as industrialization, make the former much more vulnerable to the intrusion of such actors into their domestic politics and less able to have a similar impact on the politics of other nations.

Preeminent among the wide variety of foreign actors with a significant impact on Colombian politics has been the government of the United States and its various programs, agencies, and representatives. Its most visible arms have been the embassy in Bogotá, the military and economic aid missions that have from time to time operated within the country, the Peace Corps, and occasional consultative teams (such as advisers on the suppression of the drug traffic). While the United States has been by far the most active and influential foreign government, it is by no means alone. A Chilean mission helped establish the first permanent military academy in Colombia (1907); it had been preceded by a less successful French mission in the 19th century. And the Dutch and British have sent members of their volunteer corps to assist with community development.

Various international agencies have been important actors in the Colombian political arena, notably such economic bodies as the World Bank, the International Monetary Fund (IMF), the Interamerican Development Bank, and the International Labor Organization. One consequence of Colombia's ties to such organizations has been the formation of a "transnational technocratic elite" of Colombians with experience in both national and international posts; its members have often served as interpreters and legitimizers of the policies of the international agencies in Colombian policy debates.[45]

Transnational corporations and private banks have had a similar influence in the sense that, besides the potential impact of economic decisions made by parent firms located abroad, the Colombians among their top management can represent the views of their companies within the Colombian political process. The Colombian government has on occasion found it convenient to involve foreign corporations in its economic development projects. For some years after 1951, when Exxon's oil concession reverted to the Colombian state, there was a close advisory relationship between Exxon and the newly formed Colombian Petroleum Enterprise (ECOPETROL). And during the early 1980s a subsidiary of Exxon entered into a joint venture with the Colombian Coal Company (CARBOCOL) to develop large coal reserves in the El Cerrejón area of northeastern Colombia.

Still other international actors with important influences on Colombian political processes have included private (mostly U.S., but some western European) foundations and universities, the Vatican, the government of Cuba (through training and other assistance to guerrilla groups),[46] and Colombia's colleagues (Venezuela, Ecuador, Peru, and Bolivia) in the regional economic organization called the Andean Pact.

Finally, a number of Colombia's domestic political actors receive financial, advisory, or other support or direction from abroad. These obviously include the Church, some businesses and banks, and guerrilla movements (to a varying and debatable extent). They also include however, both the CTC and the UTC, both of which have been members of the Interamerican Regional Organization of Workers (ORIT) and the International Confederation of Free Trade Unions (ICFTU), and have received modest levels of financial support and leadership training from them or from their affiliated unions in other countries. The peasant organization ANUC also received material support from external sources such as the World Council of Churches and the government of Sweden, which was a matter of considerable controversy within the organization.[47]

The arenas of influence of such international actors have included macroeconomic policy and capital investment, the professionalization of the military (including its doctrines and tactics), education,[48] community development, the Church, the labor movement, social security legislation, transportation policy, agrarian reform, and a great many more. Most such influences are confined to specific institutions or policy sectors. However, such arenas as development planning and macroeconomic policy are clearly broader in scope, while policies of the U.S. government (counterinsurgency training for the military, for example, and the Alliance for Progress) may be quite explicitly directed at political stability or the survival of a particular regime (for instance, the National Front).[49]

International actors are, then, in all their variety, a collectively important component of the Colombian political process. Yet it would be a considerable misconception to regard them—or any segment of them, such as the U.S. government or the IMF—as somehow determining the course of Colombian politics. They are, in the first place, hardly monolithic in their impact, sometimes differing among themselves (even as among agencies of the same government) or over time in the policies they seek to pursue.[50] Most important, there are quite real barriers thrown up by other actors or aspects of Colombian society and politics that often prevent the adoption or implementation of the preferences of even powerful international actors. When in 1975 President López Michelsen asked the Agency for International Development mission to withdraw from Colombia, he eliminiated an important source of leverage for the U.S. government. And in 1966 President Lleras Restrepo successfully resisted the IMF's pressures for devaluation of the peso, thereby strengthening his domestic prestige into the bargain.[51] As one knowledgeable Colombian commented:

> [My impression of the relationship between international agencies and Colombian government officials] is of a mixture of successes and

failures; of agreement and conflict; of actions and omissions; of trust and distrust; of effective, impossible and difficult alliances; of incomprehension, of rejection, failure, coolness and enthusiasm. In short, the interaction among these actors in the political process doesn't appear to be . . . that of a uniform, unilinear, stable, invariable relationship, but, rather, a relationship subject to the interplay of personalities, of opportunities, of inescapable exigencies that create a [very] complex relationship. . . .[52]

While international actors play a prominent part in Colombia's internal political life, they are merely one set of actors among many (admittedly of unequal weight) rather than a necessarily predominant or controlling one.

CONCLUSION

The array of Colombia's political actors—parties and guerrilla groups included—does indeed constitute a kind of "living museum," forming a political system where new actors are added to old without replacing them or the particular political resources they employ in the political arena. The political currency of some is economic power; of others, armed force; of others, the ability to mobilize or stir constituents; of still others, the capacity to strike or demonstrate.[53]

Is Colombia in the end, though, a society whose interest-group structures and behavior can be described as pluralist or corporatist? If pluralism signifies free and voluntary association independent of restriction (or support) by the state, without structured association with the state, Colombia is clearly far from purely pluralist. The constraints of *personería jurídica* (even though not always invoked) and other restrictions on group organization and behavior, the initiatives of the state in organizing or subsidizing certain groups, and the structured interrelationships between government and a variety of political actors argue otherwise.

And if corporatism means a system of representation whereby the state officially sanctions an array of legally prescribed, noncompetitive interest associations, controlled and subsidized by the state, Colombia only very partially fits this pattern. A number of groups have been organized outside the purview of the state, state subsidies are limited and sometimes absent, and competing groups often operate within the same arena (as with labor, peasant, financial, and some agricultural associations). There is also considerable intergroup dialogue apart from government structures.

Such a conceptualization ignores other important distinctions. On the one hand, there are the mass organizations that the state seeks to co-opt in order to constrain their potential threat to the system or to mobilize them on behalf of its programs. They tend to be the groups, like workers or peasants, weakest in organization and resources. In contrast with this "state corporatism" there is a second subspecies, "societal corporatism," found more often in western Europe, that entails the penetration of the state by interest groups.[54] FEDECAFE is the clearest Colombian instance. The pervasiveness of group membership on the boards of governmental agencies and on special commissions is another. Although this variety of corporatism may be most clearly applicable to producers' associations or the Church, labor and peasant representatives are also members of such boards and commissions. Still other actors do not readily fit either category of corporatism, or do so in very special ways. These include the military, the Church, and especially the various international actors that appear to lie outside any of the common conceptualizations of state-group relationships.

Altogether, then, while Colombian politics has a number of corporatist elements, as well as some characteristics of pluralism, it is perhaps best characterized as a case of limited pluralism.[55] Less pluralistic than most democracies, especially in its restriction and co-optation of labor and peasant groups, it is also much less corporatist than Mexico or Brazil. The pattern is on the whole very much in line with the functioning of an elitist quasi democracy.

At the same time, while organized groups have proliferated in number and expanded in political influence in recent decades, adding a new dimension to Colombian politics, it would be highly misleading to suggest that all of Colombian politics is channeled through formal entities with *personería jurídica.* As in any political system, but above all in one where family, patron-client relationships, and cliques have great prominence, informal ties still constitute much of the stuff of real politics. Thus the personal or family ties of the president of a firm to the president of the republic, or their common membership in the Jockey Club, Gun Club, or country clubs, may in a given instance be as, or more, important in the articulation of demands than any institutionalized relationship between an interest-group bureaucracy and a government ministry. Perhaps most important for politics, throughout the society, at the municipal, departmental, and national levels, there are often groups of leaders who confer informally when important decisions are to be made. Some Colombians aver that there is a single peak (*rosca*) of powerful individuals who make the important national decisions. While certainly an exaggeration, such a conception indicates the perceived importance of such groups or networks in Colombian political life.[56]

Finally, there is little question that the pattern of interest articulation in Colombia, whether through informal or more institutionlized channels, overwhelmingly favors those with wealth and status. Producers' associations are generally better organized, with far greater resources, than labor unions or student or peasant organizations. They also have closer interpersonal and class ties to political leaders and are less vulnerable to government repression. Not surprisingly, within the producers' associations the larger firms or owners tend to predominate. The politics of informal cliques also favors elitism. At the same time, nonelite groups, particularly labor unions, do have a measure of structured access to government and do sometimes have an impact on policy, albeit at times through the use of direct action.[57] Almost all groups, even peasants, are to some degree organized and active in the political arena, whether through contacts with congressmen or land invasions. Clearly elitist in nature, the Colombian political system is in some degree genuinely pluralist as well.

Notably, while all organized groups from time to time oppose government policies or the manner of their implementation, since the 1960s most have at moments of crisis supported Colombia's regime of quasi democracy. This has been true for the producers' associations and for the two major labor confederations, as well as for the armed forces, the Church, and most international actors. True, students (the activists among them), some unions, elements of ANUC, and a few dissident priests or army officers have at times appeared to challenge the regime or have called for major structural reforms. So far, most have been marginal to their own groups or institutions, or have been easily contained by government counteraction, whether this be the arrest of student leaders or the dismissal of outspoken military commanders. The increasing militance of students, peasants, and workers over the last several decades, not to mention the simultaneous role expansion on the part of the military, are nonetheless signs that the future stability of the regime can hardly be taken for granted.

NOTES

1. Fabio Hernán Gómez, *Concentración del Poder Económico en Colombia* (Bogotá: Centro de Investigación y Acción Social, 1974), pp. 51–52.

2. Jonathan Hartlyn, "Producer Associations, the Political Regime and Political Processes in Contemporary Colombia" (MS, Vanderbilt University, 1984), p. 16.

3. See, for instance, Pierre Gilhodes, *La Question Agraire en Colombie, 1958–1971* (Paris: Armand Colin, 1974), pts. 1 and 2, passim.

4. John J. Bailey, "Pluralist and Corporatist Dimensions of Interest Representation in Colombia," in James M. Malloy, ed., *Authoritarianism and Corporatism in Latin America* (Pittsburgh: University of Pittsburgh Press, 1977), n. 56. For similar overlap in a more recent cabinet, see *Latin American Regional Reports. Andean Group Report* (London), July 27, 1984, p. 5.

5. Harvey F. Kline, "Interest Groups in the Colombian Congress," *Journal of Interamerican Studies and World Affairs* 16, no. 3 (August 1974): 274–99.

6. Several instances to the contrary are cited in Miguel Urrutia, *Gremios, Política Económica y Democracia* (Bogotá: Fondo Cultural Cafetero, 1983), pp. 42–43.

7. In 1981 President Turbay felt able to ignore the recommendations of a coalition of interest group leaders, the so-called Frente Gremial; see ibid., pp. 162ff.

8. See Bruce M. Bagley, "Political Power, Public Policy and the State in Colombia: Case Studies of the Urban and Agrarian Reforms During the National Front, 1958–1974" (Ph.D. diss., University of California, Los Angeles, 1979), chaps. 4–6.

9. The Bankers Association divided in 1974 with the formation of the National Association of Financial Institutions (ANIF), SAC has over the years spawned a number of specialty associations (beginning with FEDECAFE in 1927), and the cotton growers are divided into a number of sometimes antagonistic local and regional entities. There are also persistent differences between the more traditional landowners and those more inclined to modern commercial agriculture; see Gilhodes, *La Question Agraire*, pts. 1 and 2, passim.

10. Estimates of casualties in the banana workers' strike range from 150 to 1,500; for an authoritative discussion, see J. Fred Rippy, *The Capitalists and Colombia* (New York: Vanguard Press, 1931), pp. 182–88. For histories of the Colombian labor movement through the mid- and late 1960s, respectively, see Miguel Urrutia, *The Development of the Colombian Labor Movement* (New Haven: Yale University Press, 1969); and Daniel Pecaut, *Política y Sindicalismo en Colombia* (Bogotá: La Carreta, 1973).

11. According to official figures of the Ministry of Labor, as cited in María Teresa Herrán, *El Sindicalismo por Dentro y por Fuera* (Bogotá: Editorial La Oveja Negra, 1981), pp. 19–21. Percentages should be taken as rough estimates only. Other, more recent, estimates consider the CSTC to have gained notably in relation to the UTC and perhaps to have surpassed it in the number of affiliated members; *Latin American Weekly Report* (London), March 16, 1984, p. 4.

12. See Jonathan Hartlyn, "Consociational Politics in Colombia: Confronta-

tion and Accommodation in Comparative Perspective" (Ph.D. diss., Yale University, 1981), pp. 351-52; see also Urrutia, *Development of the Colombian Labor Movement*, p. 184.

13. The government can also suspend a union's *personería*. Once granted, however, *personería* is difficult to remove altogether.

14. The consequences of illegal strikes can include the freezing of union funds and permission for an employer to dismiss union leaders. Illegal strikes, especially among public service workers, are nonetheless numerous.

15. See Gustavo Gallón Giraldo, *Quince Años de Estado de Sitio en Colombia: 1958-1978* (Bogotá: Editorial América Latina, 1979).

16. See Bailey, "Pluralist and Corporatist Dimensions," pp. 288–89, for an illustrative list of private representatives on the boards of public corporations; see also Herrán, *El Sindicalismo*, chap. 13.

17. For examples of some of these, see Bailey, "Pluralist and Corporatist Dimensions," p. 284; see also Herrán, *El Sindicalismo*, chap. 3.

18. For the distinction between political bargaining and collective bargaining, and the predominance of the latter in Colombia, at least until recently, see Urrutia, *Development of the Colombian Labor Movement*; and James L. Payne, *Patterns of Conflict in Colombia* (New Haven: Yale University Press, 1968), pp. 254–86.

19. See John J. Bailey, "Bureaucratic Politics and Social Security Policy in Colombia," *Inter-American Economic Affairs* 29, no. 4 (Spring 1976): 16–18, for one such successful instance.

20. In late 1977, for example, the leaders of both the UTC and the CTC supported a call for a general strike even while continuing to back one or another of the party candidates for president, each of whom condemned the strike; see Hartlyn, "Consociational Politics," p. 381.

21. Ibid., pp. 359–61. Hartlyn suggests that different levels of labor militancy may account for the military's overthrow of the government in Uruguay (1973) and the failure of the same to occur in Colombia.

22. Urrutia, *Development of the Colombian Labor Movement*, p. 133; Bagley, "Political Power, Public Policy and the State," p. 193n.

23. The following discussion of Acción Comunal relies largely on Bruce M. Bagley, "The State and the Peasantry in Contemporary Colombia" (paper prepared for the annual meeting of the Latin American Studies Association, March 1982); and Bruce Bagley and Matthew Edel, "Popular Mobilization Programs of the National Front: Co-optation and Radicalization," in R. Albert Berry, Ronald G. Hellman, and Mauricio Solaún, eds., *Politics of Compromise* (New Brunswick, N.J.: Transaction Books, 1980), pp. 257–84.

24. Bagley, "State and Peasantry," p. 21; see also Bagley and Edel, "Popular Mobilization Programs," pp. 269–70. For a similar conclusion, see Elisabeth Ungar, "La Organización Popular y los Servicios Públicos: Política de Concertación o Política de Confrontación? El Case de Acción Comunal," *Carta Financiera* (Bogotá) no. 49 (April-June 1981): 217–31. Ungar also notes (p. 229) that AC's satisfaction of immediate needs has tended to preempt redistributional claims.

25. The following discussion of ANUC derives largely from Bagley, "State and Peasantry"; and Bagley and Edel, "Popular Mobilization Programs." The

usuarios (users) were those campesinos who benefited from, or made use of, government agrarian services.

26. See Anthony Maingot, "Colombia," in Lyle N. McAlister et al., *The Military in Latin American Sociopolitical Evolution: Four Case Studies* (Washington, D.C.: Center for Research in Social Systems, 1970), pp. 127–95, for a detailed history of the Colombian military. For the size of the military at various points during the 19th century, plus comparisons with Ecuador and Peru, see Payne, *Patterns of Conflict*, pp. 119–21.

27. As of 1932 the Colombian army remained the smallest in the western hemisphere in proportion to population; J. León Helguera, "The Changing Role of the Military in Colombia," *Journal of Inter-American Studies* 3, no. 3 (July 1961): 352–53.

28. Maingot, "Colombia," p. 127 and n. 4.

29. For this argument applied specifically to Colombia, see Payne, *Patterns of Conflict*, chap. 7; for a general argument along similar lines, see Eric Nordlinger, *Soldiers in Politics* (Englewood Cliffs, N.J.: Prentice-Hall, 1977).

30. For this period of Colombian military development, see in particular Francisco Leal Buitrago, "Política e Intervención Militar en Colombia," in Rodrigo Parra Sandoval, ed., *Dependencia Externa y Desarrollo Político en Columbia* (Bogotá: Imprenta Nacional, 1970), pp. 178–79.

31. Retired General Valencia ran an independent campaign for president in 1978 but received only 1.3 percent of the vote.

32. *Latin America Weekly Report*, February 3, 1984, p. 5, and February 17, 1984, p. 7. In the wake of Landazábal's removal, the CONFECORE (Confederation of Retired Officers) spoke out in agreement with him, thus effectively circumventing the ban on political statements by serving officers; *Latin America Weekly Report*, March 16, 1984, p. 12.

33. By 1980 the Colombian military numbered some 65,000 men, 55,000 of whom were in the army. The national police, under military control since 1960, numbered another 50,000; Daniel L. Premo, "The Colombian Armed Forces in Search of a Mission," in Robert Wesson, ed., *New Military Politics in Latin America* (New York: Praeger, 1982), p. 173. In comparison with most other major Latin American countries, Colombia's military remained small and underfinanced, especially given its problems with internal order; J. Mark Ruhl, *Colombia: Armed Forces and Society* (Syracuse, N.Y.: Syracuse University, Maxwell School of Citizenship and Public Affairs, 1980), p. 31.

34. Howard I. Blutstein et al., *Area Handbook for Colombia* (Washington, D.C.: U.S. Government Printing Office, 1977), pp. 134–35. In the mid-1970s all but 5–6 percent of diocesan priests were Colombian, although more than a third of male religious in orders were non-Colombian (mostly Spanish). There were almost 18,000 female members of religious orders divided among nearly 90 religious communities. According to Alexander W. Wilde, "A Traditional Church and Politics: Colombia" (Ph.D. diss., Columbia University, 1971), p. 164, Colombia has the largest number of nuns in proportion to population of any country in Latin America.

35. J. Lloyd Mecham, *Church and State in Latin America* (Chapel Hill: University of North Carolina Press, 1934), p. 141; see Wilde, "A Traditional Church," for a somewhat more balanced judgment.

36. For some striking comparisons between the Colombian and Venezuelan churches, see Daniel H. Levine, *Religion and Politics in Latin America* (Princeton: Princeton University Press, 1981); and his "Church Elites in Venezuela and Colombia: Context, Background and Beliefs," *Latin American Research Review* 14, no. 1 (1979): 51–79.

37. Blutstein et al., *Area Handbook*, p. 139.

38. Daniel H. Levine and Alexander W. Wilde report in "The Catholic Church, Politics and Violence: The Colombian Case," *The Review of Politics* 39, no. 2 (April 1977): 235, that fewer than 20 percent of Colombia's bishops sanctioned direct political and social action by the clergy on behalf of social change. According to the *Encyclopedia of the Third World* (New York: Facts on File, 1978), vol. 1, p. 320, some 10 percent of Colombia's priests belong to radical clerical groups. In the face of pressure from the Church hierarchy, the Golconda Group went out of existence after two years, although it has had several successors; see Kenneth N. Medhurst, *The Church and Labour in Colombia* (Manchester: Manchester University Press, 1984), pp. 195–96.

39. See Levine and Wilde, "The Catholic Church, Politics and Violence," for a good discussion of this general point.

40. See E. Wight Bakke and Mary S. Bakke, *Campus Challenge: Student Activism in Perspective* (Hamden, Conn.: Archon Books, 1971), pp. 383–91.

41. Francisco Leal Buitrago, "La Frustración Política de una Generación. La Universidad Colombiana y la Formación de un Movimiento Estudiantil 1958–1967," *Desarrollo y Sociedad* no. 6 (July 1981): 299–325 stresses this point.

42. For details and examples of student militance and government counteraction, see ibid.; see also Gallón Giraldo, *Quince Años*, passim.

43. According to a 1935 law, two students could be elected to the University Council of the National University, which included seven other members. Following a confrontation with students in 1969, President Lleras Restrepo abolished student elections for the university council; see Bakke and Bakke, *Campus Challenge*, p. 144.

44. Samuel Huntington, *Political Order in Changing Societies* (New Haven: Yale University Press, 1968), p. 290.

45. See Fernando Cepeda Ulloa and Christopher Mitchell, "The Trend Towards Technocracy: The World Bank and the International Labor Organization in Colombian Politics," in Berry et al., *Politics of Compromise*, p. 240.

46. Bagley, "The State and the Peasantry," pp. 71–72, offers a rather skeptical view of the extent of Cuban assistance to Colombian guerrilla groups.

47. For labor see Urrutia, *Development of the Colombian Labor Movement*, p. 215n; and Medhurst, *The Church and Labour*, p. 157; for peasants see Bagley, "The State and the Peasantry," p. 44.

48. During the National Front years several international agencies and foreign governments selected Colombia as a "showcase" of educational innovation

and poured tens of millions of dollars into the country for the purpose; see Robert F. Arnove, "Education Policies of the National Front," in Berry et al., *Politics of Compromise*, pp. 381–411, passim.

49. See, for example, U.S. Senate, Subcommittee on American Republic Affairs, Committee on Foreign Relations, 91st Congress, 1st Session, *Colombia – A Case History of U.S. Aid* (Washington, D.C.: U.S. Government Printing Office, 1969).

50. In 1981, at the initiative of the World Bank, the Colombian government hired a team of international consultants to help the National Coal Company (CARBOCOL) keep Exxon "honest" in their joint collaboration on developing a new coalfield; Harvey F. Kline, *Colombia: Portrait of Unity and Diversity* (Boulder, Colo.: Westview Press, 1983), p. 136.

51. Richard L. Maullin, *The Colombia-IMF Disagreement of November– December 1966: An Interpretation of Its Place in Colombian Politics* (Santa Monica, Calif.: RAND Corp., 1967); see also Cepeda and Mitchell, "The Trend Towards Technocracy," concerning the respective successes and failures of the International Labor Organization in Colombia.

52. Fernando Cepeda Ulloa, "La Influencia de las Agencias Internacionales en el Proceso de Desarrollo de Colombia, 1950–1974," *Estudios Internacionales* (Santiago) 11, no. 43 (July–September 1978): 59; for a comparable view see Richard A. Hartwig, *Roads to Reason: Transportation, Administration and Rationality in Colombia* (Pittsburgh: University of Pittsburgh Press, 1983), pp. 17–18.

53. For this conceptualization of Latin American politics, see Charles W. Anderson, *Politics and Economic Change in Latin America* (Princeton: D. Van Nostrand, 1967), chap. 4.

54. For this distinction between types of corporatism, see Philippe Schmitter, "Still the Century of Corporatism?" in Fredrick B. Pike and Thomas Stritch, eds., *The New Corporatism: Social-Political Structures in the Iberian World* (Notre Dame, Ind.: University of Notre Dame Press, 1974), pp. 85–131.

55. See Bailey, "Pluralist and Corporatist Dimensions." Bailey notes (p. 27) that Laureano Gómez's proposals for a corporatist state in the 1950s proved to be a minority position within the minority party.

56. See Edwin G. Corr, *The Political Process in Colombia* (Denver: University of Denver, 1972), pp. 44–51, for an incisive discussion of the role of informal groups in the Colombian political process.

57. In fact, Miguel Urrutia argues that the threat of a general strike may well receive greater attention from the government than the plaints of the producers' associations. In just such an instance in 1981, President Turbay agreed to parley with the labor confederations while refusing to receive representatives of the producers' Frente Gremial; *Gremios*, pp. 166–68.

7

GOVERNMENT INSTITUTIONS

As Jacques Lambert suggested some years ago, Latin American polities are probably best classed not as presidential, but as systems of presidential dominance,[1] since at least in practice they eschew the sort of balance of power among the three separate branches of government that characterizes the archetypal case of presidentialism, that of the United States. Colombia has largely shared that pattern of presidential dominance, despite some periods of attempted executive constraint. Generally speaking, the president's formal and informal strength has been far greater than that of Congress or the judiciary, while departmental (provincial) and local governments have in the last analysis been dependent on him. Nonetheless, there are some real restraints on presidential powers. In fact, in comparative perspective, the limits on presidential domination have been historically greater in Colombia than in almost any other Latin American country.

Historically dominant in comparison with the other institutions of government, but at the same time traditionally weak in its ability to effect policy and carry out its decisions, the Colombian presidency has undergone some important changes since the mid-1930s, and notably since the late 1960s. Such changes suggest that the presidency is becoming even more dominant and the state stronger.

THE ROOTS OF PRESIDENTIAL DOMINANCE

The difference between presidential dominance and a presidential system like that of the United States is of course a distinction of degree rather than of kind, and subject in any political system to the vagaries of presidential personality and political circumstance. Nevertheless, presidential dominance is manifest in the authority that the Colombian constitution (in common with most other Latin American constitutions) grants the chief executive. As one Colombian legal scholar has put it, "In Colombia the president is almost the whole state."[2]

Colombia had 10 constitutions during its first 75 years of independent life, beginning with that of 1811. Some of these gave considerable power to the central government and to the president; others were highly federal—even confederal—in nature and tended to weaken the power of the president (by limiting him to a two-year term, for example). The last of these ten constitutions, that of 1886, is still in force, albeit with major amendments or "codifications."[3] That constitution establishes Colombia as both unitary in form and distinctly presidential.

Under the constitution of 1886 the president's appointive powers are much more extensive than those in the U.S.-style presidency. The president can appoint cabinet ministers and most other high officials, including the heads of the "decentralized institutes," without the approval of either house of Congress. Since the system of government is unitary rather than federal, the president appoints the departmental governors (who in turn appoint the mayors of *municipios*),[4] thus giving the president direct and indirect control over positions high and low throughout the national, departmental, and even municipal bureaucracies. Additional appointive authority accrues to the president through the extensive government intervention in the economy and in other aspects of national life (such as, education) either directly or through his ministers or governors.

Authority to issue decree-laws or decrees with the force of law is likewise considerable. The constitution gives Colombia's Congress authority (not infrequently exercised) to grant the president extraordinary powers for specified periods "when necessity demands it or the public convenience advises it" (Article 76). In addition, it is common for Congress to pass laws in quite general terms, thus granting the president unusually broad power (compared with the United States) to implement the legislation by decree. The executive's powers are further enhanced by his constitutional authority to declare certain matters "urgent," thus requiring priority congressional attention

(Article 91), and by the stipulation that cabinet ministers shall participate in congressional debates (Article 134).

Provision for the presidential assumption of extraordinary power in crisis situations is also a prominent part of the Colombian constitution, as it is in the rest of Latin America. Article 121 permits the president to declare the public order disturbed in all or part of the country and to issue the requisite decrees, as well as to suspend (though not rescind) existing laws. Every administration since World War II has found it either necessary or convenient to invoke a state of siege over all or part of the country, for all or part of its term in office, in the name of countering rural violence, domestic unrest, or the traffic in drugs.[5]

Yet another constitutional provision, Article 122, added in 1968, grants the president authority to declare an economic emergency, thus not requiring him to declare or prolong a state of siege for the purpose, and permitting him to legislate by decree (subject to subsequent congressional oversight), though such authority is limited to 90 days a year. Article 122 has since been invoked to decree significant legislative changes, such as President López Michelsen's tax reforms in 1974.

A final major constitutional basis of presidential authority rests with his control over legislation and the budget. The president has the item veto, and in 1968–a few years before the powers of the U.S. Congress were being strengthened with regard to the budget–the budgetary controls of the Colombian Congress, as well as those over credit and over the national debt, were being loosened. Thus Congress can reduce the executive's proposed budget but cannot add to it without government assent. Likewise, in 1968 the authorization for Congress to mandate specific public works was eliminated and a more general supervisory clause substituted; the result was to weaken somewhat one of congressmen's principal claims to the support of their local constituents.

In short, in such crucial areas as appointments, decree-laws, emergency powers, legislation, and the budget the Colombian president clearly has greater constitutional authority within his political system than the president of the United States has within his.

The real sources of presidential power in Colombia nevertheless lie deeper than constitutional authority. One such source is Colombian political culture. One study suggests that early socialization patterns place constraints on the extent to which Colombians perceive the relevance of impersonal institutions for problem solving and task management. This may partially explain the relative weakness of Congress and the comparative strength of the obviously more personalized presidency in Colombia.[6] In fact, the entire tradition inherited from the Spanish imperial system, including its emphasis on administrative and civil law, provides the cultural and historical underpinning for the nature of Colombia's republican presidency.

Perhaps even more important are the structural reasons for presidential dominance. In Colombia, as in most developing societies, the budget of the central government and the jobs government can provide are critical to the well-being of a great many people. In a society where status has traditionally accrued to governmental rather than to commercial employment, where socially acceptable jobs in the private sector have (at least until recently) not been very numerous, and where the system of spoils and patronage prevails, the president's constitutional authority looms as that much more important. The fact that societies like Colombia's are relatively so vulnerable or dependent on the international environment, and on economic and other factors beyond the confines of their own boundaries, similarly gives the government, and with it the chief executive, an unusually critical role. In short, in developing societies generally, where other structures or networks of relationships are weak or inadequate to integrate the society, the president, as head of government, tends to assume an importance compared with other institutions that is markedly greater than in the more developed nations.

The fact that the president is commander in chief of the armed forces and of other security services is yet another source of presidential power. To be sure, the constitution in any presidential system, including that of the United States, customarily gives the president this authority. The distinction in Colombia and comparable Latin American nations is that the armed forces, by custom and function, play a different role than they do in North America. Except nominally, they have usually played an insignificant role in external defense. Rather, their preeminent role has been one of internal security. As long as the president can retain the political loyalty or at least neutrality of the military—and most especially if the country is under a state of siege in which some of the normal constitutional inhibitions on governmental action are suspended—he has a weapon that can be formidable indeed. This has been particularly evident in

Colombia since the early 1950s, when politically derived violence has seemed almost endemic.

The executive branch has been strengthened in recent years by the emergence of a group of technocrats (*técnicos*)—economists, agronomists, engineers, and the like—who have come to staff such important government organs as the National Planning Department, the Monetary Council, and the Colombian Institute for Agrarian Reform (INCORA). These technocrats have goals and attitudes that contrast markedly with those of most Colombian *politicos*. Many have advanced degrees from foreign universities, and in their careers move readily among government, the university, and business. Their goals tend to be those of development and policy enactment, not partisan or factional or regional enhancement, and they are on the whole younger than executives in the private sector.[7] They provide a reservoir of expertise that enhances presidential capabilities in such complex areas as modern economics, and that both supports and helps to generate presidential initiatives in areas of social reform. In some ministries and agencies, they tend to form a barrier between the demands of interest groups and direct access to the more politically attuned ministers or to the president.

Concomitant with the growth of technocracy has been the increasing institutionalization of the office of the presidency. Early in the National Front years, the National Planning Department was created to help the president formulate economic plans and to assist in the coordination of policy in the increasingly multiheaded bureaucracy. Its staff has expanded over the years, and some presidents have used it quite effectively to strengthen both the presidency and the state. There is also the National Council of Social and Economic Policy (CONPES), whose membership includes the president, several of the economic ministers, the foreign minister, the manager of the Banco de la República, and the head of the National Planning Department. Among its purposes is supposedly the coordination of economic policy. Frequent turnover in personnel in both the Planning Department and CONPES, and the varying commitments of successive presidents to planning and coordination, have nonetheless often detracted from the purported functions of both bodies.[8] Finally, the president can use his control of his party or faction, or threats to restructure the factional composition of the governing coalition, to bring Congress into line.

There are, then, a variety of factors, reflected in the provisions of the Colombian constitution and deeply rooted in the political culture and nature of the political system, that help to make the Colombian presidency predominant among the institutions of government. Many of these factors are similarly evident in other Latin American countries, where presidential predominance is also the norm.

LIMITS ON PRESIDENTIAL POWER: INSTITUTIONAL CHECKS

Nonetheless, the president is far from all-powerful; in fact, from the beginning the constraints on Colombian presidents have generally been greater than in most other Latin American countries.

In the first place, as is true of most of Latin America, presidents cannot constitutionally succeed themselves after their four-year terms, although in Colombia they may do so after an intervening term, as former president Alfonso López Michelsen (1974–78) sought unsuccessfully to do in 1982. Nor has the president generally been able to play a determining role in choosing his successor. He is also limited by the constitutional stipulation that, following the end of the National Front, he give due representation in his cabinet to the principal minority party (Article 120). There are also some rather explicit limits on the president's powers under the state of siege or emergency, even if in practice they have often had limited meaning. The civil rights (free press, free speech, and so on) enumerated in the constitution place further legal constraints on government; certain social guarantees, such as protection of labor, are also spelled out.

Exceptionally in Latin America, there has been a functioning bicameral Congress throughout most of Colombia history. It by no means compares with, say, the U.S. Congress in its impact on legislation or in its ability to check presidential power. Its Colombian critics (and they are many) regard it as ineffectual. Yet it does perform some important functions in the Colombian political system.

Terms for both senators and members of the House of Representatives are four years. Since Colombia is not a federal system, members of both houses are selected on the basis of population; the only difference between them is size. Each Colombian department has a minimum of two senators, plus an additional one for each 200,000 population; the constitution also allots two House members to each department, plus an additional one for each 100,000 persons.

Elected at the same time are alternates (*suplentes*) equal to the number of legislators on each party's (or faction's) list; they take the place of a legislator whenever the latter chooses not to occupy his seat. This occurs rather frequently, since congressmen seem to be more interested in being in Congress than in serving in a relatively powerless body, and because some congressmen simultaneously hold office (legally) in departmental assemblies, municipal councils, or even the executive branch.[9]

Congressional powers are hardly insignificant. In fact, there have been several instances in Colombia's history when former presidents have been placed on trial before Congress or the Senate for their actions while in office; the most recent of these was Rojas Pinilla's conviction for malfeasance in 1959. Likewise, since Colombia has no vice-president, Congress every two years elects a *designado*, a person designated to take the president's place in the case of the latter's absence or resignation; that person may hold some other position in government at the same time.

Congress's powers to interpellate government ministers and other officials makes the executive aware that its performance is open to institutionalized scrutiny, and therefore presumably affects the president's behavior and that of his officials. INCORA has been a particular target of this kind of oversight.

Of generally greater significance, Congress has often been able to delay, reject, or otherwise thwart the legislative initiatives of the president—although seldom has it been able to exercise its own initiative with regard to major legislation. Thus Congress was able to stall, and in the process to modify, a major agrarian reform bill, finally passed late in 1961, for well over a year, and to do much the same with respect to the 1968 constitutional reform. It has generally frustrated further attempts at (modest) agrarian reform in the years since, and has so far impeded attempts at a comprehensive urban reform, despite the efforts of several presidents. Congress does not necessarily have to reject the president's proposals to accomplish such an end; perhaps more often, it merely fails to act. Two of the strongest, most reform-minded presidents in modern Colombian history—Alfonso López Pumarejo (1934–38, 1942–45) and Carlos Lleras Restrepo (1966–70)—have had to threaten resignation, and thus a crisis in the system, in order to get key legislation passed.

Legislation, however, is not Congress's strongest suit. It rather readily grants broad powers to the president (in the event he does not assume them himself under Article 121 or 122). Congress has in fact often failed to exercise powers it has been expressly granted, such as the right to veto foreign loans; it was many years before it constituted a commission to participate in the process of economic planning as envisioned by the 1968 constitutional reform. Congress has little staff; the standing committees seldom meet and do not use subcommittees. Congressional absenteeism is chronic, and turnover in office has been very rapid.[10] Acquisition of specialized knowledge with which to confront the bureaucracy is therefore very difficult.

In any case, congressmen have seldom been much interested in the making of laws. Their reason for being seems largely, in their own view, to assure that their particular localities or departments receive their due share of the material largesse that the government budget has to distribute. Thus a frustrated President Lleras Restrepo complained at one point, "Not a single executive bill has been passed by Congress, while in four months of government I have had to sign numerous regional aid laws . . . which if totaled up would represent the national budget for ten to twenty years."[11]

Whereas Congress is highly unrepresentative in terms of education and occupation, it is representative in terms of geography. In fact, the Colombian Congress has been adjudged more regionalist in orientation than the legislature of either the United States or Canada.[12] Congressmen also serve a vital brokerage role between their constitutents and government agencies and offices in Bogotá. Congress has thus served "as a key political institution in the territorial and political integration of the country by providing a forum where regional politicians interact and relate to political party and governmental activity."[13] In addition, the composition of the Congress tends somewhat to overrepresent the economically deprived departments (in contrast with the cabinet and the executive branch generally), thus providing something of a balance in this respect in the Colombian political system.[14] Indeed, even while municipal and departmental governments tend to be weak and to lack adequate resources to carry out their functions, one of the major activities of these levels of government is to serve as petitioners and brokers between local interests and a highly centralized government. Their representatives are among those having the most frequent contact with congressmen.[15] By the same token, the inadequacy of municipal financial resources leads to a dependence on Congress for subventions and subsidies for local projects.

In addition, Congress serves as a key arena in the battle among political parties (and factions of parties), with those left out of the government coalition seeking to use the congressional forum to harass the president either in preparation for future electoral battles or as a device to force upon him their claims to greater patronage. In fact, when Congress does finally act on an important piece of legislation, it is because leaders of the various parties and factions, who often are not congressmen, have come to an understanding. It is therefore the parties, as much as the executive, that circumscribe Congress's legislative role. Thus, "legislative conflict [during the National Front] did not revolve so much around specific governmental policies related to economic and social matters. Rather, it centered on legislative action directly affecting *el país político* – that is, politically strategic measures impinging upon the perceived growth or survival of political parties or factions thereof."[16] Although the artificial constraints of the National Front might have heightened such tendencies, much the same could be said of congressional behavior since the formal end of the Front. For instance, Congress proved willing to pass the core of President Betancur's economic program while it resisted the president's proposals concerning campaign financing.

Last—and its importance is not to be overlooked—the existence of Congress and the regularity of its convening (at present 150 days a year plus any extraordinary sessions) throughout most of Colombia's history have served a legitimating function for the country's version of democracy, a function that only a few other Latin American congresses have performed so consistently (Costa Rica's, Chile's and Uruguay's before 1973, and perhaps Brazil's come to mind).

Rather than in the passing of laws or the occasional spectacular callings to account of ex-presidents, the principal functions of Colombia's Congress therefore lie in such areas as regional representation and national integration, political criticism and government oversight, and legitimation.

The Supreme Court plays a relatively minor role in constraining presidential power in Colombia; thus it was unable (or unwilling) to do much to prevent the breakdown of democratic institutions in the years after 1949. Thus, too, it has generally interpreted its role with respect to the state of siege as the review of the legality of the procedures for its declaration, rather than of the substance of the decrees issued under it. This is not just a matter of personal or institutional timidity, but a seeming recognition of the fact that, in a country prone to crises of internal order, only the president can act to ensure the system's survival. In the economic arena the Court has generally given the president considerable leeway under Article 122, quite possibly because it has recognized that Congress has become a redoubt of established economic interests and that only executive action to further development objectives can save the system.[17]

Still, the Court is not wholly irrelevant as a check on the executive. Its members serve for life and since 1958 have been selected by the Court itself on the basis of parity between the parties, thus giving it a measure of independence. It has the power to rule on the legality of presidential decrees and on the constitutionality of laws. It has in recent years on several notable occasions exercised such powers to discomfit the president. In 1981 the Court ruled the constitutional reform of 1979 (designed to redress to some degree the 1968 enhancement of presidential powers) unconstitutional, thus negating a variety of government actions. Even though President Turbay reacted angrily and there were implied threats against the Court, the decision stood. And early in 1983 the Supreme Court declared unconstitutional aspects of the tax reform decreed by President Betancur under the economic emergency powers of Article 122; the president accepted the decision in accord with "the state of law that reigns in Colombia."[18]

In addition to the Supreme Court, there is the Council of State, which both advises the president on administrative matters (even drafting bills relating to administrative reform) and acts as the supreme tribunal for a hierarchy of administrative courts where complaints against the government and its officials may be brought. Its members are chosen in the same manner as those of the Supreme Court.

The most important constraints on the presidency, though, are political in both the broad and the narrow senses. Potentially powerful interests can have an important impact on policy, and of course they may also be mobilized on behalf of presidential policies. At the extreme and especially, though not exclusively, in the case of the military, they can pose a threat to a president's survival in office. The play of party and factional politics can also effectively limit a president's ability to achieve his goals. While personal, factional, and party loyalties often enable a president to mobilize others behind his programs in Congress or elsewhere, this is far from certain; they can just as readily generate "opposition for opposition's sake." The president is not necessarily able to control even his own party, and congressional discipline has varied in effectiveness. Even the president's cabinet ministers—whom he is legally free to remove—on occasion pursue policies at odds with those of the president if, by removing a minister, the president might alienate a political faction whose support he needs. In fact, one of the important limitations on the pursuit of presidential program initiatives is the recurrent need to give priority attention to the immediate political concerns and objectives of the various factions. In this sense it might even be said that Colombia bears some resemblance to a multiparty parliamentary system, with the president dependent on assuaging various factions in order to avoid a cabinet crisis.

Without question, then, the president is the key actor in the Colombian political process, but also without question he operates under a number of formal and informal constraints that over time have generally been more meaningful than in the great majority of political systems both in Latin America and in the developing world at large.

LIMITS ON PRESIDENTIAL POWER:
THE BUREAUCRACY

It is of course one thing to be the dominant institution within a political system, as the Colombian presidency tends to be, and another to be able to implement policy and effect one's political will in the society at large. It is in this sense that a president of the United States is usually stronger than a Latin American president, even if he is less dominant over the other institutions in the political system.

To begin with, while the Colombian president has at his disposal a sizable bureaucracy, the appointments to which he substantially controls, its neutrality and effectiveness are often in serious question. Appointments tend to be made with an eye to the partisan allocation of posts, with personnel added, rather than removed and replaced, at least since the onset of the National Front parity arrangement. Many government offices therefore tend to be overstaffed, at least in terms of those who effectively carry out the tasks of the ministry or agency concerned. Loyalties tend to be accorded to persons rather than to institutions in a political culture that stresses the patron-client relationship and other forms of particularistic attachments. Although financial scandals in recent years have touched such figures as the president of the House of Representatives and the comptroller general, government in Colombia is said not to have been particularly corrupt, at least until the advent of the drug trade, and presidents and other high officials have not typically used political office to enhance their fortunes,[19] as is reputedly true in Mexico, for example. Nonetheless, nepotism, *palancas* (connections), petty bribery, and similar means of acquiring private influence and advantage are fairly widespread. The consequence is that the president often has had difficulty in carrying out policies that will serve the general public, as distinct from dispensing favors to particular persons or localities.

A highly legalistic approach, rooted in a lack of mutual trust, also hampers the operations of government. Public officials tend to be held "accountable not for the effective administration of their programs, but rather for conformance to detailed and often time-consuming legal formalities."[20] Red tape abounds, with every official act requiring numerous signatures and seals of approval. Bureaucratic multiplication and complexity may be rooted in the administrative traditions of the Spanish Empire, but they also serve the purposes of expanded political patronage, and of additional income for minor (and greatly underpaid) officials who make it a practice to expedite paperwork for a fee. Such procedures are also inspired by a deep-seated mutual distrust that goes beyond ordinary precautions seeking to prevent misuse of public funds. Conformity, in short, tends to supersede performance. The consequences include the slowing of government operations, a proliferation of government personnel beyond realistic needs, and an encouragement of time-serving and a discouragement of initiative, as well as a search for various informal means of influence as a way to circumvent bureaucratic rigidities.[21] A further result is to promote a general cynicism toward, and lack of confidence in, government.

The rapid turnover of cabinet ministers and other key personnel likewise inhibits governmental performance. Very seldom does a cabinet minister last out a presidential term: more often a given post sees several incumbents come and go during one administration.[22] An established career service might partially compensate for such rapid turnover, as it has in France, for example. But despite sporadic efforts to establish such a service and the founding of the Higher School of Public Administration (ESAP) to train public servants, the results have been minimal. At most some 15 percent of Colombian government employees are part of the civil service,[23] the rest being patronage appointees. In the end, the desire of politicians to have such appointments at their command has usually overridden other concerns. Writing in 1982, a student of Colombian public administration observed, "Today we are farther from the administrative career than in 1960."[24]

In yet another sense the dominance of the president works against his ability to govern effectively. Given the weakness and lack of resources of departmental and municipal governments, and a political culture that eschews the assumption of responsibility at lower levels, there is a tendency to buck even minor decisions toward the top. The president, or at least his ministers, are frequently called upon to mediate workers' or student strikes and the like, with the result that presidential time, energy—and precious political capital—must often be expended on matters that might be handled elsewhere in a less centralized system.

Noncompliance with the law carries forward the tradition of "*se obedece, pero no se cumple*" (one obeys, but does not comply) from the days of royal rule from distant Spain. Tax evasion has been routine, as has a clandestine cross-border trade in coffee, cattle, arms, and, more recently, drugs. Not only can tax collections and economic policy be threatened by such actions but—particularly in the case of drugs, considering the vast amount of wealth involved and the association with violence—the authority of the state can be seriously undermined in certain regions of the country. During the years of *la violencia*, the authority of the state was unable to reach certain parts of the country and was considered illegitimate when it did. Today there are still regions of Colombia's rugged terrain where guerrillas are able to defy government authority, even on occasion briefly occupying a town. The government's frequent resort to the state of siege is yet another reflection of the sometimes tenuous nature of authority in Colombia today.

There is one final sense in which the actions of the Colombian state may be limited: it must function in an international environment of great powers and economic forces over which it can exert little direct influence. Actors such as foreign governments, international banks, and transnational corporations—the decisions of which have a very important impact on Colombian prosperity and even, potentially, on the survival of a government—are substantially, though not entirely, beyond the control of any president.

Taken together, the constraints on governmental effectiveness have an impact on the real exercise of presidential power at least as great as constitutional restrictions or institutional obstacles. There has nonetheless been a tendency for the Colombian state, and with it the presidency, to grow in strength over the last several decades. The process, if a date has to be set, began with the reforms of the *revolución en marcha* in the mid-1930s; it received new life with the onset of the National Front and particularly with the presidency of Carlos Lleras Restrepo and the constitutional reforms of 1968. While the reforms of the 1930s accorded the state an expanded role in the social and economic life of the country, the National Front both enabled the state to regain much of the autonomy and neutrality it had lost to the claims of partisan hegemony, and instituted a number of institutional and policy reforms (the National Planning Office, for example, and the Agrarian Reform Institute) designed to enhance the state's role in development. Lleras's 1968 reforms further strengthened the position of the president and the role of planning.

In yet other ways the process of state growth has been a more or less continuous one since at least the 1930s. Thus a series of decentralized institutes and corporations, now numbering more than 100, has been created to carry out specialized functions and to enable parts of the public administration to operate at least one step removed from the day-to-day play of party politics. Their number more than doubled in the years 1960–75. Considering the high salience of partisan politics in Colombia, a number of them have had a substantial degree of freedom to function on a strictly technical basis, although politics does sometimes intrude.[25] Their directors, though appointed by the president and in most cases nominally responsible to the appropriate minister, answer to boards of directors made up of those groups most directly interested in the area of the agency's jurisdiction. Prominent examples of decentralized institutes include the Institute of Territorial Credit (ICT) in the housing field, the Colombian Institute of Social Security (ICSS), and the Industrial Promotion Institute (IPI). Still others embrace such diverse fields as agricultural research, school construction, and export promotion. There are also regional development corporations, such as the Cauca Valley Corporation (CVC), patterned after the Tennessee Valley Authority in the United States,[26] and a variety of state enterprises, such as the Colombian Petroleum Enterprise (ECOPETROL). These agencies have enabled the Colombian state greatly to expand its role in the country's economic and social life, in the process serving the significant purpose of national integration in an otherwise regionally and socially fragmented society.

In an important sense these institutions strengthen the powers of the central government, and weaken the power of local and departmental governments whose functions and resources they sometimes absorb. The fact remains, however, that the Colombian government is still less directly involved in economic ownership and management than are the governments of most other Latin American countries.

Many factors continue to restrict the effective powers of the president. Nevertheless, it is fair to say that while the Colombian state is not nearly as strong as, say, its Mexican or Brazilian counterpart, it has grown considerably in strength, and in relative autonomy from partisan and group pressures, particularly since the inception of the National Front. Its institutions have taken on more functions and are more expertly staffed. They also more effectively penetrate the society—for instance, in the rural areas, with the Institute of Agrarian Reform, Acción Comunal, and the program of civic-military action of the army. Meanwhile, the augmented capabilities of the government, especially in the economic realm, have helped to reduce Colombia's external dependence.

CONCLUSION

Colombia has shared with much of the democratic world a tendency toward increased executive and state power, and an attendant "decline of the legislature," beginning at least in the 1930s and enhanced significantly by the constitutional reform of 1968. Strongly promoted by President Carlos Lleras Restrepo, this reform signaled a marked shift in the legal basis of the balance of power between Congress and the executive, enhancing the president's power in such areas as the budget and economic planning, and granting him the authority to declare an economic emergency. That the Congress would accept such changes—and that its major preoccupations during the extended debate over the reform centered on certain electoral arrangements having to do with the prospective phasing out of the National Front, rather than on the alteration in that balance[27] —says a great deal about the preexisting realities of power in the Colombian system. A constitutional revision such as that of 1968 would be unthinkable in a presidential system like that of the United States.

Above all, the 1968 reform was an institutionalization of a trend toward an increasing role for the central government in economic planning that had been evident for some time. What the reform did was to narrow the difference between the norms of the system and its actual behavior.

A Colombian president must still mobilize political support and reckon with potential congressional obstruction in order to pursue policy initiatives; the 1968 reform was not sufficient to permit arbitrary rule on his part. Nevertheless, most observers, as well as many congressmen, seem to agree that the reform of 1968 marked a signal decline in the power of the legislature and a corresponding increase in the legal basis of presidential authority.[28] It therefore seems fair to say that both the Colombian state and Colombian presidents have in recent years increased their powers to effect their wills. The result has been to enhance the presidential dominance over the other institutions of government that has long existed, and to counteract somewhat those rather special factors that have made Colombia's dominant president less dominant than in most of the rest of Latin America.

To be sure, there have been some countertrends. For example, in the 1968 reform Congress was granted more explicit and institutionalized review powers over the economic plans of the government. Yet such powers have hardly been utilized. Congress seems little interested in playing such a role and, given its inadequate staffing and access to expertise, is probably incapable of it. Nor has Congress made much use of a power granted to it in 1970 to veto executive actions regarding foreign credit. Talk of the need to decentralize the administrative machinery of the state, and even occasional federalist rumblings from departments such as Antioquia, have likewise borne little fruit, although the prospective change to direct election of mayors may have some input. More important has been the seeming tendency for the army, amid persistent problems of public order that have accentuated its role, to once more assert itself in ways that have potentially important political implications.

Despite such possibilities, and despite a stronger presidency and a stronger state—all consonant with recent trends throughout Latin America—Colombia's president seems unlikely to become a dictator during the immediate future. For he remains circumscribed, though to a lesser extent than formerly, both by the political realities of a genuinely constitutional system and, above all, by the historic bonds of the country's elite-directed political factionalism.

NOTES

1. Jacques Lambert, *Latin America* (Berkeley: University of California Press, 1967).

2. Alfredo Vásquez Carrizosa, *El Poder Presidencial en Colombia* (Bogotá: Sociedad Ediciones Internacionales, 1979), p. 15.

3. William Marion Gibson, *The Constitutions of Colombia* (Durham, N.C.: Duke University Press, 1948), contains the Colombian constitutions and codifications through 1948. For the provisions of the 1968 constitutional reform and a discussion, see Jaime Vidal Perdomo, *Historia de la Reforma Constitucional de 1968 y Sus Alcances Jurídicos* (Bogotá: Universidad Externado de Colombia, 1970). The normal method of amending the constitution is by the debate and approval of the proposed amendment in two consecutive ordinary sessions of Congress.

4. A *municipio* is very roughly equivalent to a country, in that it typically encompasses an urban center surrounded by a more rural area that includes several other settlements (*veredas*). Late in 1985 a bill providing for the direct election of mayors beginning in 1988 passed the Congress. For a portrayal of the weakness and futility of local government in one community, see Michael Whiteford, *The Forgotten Ones* (Gainesville: University of Florida Press, 1976), chap. 7.

5. Between 1949 and 1957 the country was continually under a state of siege. Since 1958 the state of siege has been imposed and revoked several times, having been in effect in all or portions of the country approximately 75 percent of the time.

6. Reid Reading, "Early Socialization to Impersonal Political Institutions: Some United States-Latin American Comparisons" (MS, University of Pittsburgh, n.d.). This is not to say that the president is necessarily regarded as benevolent, however; cf. Reading, "Political Socialization in Colombia and the United States: An Exploratory Study," *Midwest Journal of Political Science* 12 (1968): 352–81.

7. Fabio Hernán Gómez, *Concentración del Poder Económico en Colombia* (Bogotá: Centro de Investigación y Acción Social, 1974), pp. 62–63.

8. An illustrative instance occurred shortly after President Misael Pastrana took office in 1970. The head of the Planning Office and several others on the staff resigned when the president decided to structure priorities according to the recommendations of his political advisers rather than of his planners; see Steffen W. Schmidt, "Bureaucrats as Modernizing Brokers? Clientelism in Colombia," *Comparative Politics* 6, no. 3 (April 1974): 425–50.

9. Julio César Turbay Ayala, who eventually became president (1978–82), was at one point simultaneously a senator, presidential designate (see below), ambassador to the United Nations, and a director of the Liberal Party.

10. Gary W. Hoskin found in 1968 that some two-thirds of the representatives had not served more than four years; he attributes rapid turnover largely to political infighting at the local and departmental levels; see his "The Impact of the National Front on Congressional Behavior: The Attempted Restoration of El País Político," in R. Albert Berry, Ronald G. Hellman, and Mauricio Solaún, eds.,

Politics of Compromise (New Brunswick, N.J.: Transaction Books, 1980), pp. 114, 123. James Payne also pointed up high congressional turnover in his *Patterns of Conflict in Colombia* (New Haven: Yale University Press, 1968), chap. 11; however, he ascribed turnover to Colombian politicians' concern with status (the prestige of having been in Congress) rather than with the promotion of programs. Turnover on committees is also very high; see Harvey F. Kline, "Committee Membership Turnover in the Colombian National Congress, 1958–1974," *Legislative Studies Quarterly* 2, no. 1 (February 1977): 29–43.

11. Quoted in Richard Maullin, *The Colombian-IMF Disagreement of November-December 1966* (Santa Monica, Calif.: RAND Corp., 1967), p. 10. Article 69 of the constitution specifically allots congressmen funds to "encourage useful and beneficial works."

12. Gary W. Hoskin, "Dimensions of Representation in the Colombian National Legislature," in Weston Agor, ed., *Latin American Legislatures: Their Role and Influence* (New York: Praeger, 1971), p. 430.

13. Hoskin, "Impact of the National Front," p. 120.

14. Fernando Cepeda Ulloa, "La Desigualdad de Representación en el Congreso y en la Constituyente," *Separata de la Revista de la Cámara de Comercio* (Bogotá: n.d.), pp. 39–44. There is also some evidence that congressmen are of somewhat lower (though still high) social status compared with ministers and upper-level bureaucrats; cf. Rodrigo Losado, *Perfil Socio-Político del Congresista Colombiano* (Bogotá: Universidad de los Andes, 1972).

15. Harvey F. Kline, "Interest Groups in the Colombian Congress," *Journal of Interamerican Studies and World Affairs* 16, no. 3 (August 1974): 288–89.

16. Hoskin, "Impact of the National Front," p. 106; see also Payne, *Patterns of Conflict*, for a similar interpretation of Colombian politics generally.

17. This was in fact the Council of State's expressed opinion; cf. Roger W. Findley, "Presidential Intervention in the Economy and the Rule of Law in Colombia," *American Journal of Comparative Law* 28 (Summer 1980): 450–56.

18. *Visión* (Mexico City), March 21, 1983, p. 21.

19. Corruption of the police and the army, up to and including high-ranking officers, by drug traffickers has allegedly been extensive in recent years; see Peter A. Lupsha, "Drug Trafficking: Mexico and Colombia in Comparative Perspective," *Journal of International Affairs* 35, no. 1 (Spring–Summer 1981): 110. The principal prior example of high-level corruption was General Rojas Pinilla, who, with his family, is reputed to have increased his wealth considerably during his years in office. Even so, the alleged corruption of the Rojas regime pales when compared with that of, say, Juan Perón of Argentina or Marcos Pérez Jiménez of Venezuela. For the charges against Rojas, see Senado de la República, *El Proceso Contra Gustavo Rojas Pinilla* (Bogotá: Imprenta Nacional, 1960).

20. Lynton Caldwell, "Technical Assistance and Administrative Reform in Colombia," *American Political Science Review* 47, no. 2 (June 1953): 501. The powerful office of the *contraloría* is specifically assigned the task of bureaucratic oversight, especially with regard to public expenditures.

21. For a case study of such problems in the Colombian bureaucracy, see Richard E. Hartwig, *Roads to Reason: Transportation, Administration, and*

Rationality in Colombia (Pittsburgh: University of Pittsburgh Press, 1983), esp. chap. 7.

22. Almost three-quarters of the ministerial changes studied by Richard Hartwig occurred as parts of ministerial crises involving changes in at least three cabinet positions on the same date, suggesting that such factors as factional conflict and coalition building were at the root of the problem; see Hartwig's "Cabinet Instability and the Colombian Political System" (MS, Vanderbilt University, 1971), p. 12; see also Payne, *Patterns of Conflict*, pp. 227–29, 287–89.

23. Harvey F. Kline, *Colombia: Portrait of Unity and Diversity* (Boulder, Colo.: Westview Press, 1983), p. 69.

24. Jaime Vidal Perdomo, "The 1968 Administrative Reforms in Colombia," *International Review of Administrative Sciences* no. 1 (1982): 84.

25. INCORA's budget was systematically reduced, and political appointees named to replace professional personnel, in an effort to eviscerate agrarian reform projects in favor of other rural programs; see Robin Ruth Marsh, *Development Strategies in Rural Colombia: The Case of Caquetá* (Los Angeles: University of California, Latin American Center, 1983), p. 123.

26. David Lilienthal of TVA fame was a consultant to the project in its formative stages. For a study of the establishment and functioning of the CVC, see Antonio Posada and Jeanne de Posada, *The CVC: Challenge to Underdevelopment and Traditionalism* (Bogotá: Ediciones Tercer Mundo, 1966).

27. Cf. the comment in Hoskin, "Dimensions of Representation," pp. 416–17; and the discussion in Armando Borrero, "El Porceso Legislativo," in Gary Hoskin et al., *Estudio del Comportamiento Legislativo en Colombia*, vol. 2 (Bogotá: Universidad de los Andes/Cámara de Comercio de Bogotá, 1975). Alfonso López Michelsen, then head of a dissident Liberal faction that had just rejoined the main body of the party, commented that his support of the constitutional reform was a political concession designed to help reunite the Liberal Party; see Vidal Perdomo, *Historia de la Reforma Constitucional*, p. 75.

28. For the opinions of congressmen to this effect, see Harvey F. Kline, "Orientación hacia el Ejecutivo," in Hoskin et al., *Estudio del Comportamiento Legislativo*, pp. 358–59.

8

PUBLIC POLICY

Every political system effectively excludes certain issues from the agenda of public decision making, and Colombia is no exception. Proposals that would significantly restructure the society, the economy, or the polity are not seriously addressed, except by groups such as the guerrillas at the margins of the system. The entire pattern of Colombia's elite-dominated politics works toward such exclusion, as reinforced by ties of clientelism, loyalties to the established parties, and many aspects of Colombian political culture. When necessary, coercion is employed to restrict the policy agenda. An example was the special security statute, in effect from 1978 to 1982, that permitted the arrest of certain vocal critics of the government and placed restrictions on the press when matters defined as relevant to national security were concerned. It is therefore within parameters that do not challenge the fundamentals of the system, and for the most part among actors who already hold dominant positions within that system, that Colombian public policy is debated and enacted.

THE POLICY-MAKING PROCESS

Among those issues that do make their way onto the agenda of Colombia's decision makers, there is little question that the policy initiatives that have any real chance to prosper mostly originate with the president and his chief aides and ministers. As we have seen, the president has rather wide discretionary powers to enact legislation in areas such as the economy (for instance, President López Michelsen's 1974 tax reform) or national security (for instance, President Turbay's 1978 security statute). Most ordinary legislation of any real importance also originates with the president and his advisers.

Working to the same end in recent years has been the emergence of the technocrats. Of the series of urban reform bills proposed by several presidents during the late 1960s and early 1970s, most were developed by these officials without prior consultations with party directorates or private interest groups.[1] There are nonetheless real limits on the role of these *técnicos*. The views of technocrats in the Planning Office, the Ministry of Mines, and the Colombian Coal Company (CARBOCOL), the decentralized institute responsible for the development of the country's coal reserves, were largely ignored by President Turbay when he made the very important decision to proceed with the development of the El Cerrejón coalfields in association with Exxon.[2] It is above all in those areas that do not require major policy agreement, because they do not challenge such basic principles as private property, that the technocrats maximize their contribution to policy making.

Occasionally, ad hoc commissions and conferences composed of government, party, and interest group representatives have played key roles in the initiation of policy proposals. One, more formalized, version is the presidentially appointed commission expressly charged with formulating policy recommendations. A striking example was the Agrarian Reform Commission of 1960, whose recommendations were adopted wholesale as the initial government proposals to Congress.[3] A second, more informal, version is the occasional "summit conference" of employer and worker representatives, and others, to seek accommodation on wage-price policy or to make proposals to the government designed to alleviate immediate economic and social crises. A recent example was the conference convoked in October 1981 by President Turbay in an effort to head off a threatened general strike and to confront other national problems. It included representatives of the producers' associations, the unions, the Church, and the armed forces. Mixed commissions of a more permanent nature have been utilized from time to time to formulate policy proposals—the National Salaries Council and the National Work Council attached to the Ministry of Labor, for example—but they have functioned only sporadically and disputes among their constituent sectors have often led the government to impose its own decisions.[4]

Once a president has decided on a policy initiative, he will normally ask one of his cabinet ministers to draw up the specific legislative proposal. The latter may consult representatives of interest groups particularly concerned with the area of legislation. Cabinet ministers, although they hold their posts at the president's discretion, often have some "initiative space" of their own.[5] The president, after all, cannot interest himself in every matter, and in any case may prefer that a minister take the lead so that if opposition to a policy mounts, he can subsequently be repudiated, or even removed, by the president, thus deflecting responsibility from himself. A minister may represent a political faction whose support the president needs and thus must be allowed a degree of independence. He may also have presidential ambitions and wish to use his position to promote policies that will work to his own future acclaim.[6] Use of the high-level ministerial Council of Economic and Social Policy (CONPES) is apparently sporadic or at times perfunctory; the decision on the Exxon contract, for example, was reportedly taken after a debate of only ten minutes.[7]

Once formulated by the executive, a bill goes to Congress, where it is debated in committee and on the floor, as well as in the press. On items of major policy importance, the congressional role in the policy process is very largely the approval, delay, or veto of executive branch initiatives. Sometimes that role seems virtually irrelevant. For instance, congressional debate on the Exxon contract took place mainly after the president and CONPES had agreed to it.[8] For the most part, the concerns of Congress are distributive, that is, the allocation of budgetary resources among the various departments and localities, or the political advantage to be gained by the support or defeat of a government proposal. Not only does Congress distrust the technocrats of the executive branch, but broad, impersonal plans have little direct relevance to the budgetary resources congressmen can acquire for their constituencies (on which their careers depend). Only on markedly redistributive questions that involve the concerns of major producer interest groups may Congress take a genuine interest in the content of proposed legislation, usually by resisting the reformist intentions of the executive. This has been particularly true of agrarian reform legislation, where congressional ties to landowners in the departments has been notable. It has been much less true of tariff and monetary policy.[9]

Interest groups play primarily a reactive role in the Colombian policy process, seldom initiating policy changes (although they are sometimes consulted in drawing up specific legislation) but seeking to amend or defeat legislation proposed by the executive. That failing, attempts may be made to delay or impede implementation by bringing court challenges, or by getting Congress to eviscerate the budget of the agency charged with the law's implementation. Thus the Society of Colombian Agriculturalists (SAC), while giving lip service to the principle of agrarian reform, attacked many of the specific features of the 1961 and 1967 laws as they were being debated and resisted their implementation thereafter.[10] Similarly, the two key urban business groups adopted a reactive strategy vis-à-vis executive proposals for urban reform. Only when their interests were threatened did they put forward any counterproposals. Moreover, only those groups directly threatened by the government's reform proposals reacted. Potential beneficiaries of the reform, such as labor unions, did not rally in support; nor did landowners rally in defense of urban property interests. When a president does consult interest groups before proposing or enacting a policy, it is as likely to be in order to mobilize support as to request suggestions.[11]

Overall, it has been much easier to thwart reform than to promote it. This tendency is accentuated by the fact that a reformist executive can seldom rely on much organized support for reform. Labor and peasant organizations have been weak, divided, and co-opted; they simply do not have the political weight to counter those opposed to reform.[12] President Lleras Restrepo's recognition that such support was necessary if agrarian reform were to succeed was a major reason for the creation of the National Association of Peasant Users (ANUC), although it failed miserably in its purpose.

It would nonetheless be erroneous to conclude that public opinion, or at least the anticipation of its reaction, is irrelevant to policy making in Colombia. The near defeat of the National Front candidate by Rojas Pinilla in 1970 quite clearly precipitated the urban reform initiatives that followed (even though none of them passed the Congress), and the upcoming midterm elections brought the convoking of a special session of Congress and the reintroduction of a reform program early in 1972. Similarly, both rural violence and the anticipation of electoral advantage have helped to spur the various efforts at agrarian reform. Foreign exchange policy is another good example of the constraints of public opinion, with the government hesitating to engage in unpopular devaluations of the peso. In fact, as might be anticipated in a democratic system, presidents and cabinet ministers frequently initiate policies with an eye to their own or their government's popularity, and out of concern for the regime's popular legitimacy.

A very different component in the policy making process encompasses pressures and inducements from actors external to Colombia's political institutions. They have been a prime element in inducing or facilitating policy changes, especially but not only during the period of the National Front. This was the case with various tax and administrative reforms in the early 1960s, a wholesale revision of foreign exchange policy in 1967, and urban planning in the 1970s.[13] The United States, through the Alliance for Progress, was a major stimulus to agrarian reform in the early 1960s as a putative means of countering the appeals of the Cuban revolution. The Alliance also provided significant funding for low-income housing. Population policy was yet another focus of international influence and funding; in this case AID and other international agencies and foundations clashed in their policy objectives with another actor having international ties, the Roman Catholic Church.[14]

The impact of the Alliance and of the World Bank, the International Labor Organization (ILO), and other international agencies has been not merely on the substance of policies and the resources available to pursue them. They have also fostered the development of an institutional structure, preferring to operate through planning offices, "de-partisanized" decentralized institutes, and technocrats much like their own personnel. In the process, the more strictly political institutions like the parties and Congress have been deemphasized, and popular initiatives and responses have become less relevant to policy making. Coherence, efficiency, and technical criteria increasingly have taken precedence over regional considerations, and politicians have become more and more cut off from the possibility of basing campaigns on the government's achievements.[15]

It is, however, doubtful that international lending authorities have substantial leverage in inducing a country to make policy changes it would not otherwise undertake; in fact, at times the influence has run the other way, with the Colombian government convincing foreign agencies or governments that a particular project was feasible for funding.[16] What they have done is to facilitate technocratic trends already under way, and to further, and in a sense legitimize, the enactment of policies that Colombia's leaders in any case sought to undertake. International influence may well have peaked; the U.S. AID program has been terminated, and the Colombian state is considerably stronger in the mid-1980s than it was in 1958. Still, the very fact of that strength is in part a tribute to those international influences.

As might be supposed from the foregoing account, the role of the parties in policy making has declined noticeably in the wake of the augmented role of the technocrats, the interest groups, and international agencies. One or more party factions may oppose a government bill in Congress for reasons of presumed political advantage. But the parties as such play only a minimal role in policy making and almost none in policy initiation.

The *jefes naturales* of the parties (or factions thereof) do, however, on occasion play a key policy role, whether or not they hold a formal party position. Thus it sometimes happens that the only way to resolve policy questions proposed by the executive and blocked or delayed in Congress through the actions of pressure groups, political factions, and regional interests is to hold a kind of summit meeting between representatives of the government (often the president), on the one hand, and leaders of key political factions, congressmen, or interest groups, on the other. When an agrarian bill was stalled in Congress in 1972 as the result of resistance from landowners and various political factions, such a meeting produced the Declaration of Chicoral and eventuated in the passage of the legislation in considerably modified form.[17] The "ex-presidents" club including viable presidential aspirants, plays a like role on occasion. "Given the decentralized and factionalized nature of the party system, the weight of their support has been crucial to passage of any major political or social reform."[18] Not least, the "club" has ready access to the national press, which in Colombia is a (if not the) main channel of communication.

The court of last resort for the resolution of major conflicts in the Colombian policy process is therefore not primarily interinstitutional—that is, between the president and the Congress—or between the parties as such, but among the nation's very top political leadership, whether or not those leaders hold any formal position in government or party leadership.

In the end, both in the way policy choices have manifested themselves, and in the ways they have been addressed by presidents with their varying styles and imperatives, the modern Colombian policy-making process is clearly transitional (or mixed) between what have been called "two different systems of influence and obligation." The first, the traditional or classic, is dominated by the time-honored values and concerns of social status, regionalism, partisan rhetoric, and the formalistic courtesies and "romanticism" of Hispanic culture. The style of power in the second system is more pragmatic or "industrial," with the stress on instrumental and "scientific" solutions to problems of productivity and social change. Consequently, "the chief executives of Colombia find that the promotion of a transitional or developing economy resolves itself into the difficult political job of providing leadership for two worlds that are often poorly connected and from time to time in direct conflict."[19] Even a more powerful Colombian president, rooted in a state stronger than at any time in the past, must ultimately base much of his ability to accomplish his goals not on his newfound constitutional prerogatives or on the expertise of his technocrats, but on his capacity to manage the pressures and manipulate the symbols of the traditional "political country" from which many of the fundamental constraints on Colombian presidents have always emanated. As a matter of fact, the technocrats are not immune from politics; the permissible limits of their actions are set elsewhere, and they are often the implementors and executors of policies established by the president and the elite interests he tends to reflect and represent.

ECONOMIC POLICY

The private sector remains dominant in the Colombian economy, and international market forces continue to be a major determinant of the country's economic health. Yet government has played an ever increasing economic role. It has long been a co-participant with the Federation of Coffee Growers (FEDECAFE) in the promotion of coffee exports, and provides credit and varied assistance to other sectors of agriculture.

However, it is in the promotion of industrialization and in overall economic coordination and planning that the government's role has grown markedly since the mid-1930s. At first using such devices as protective tariffs in the 1930s, the government began to take a more direct role by establishing the Institute for Industrial Promotion (IFI) in 1940, which helped to spur the creation of a number of industries. Today energy and transportation development is largely in government hands, the exploitation of mineral resources requires a contract with the government, and the National Planning Department plays a major role in economic planning and coordination, including the approval of major foreign investments. Exchange controls, tax policies, and a variety of other devices also play crucial parts in government's efforts to promote economic growth. While the economic role of government remains less than in most Latin American countries, the technical input to economic policy has risen notably, to a point perhaps superior to that in most Latin American nations.[20]

The first comprehensive plan for Colombia's economic development, contained in a report by a mission of the World Bank headed by Lauchlin Currie (1950);[21] the establishment of the Paz del Río steel mill (1951); and the creation of the Cauca Valley Corporation (CVC) during the military regime of Rojas Pinilla were highlights on the path to Colombian economic development. But it was the governments of the National Front that provided the first truly concerted, and bipartisan, attack on the problems of economic development. The blueprint for the government's efforts was to be the ten-year General Economic and Social Development Plan for 1961–70, the first such plan to be presented by any Latin American country in express fulfillment of one of the goals of the Alliance for Progress.[22] Among other things, the plan set targets for economic growth, and for public and private investment. While not entirely measuring up to those goals, growth rates thereafter were moderately good (as they had been before the onset of the Plan), while the share of the national budget allotted to public investment rose from some 25 percent in 1958 to more than 40 percent by the early 1960s.[23]

Prior to the late 1960s, Colombia had relied primarily on coffee exports and import-substitution industrialization (the domestic manufacture of consumer goods previously imported) to stimulate economic growth. But under President Carlos Lleras Restrepo (1966–70) a new strand was added to economic policy: export diversification, that is the promotion of "minor" exports other than coffee (and petroleum). This was to be accomplished through a variety of tax credits and the establishment of the Export Promotion Fund (PROEXPO) to grant credit and to insure against export risks. The establishment of a "crawling peg" exchange rate in place of more infrequent, but large, devaluations of the peso in order to minimize financial uncertainties worked to the same end. The result was a significant increase in the export of sugar, cotton, tobacco, bananas, meat, hides, and other agricultural products, as well as the very modest beginnings of such industrial exports as textiles.[24]

Also under the Lleras administration, multinational corporations came to be more systematically controlled through new regulations, including government approval for significant new investments. The objective was to provide a measure of protection for Colombian businesses, as well as some control over the repatriation of profits. It was also during the Lleras administration (1967) that Colombia signed the Andean Pact, seeking a measure of regional economic integration with its neighbors (see below).

Each of the last several Colombian presidents has continued to foster industrialization, export diversification, the simultaneous encouragement and control of foreign investment, regional integration, and the all-important trade in coffee. However, each has contributed his own variations to economic policy, typically prescribing his own four-year "plan," and each has faced his own particular set of constraints as well as some common ones—in particular, inflation—that have prevented him from fulfilling his original goals.

President Pastrana (1970–74) in his "new strategy" approach declared urban construction to be the key that would both provide employment for the unskilled and serve as a "leading sector" for economic growth at relatively little cost in foreign exchange.

President López Michelsen (1974–78), soon after his sweeping electoral victory in the first post-National Front election, inaugurated a rather different plan, "To Close the Gap," that is, the gap between rich and poor, urban and rural. In intention it had the most redistributive emphasis of any recent presidential strategy, although its central feature—reform of the tax system—was partially frustrated by Supreme Court decisions and tax evasion.

President Turbay (1978–82) pursued a Plan of National Integration (PIN), promoting such goals as economic decentralization, development of transportation and communications networks, and development of the energy and mining sectors.

In line with other recent presidents, Belisario Betancur presented a development plan to Congress, "Change with Equity." Among other things he proposed to accelerate urban housing construction to provide 400,000 new units between 1983 and 1986, in part to provide jobs; he also promised houses without down payments. However, the president's first policy priority proved to be economic crisis management, in particular taking measures to lower the inflation rate, reduce the balance-of-payments gap, and lower interest rates. He also sought to generate new foreign loans and new foreign investment. For the purpose he declared a 60-day state of economic emergency in December 1982. When some of the resulting decrees were pronounced unconstitutional, he was forced to pursue the more time-consuming course of working with Congress to pass the requisite legislation.

Energy policy came to be a key question for both the López and the Turbay administrations in the wake of the world oil crises of the 1970s.[25] Petroleum had for many years been Colombia's second largest export, but by the early 1970s increasing consumption and the declining output of existing fields required the country to begin importing oil and to expend precious foreign exchange for the purpose. Heretofore Colombian petroleum had been developed under concession contracts with foreign corporations.[26] Under this system the corporation made the investments; controlled production, refining and marketing; and reaped the profits, with a modest share going to the government in the form of taxes and royalties. Some argued that this system gave the companies undue rewards and undue control over decisions concerning the amount of petroleum to be produced. In any case, President López Michelsen decreed that all new petroleum agreements were to be "association" contracts in which the foreign corporation would conduct the exploration at its own risk, with the government and the corporation thereafter sharing more or less equally in both the governance and the profits of the enterprise (with royalties and taxes additional). Whether because of these changes or not, both the exploration for and the production of petroleum increased in the early 1980s, with major contracts signed by ECOPETROL, the government oil corporation, with Occidental Petroleum and a subsidiary of Texaco.

In 1976 the Colombian Coal Company (CARBOCOL) was created; it soon signed a contract of the "association" type with a subsidiary of Exxon to develop a major coalfield in northeastern Colombia. Four years later the Turbay administration accepted the company's reports on the feasibility of massive investments and agreed to go ahead jointly with the project. Development of some smaller coalfields went forward at the same time under a variety of arrangements. Considerable investments funds were also being allotted to hydroelectric development.

Energy policy, then, like the rest of economic policy, envisaged a key role for foreign capital that nonetheless gave the state a considerably stronger hand than under the former (and in some cases, continuing) concession contracts

Prior to the 1980s, while Colombia was certainly not immune from inflation, deficits, and balance-of-payments difficulties, its macroeconomic policies had a real measure of success in promoting (or at least not hindering) economic growth, particularly when viewed in comparative terms. However, problems of inflation, deficits, and international (especially private) debt then began to mount, in good part because of circumstances beyond government control, including low foreign prices for coffee and other exports, and a drug traffic that, while enhancing the country's income, has helped fuel inflation. Economic growth has at the same time declined to the lowest levels in a long time, to resume a modest 3 percent annual increase in the GNP for both 1984 and 1985.

Conflict over economic policy has accordingly increased. Nonetheless, and despite a series of differing presidential economic "plans," over the years there has been a rather high degree of elite consensus concerning the desirability of policies stressing economic growth. Such has not been the case, however, with policies aimed at structural changes or the redistribution of the country's resources.

AGRARIAN REFORM

Agrarian policy is in a sense the touchstone for judging the reformist (or revolutionary) intentions of any Latin American regime. It was Law 200 of 1936 that in modern times first addressed Colombia's agrarian problems in a serious way. Part of Alfonso López's *revolución en marcha*, it sought in particular to relieve the rural unrest of the late 1920s and early 1930s by dividing unproductive lands and granting titles to campesinos whose legal right to the land they worked was unclear. Law 200 may have helped to dampen rural unrest at the time, but over the long run it was rendered largely inoperative, or even counterproductive, both by the enactment of legislation (such as Law 100 of 1944) modifying its provisions and by the actions of landlords to expel their tenants before they could obtain title to lands that might otherwise be due them.[27]

At any rate, at the outset of the 1960s Colombia had a highly skewed pattern of land tenure in which some 76.5 percent of the holdings comprising ten hectares or less constituted only 8.8 of the land in agricultural production or pasturage, while 0.6 percent of the total landholdings comprising 500 or more hectares occupied 40.4 percent of the land.[28]

Several factors converged to induce the first National Front government of Alberto Lleras Camargo to address the question of agrarian reform. One was the carry-over of rural conflict and unrest from the days of partisan violence; another, the rural strength of a dissident Liberal faction, the Revolutionary Liberal Movement (MRL) of Alfonso López Michelsen, in the mid-term elections of 1960. There was also considerable concern on the part of the Lleras government over the need to modernize Colombian agriculture and increase its productivity in order to feed the burgeoning cities and to finance the imports needed for industrialization. Finally, the Alliance for Progress offered assistance and stimulus to agrarian reform programs throughout Latin America as a means of countering the appeals of the recently victorious Cuban revolution. Notably, direct pressure from campesinos, or from organizations purporting to speak for them, was almost entirely absent.

Among the results of such concerns were the Acción Comunal program (see chap. 6) and Law 135 of 1961. The latter stressed the distribution of large landholdings to campesinos who lacked land or held only very small parcels (minifundios). Public lands, where available, were to be divided first, followed by uncultivated and poorly cultivated private properties. Only in special cases—for example, in areas of extensive cattle grazing where minifundios needed to be enlarged—were adequately used lands to be touched. Compensation for expropriated lands was to be in the form of cash or bonds in accordance with the degree of land utilization. Law 135 also provided for the consolidation of excessively small parcels, and for credit and other forms of assistance to the farmer. Crucially, the law created the Colombian Institute of Agrarian Reform (INCORA) with broad powers to administer and implement the law.

The practical results of Law 135 did not measure up to its original intent. Initial shortages of competent administrative and technical personnel, as well as fiscal limitations, played a part in the fundamental failure of Colombia's principal attempt to date at agrarian reform. Most important was the resistance of landowners and their political allies, particularly among the Laureanista faction of the Conservative Party. Direct pressure on the government, plus deliberate restrictions on INCORA's budget, limited the latter's ability to expropriate land; and landowners' use of the cumbersome legal procedures required for expropriation often made it possible to delay or even avoid expropriation.[29] Even had the original intent of Law 135 been fulfilled, however, its modest and gradual approach to agrarian change would hardly have reordered the shape of economic power in Colombia.

In an effort to rejuvenate the lagging agrarian reform program, the administration of President Carlos Lleras Restrepo spurred the passage of Law 1 of 1968. Sometimes referred to as the "reform of the reform," it stressed the modernization and diversification of large-scale agriculture through the use of credits and tax incentives, as well as the acceleration of the pace of land distribution by eliminating some of the legal and financial restrictions that had hampered the implementation of Law 135 of 1961 as it applied to renters and sharecroppers. Although more than half of all negotiated land purchases, and two-thirds of all expropriations, that occurred during the ten years following the enactment of Law 135 were carried out in the wake of the new law, the overall impact of the agrarian reform remained very limited. By the end of the first reform decade, not even 1 percent of the country's agricultural land had been affected.[30] In fact, Law 1 of 1968 had unleashed a wave of expulsions of peasant sharecroppers and renters by landowners who sought to avoid expropriation. In any case, the policy emphasis had by now shifted from redistribution to the commercialization of agriculture even, most probably, on the part of Lleras himself, whose central policy concern was the promotion of economic development. By the late 1960s land distribution programs were no longer needed to stimulate the transformation of Colombia's large landed estates into productive enterprises.

Moreover, the conditions that had created the urgency for the passage of Law 135 had largely abated. The MRL had rejoined the main body of the Liberal Party, and *la violencia* was now a fading memory, as were the initial impact of the Cuban revolution and the Alliance for Progress. The country's foreign exchange problems had also been eased by a rise in coffee prices on the world market. In short, land redistribution, whether for economic or for political reasons, was a good deal less urgent in 1970–71 than it had been in 1960–61 in the eyes of Colombia's elites.[31]

The last government under the National Front dispensation, that of President Misael Pastrana Borrero (1970–74), a Conservative, undertook yet another modification of the agrarian reform. Particularly in its final form (Laws 4 and 5 of 1973), it made major concessions to landowners. INCORA's functions and budget were also cut back.

The subsequent administration of Alfonso López Michelsen continued the trend away from an emphasis on land redistribution and toward the encouragement of productivity and commercialization. Two new programs were launched, and continued by the Turbay administration: the Food and Nutrition Plan (PAN) and Integrated Rural Development (DRI). Both "were directed at reducing tensions in the countryside without engaging in a divisive and potentially counter-productive land reform."[32] PAN sought to raise nutritional levels among the poor; DRI was to help peasants raise their levels of production while encouraging the cultivation of traditional food crops. Their activities were concentrated in zones of guerrilla activity, in a conscious effort to defuse unrest. The World Bank offered major support to both programs. Together these plans sought to convert those campesinos who already possessed some land into efficient, commercial farmers by supplying credit, technical assistance, and various forms of subsidies. Enhancing political stability in the countryside while modernizing traditional agriculture was the aim.

Having initially committed itself to at least a measure of land redistribution as a partial solution to agrarian unrest and as a spur to more productive land use, first in the 1930s and again in the early years of the National Front, the Colombian government gradually switched its emphasis until, by the early 1970s, land redistribution was virtually abandoned. Instead, Colombian agrarian policy in recent years has pursued a three-track strategy: (1) to encourage large landowners to apply their underused holdings to commercial use, primarily for export, through subsidized credit, technical assistance, and tax incentives; (2) to promote migration to and the colonization of unoccupied lands on the Colombian frontiers (the eastern plains and the southern lowlands), thereby incorporating new areas into the national economy while providing land and work for at least some of the nation's rural poor; and (3) to provide a variety of services to rural families with small and medium-size farms in order to raise their productivity and improve their level of living. Problems of inadequate resources, ineffective implementation, and the noninvolvement of participants in projects affecting them nonetheless remain, and the long-term effectiveness of such programs remains uncertain.[33] In fact, there is evidence that, at least as of the early 1970s and the virtual end of land redistribution, the agrarian reform had done more to increase social mobilization and raise expectations among beneficiaries of the program than it had to increase economic and political satisfaction.[34]

There may be some prospect of a revival of efforts at agrarian reform. President Betancur included such a commitment in an August 1984 truce agreement with some of the guerrilla bands, and legislation to amend Law 135 of 1961 was put before Congress the following month. Moreover, there seems to be increasing recognition of the fact that guerrilla violence has been rooted in rural poverty and injustice, and that violence has contributed to declining agricultural production in some parts of the country. It nonetheless remains problematic whether the requisite funds will be available in a period of fiscal austerity, especially since most of the old obstacles to the passage and implementation of effective agrarian legislation remain in place.

SOCIAL POLICIES

Colombian governments have over the years addressed many other questions in the broadly defined arena of social policy. However, their outcome has seldom been any more effectively redistributive than in the case of agrarian policy.

Urban reform—essentially signifying amelioration of the housing problems attendant on massive rural migration—was proposed in 1960 by the dissident Liberal faction, the MRL. It was subsequently taken up by several of the National Front governments, and during the early 1960s the Institute of Territorial Credit (ICT), with the very ample assistance of Alliance for Progress funds, did sponsor the construction of considerable low-income housing, notably the Ciudad Kennedy project in Bogotá. But with the virtual demise of the Alliance in the mid-1960s, the ICT was forced to rely increasingly on more expensive private capital. The result was that fewer houses were built, unit prices increased sharply, and an important source of owner-occupied housing for the poor was closed off.[35]

The latter years of the National Front saw a concerted attempt to pass urban reform legislation, particularly during the administration of President Misael Pastrana (1970–74), when ANAPO posed an electoral threat.[36] Proposals both prior to and during the Pastrana administration included rent control, the creation of a housing bank to provide credit for construction, taxation schemes to increase the efficiency of land use, the expropriation of unused or poorly used properties, and the issuance of urban development bonds. One piece of projected legislation even went so far as to envision turning renters into owners of their rented homes. The proposals ranged from those stressing direct government involvement in housing markets and housing construction to those favoring the stimulation of private enterprise. Yet of six urban reform initiatives sent to Congress by the executive between 1969 and 1974, none prospered; in fact, none even came to a vote on the floor of either house. Resistance from affected interest groups, notably the Colombian Chamber of Construction (CAMACOL) and La Lonja, an association of Bogotá real estate agents, along with their allies in the political parties, was simply too great. Since the Pastrana years, no administration has shown comparable interest in urban reform.

While urban reform has had an even less successful legislative history than agrarian reform, its course was not dissimilar. In both cases rather extensive reformist proposals entailing fairly substantial government intervention evolved over time in the direction of less reform and greater reliance on the private sector and the marketplace. Reformist initiatives on the part of the executive were largely frustrated by the action of interest groups, the Congress, and factions within the political parties.

Accident and death benefits for certain groups date from 1915, but the principal thrust toward the institutionalization of these and related benefits took place during the 1930s, with social security being more or less full-blown by 1946. Still, as of the late 1960s, Colombia ranked 13th out of 18 Latin American countries in the provision of social security protection for medical care, and a decade later only about a third of the population had their health needs covered by a variety of social security programs. Indeed, despite a 1975 law requiring graduating physicians to provide two years of public (usually rural) health service, the obligation was widely evaded and about half the rural population remained without the most elementary modern health services.[37]

Historically, Colombia's educational performance has been poorer than that of most Latin American countries. In terms of enrollment in primary and secondary education as a percentage of the school-age population, Colombia in 1977–78 was 11th of 18 Latin American countries (and 61st of 119 countries worldwide). Similarly, it ranked 15th out of 18 (and 117th out of 130) in expenditures on public education as a percentage of GNP.[38] Educational expenditures have been notably biased in an elitist and urban direction. In 1970 more of the national budget was spent on the 23,000 students attending national universities than on the 1.5 million primary and secondary students in rural areas. Similarly, less than 10 percent of the primary school budget went to rural areas even though 40 percent of the public primary enrollment was rural.[39] In 1971 the private educational sector, strong in Colombia, helped defeat government measures that would have provided fellowships for poor children, established compulsory social service for all Colombian youth, and required full utilization of public and private classrooms for educational purposes.[40]

Still, one of the genuine accomplishments both of the National Front governments, and of those since, has been the quantitative expansion of Colombian education. The number of students attending school increased dramatically between 1958 and 1974, from approximately 1.7 million enrolled at all levels to more than 5 million. Primary school enrollment more than doubled, sceondary education increased sixfold, and higher education rose from 20,000 to 138,000 students.[41] Such trends have continued, and by 1981 Colombia had about 12 percent of the relevant age group (ages 20–24) enrolled in higher education, about the same percentage as Brazil and Chile.[42]

Such a rapid expansion of the educational system since the early 1960s has increased Colombian literacy rates and enabled many more children to have an opportunity for upward social mobility. The growth of higher education has also meant that young people from previously excluded groups are better placed to exert pressure for social change, and may help to account for the increased radicalism among university students in recent decades. However, the wide disparities in educational access and quality remain between the social classes and between urban and rural areas. As in 1958, the Colombian educational system continues both to reflect and to perpetuate the social stratification system.

Population policy is one area in which Colombia has been, in relative terms, at the forefront. Carlos Lleras was the only Latin American president to sign the U.N. Declaration on Population in

1966, and in the same year the Ministry of Health began a program that included family planning. The program soon had a significant rate of participation, especially in the large cities, and presumably has contributed, along with urbanization, to declining birth rates in recent years. As of 1982 the World Bank gave Colombia a "strong" or "B" rating for its family-planning policy, a rating superior to most other Third World (including Latin American) countries, although the country's level of public expenditures on family planning did not match its policy commitment.[43]

Hardly a redistributive policy in any direct sense, a strong population policy is nonetheless consonant with the central themes of public policy since the early 1960s: economic growth and social control (given the presumed potential for social unrest of Colombia's burgeoning cities). Also in keeping with other aspects of public policy during the 1960s and 1970s, Colombia's efforts to limit population growth depended heavily on advice and funding from international sources such as AID and the Rockefeller and Ford Foundations.

The years since the early 1960s have therefore seen a number of modest redistributive reforms, notably in the area of agrarian policy. Other reforms have been proposed but not enacted into law. Still others have become law but have not been implemented. The end result has been a substantial expansion of Colombia's educational system and the construction of some low-income housing, for example, but otherwise relatively little change in the markedly inequitable distribution of resources in Colombian society. Notably, an area of some success—population policy—did not challenge the social or economic position of established elites (although it did generate some modest opposition from the Church). Finally, it is worth reiterating that, although policies designed to redistribute resources among sectors or classes of the population have, in general, had a rather modest impact, the Colombian system has been quite effective at distributing the available largesse (jobs, contracts, infrastructure, subsidies) rather widely, albeit not altogether equitably, on a regional or geographic basis.

FOREIGN POLICY

Issues of foreign policy have only occasionally been of major consequence to Colombians, and the country has generally kept a low profile as an international actor, at least until very recently.

The president and his foreign minister are the key actors in the making of foreign policy.[44] The staffing of the Foreign Ministry and of embassies abroad tends to be minimal in terms of size, and to be more political than professional. Also, the ministry largely confines itself to traditional diplomatic arenas such as the presentation of Colombia's position at the United Nations and other international forums, boundary disputes, and the like. In keeping with trends throughout Latin America, the all-important arena of foreign trade tends to be largely preempted by other entities, such as the Institute of Foreign Trade (INCOMEX) and the Fund for Export Promotion (PROEXPO). Above all, the National Federation of Coffee Growers(FEDECAFE), essentially a private entity with government co-participation, not only controls the export of Colombia's principal export commodity and its promotion abroad, but also negotiates agreements with other countries. It maintains permanent representatives in a number of foreign countries independent of the Foreign Ministry.

Although there are committees on foreign relations in both houses, Congress and the parties as a rule play little role in the formulation of foreign policy; conversely, foreign policy issues seldom play a significant part in election campaigns. Apart from FEDECAFE, producers' associations are usually little concerned with foreign policy, except perhaps when a particular aspect of foreign economic policy especially concerns them.

In cases where internal subversion appears to have international linkages, or in matters of border disputes, Colombia's armed forces may become key actors in the foreign policy arena. Thus the military was apparently instrumental in pressing for a suspension of diplomatic relations with Cuba in 1981, following alleged Cuban involvement in an "invasion" of southern Colombia by M-19 guerrillas.[45] While the military has so far largely deferred to the Foreign Ministry in Colombia's ongoing boundary dispute with Venezuela in the region of the Guajira peninsula in northeastern Colombia, it has used the dispute to press for an upgrading of military equipment. Meanwhile, the Association of Retired Armed Forces Officers, led by former General Alberto Ruiz Novoa, has pressed the cause of preparation against possible Venezuelan attack in testimony before congressional committees and elsewhere.

Historically, the critical foreign relationship for Colombia has been with the United States. For the first century of Colombia's independent life, that relationship primarily concerned Panama, which until 1903 was a Colombian department. An 1846 treaty between the two countries governed transit across the isthmus, and a railroad was built for the purpose. Various attempts to build a canal came to naught, including one by a French company that went bankrupt in the midst of construction. Another treaty, drawn up after the Spanish-American War, spurred U.S. interest in the region. It stipulated that Colombia would receive $10 million, plus annual payments of $250,000 beginning ten years hence, in exchange for the rights to build a canal. After Colombia's Senate failed to ratify the treaty, alleging possible loss of sovereignty and inadequate compensation, President Theodore Roosevelt, on the occasion of one of the frequent revolts in Panama, sent U.S. warships to intercept the Colombian troops dispatched to put down the rebels. Panama immediately declared its independence, on November 4, 1903, and two days later was recognized by the United States. Shortly thereafter a treaty was signed between Panama and the United States granting the latter the right to build the canal.

For a time there was considerable resentment by Colombians toward the United States. Yet two sets of circumstances proved to be overriding. First was increasing economic ties between Colombia and the United States: Colombian coffee exports, for which the United States was the principal customer, and in the reverse direction, U.S. loans and investments that accelerated markedly during the 1920s. The second was that in 1922 the U.S. Senate finally ratified the Thompson-Urrutia Treaty, originally negotiated in 1914, which granted Colombia an indemnity of $25 million for the loss of Panama.[46]

Thereafter, there were occasional problems with U.S.-based multinational corporations, the United Fruit Company and the Tropical Oil Company in particular. But already, less than two decades after President Roosevelt "took" Panama, there was a growing closeness between the two countries, a relationship that President Marco Fidel Suárez (1918–21) described as that of the "polar star," based on the economic and military power of the United States, as well as the attraction of the United States as a political model. Indeed, as the interwar years witnessed the expansion of U.S. influence in Colombia, "the fundamental issue [became] whether Colombia would pursue a road to development independent of the United States. That it did not do so was in part a consequence of the realities of international power, in part the result of very successful diplomacy by the United States, and in part the effect of the lack of commitment to such a course among members of the Colombian political sector."[47] Colombia aligned itself with the United States in World War II, and subsequently contributed troops both to the U.N. (largely U.S.) action in Korea (1951–54)—the only Latin American country to do so—and to the U.N. peacekeeping forces in the Sinai (1956–58, and again in 1982), once more substantially in support of U.S. policy objectives.

With the advent of the Alliance for Progress in 1961, Colombia became a principal "showcase" of the program. The National Front governments of the time were democratic, reformist, and development-oriented. Agrarian and tax reform, development planning, and stimulation of the private sector were among the objectives of those governments, as they were of the Alliance, and some $750 million in U.S. aid poured into the country in the years 1961–67, along with numerous consultants and advisory missions. The impact was significant, but in the end disappointing in such areas as income distribution and structural change (including agrarian reform), and not without its costs, including an increasing debt burden. Most striking, a report of a U.S. Senate subcommittee concluded that

> ... the United States discovered that its influence was severely limited with respect to moving Colombia toward economic and social reform, especially in terms of the application of U.S. methods to institutional change.... The aid program in Colombia has bought time for Colombian institutions to work out changes which almost everybody in a position of responsibility in either country agrees must come. But Colombians have used this time at their leisure. The question which this study raises but cannot answer is: would they have moved more expeditiously if they had had less time, or would the pressures have been so great that the whole structure of the society would have collapsed into anarchy or dictatorship. The record, studied with the benefit of hindsight, indicates the former.[48]

Trade, aid, investment, and military cooperation have been at the core of Colombia's orientation to the United States. Yet there have been subtler ties as well. At bottom, it might be said that middle- and upper-class Colombians have traditionally looked to the United States as the leader of the free world and, implicitly at least, as the ultimate guardian of their values and interests. Colombians regularly travel to

Miami and New York for shopping and vacations, and many upper-class Colombians send their sons and daughters to the United States for part of their education (particularly in business and engineering). There is a considerable "brain drain" of educated Colombians seeking opportunities in the United States, as well as a considerable out-migration of the less-educated.[49] The "polar star" has thus had a deep attraction for Colombians.

Beginning in the late 1960s, however, there began to be a perceptible increase in Colombia's assertion of national autonomy, and increasing linkages with specifically Latin American and Third World causes and organizations.

Notable among these was the Andean Pact, which Colombia, along with Chile, took the lead in forming. Its original members included Ecuador, Peru, and Bolivia as well.[50] Substantially its goals were to achieve on a regional basis those objectives that the larger Latin American Free Trade Association (ALALC), which Colombia had joined in 1961, had been slow to attain. These included the reduction of trade barriers, the harmonization of economic policies, and the allocation of the manufacture of certain goods to particular countries in order to avoid duplication. The members also agreed in 1971 (the so-called Decision 24) on a common policy toward foreign investment designed to reduce over time the degree of foreign ownership in the enterprises of the member countries by such devices as offering tariff reductions to existing enterprises that were 51 percent domestically owned and by requiring new enterprises to convert to such "mixed enterprises" within a set period of time.[51]

Since entering into the Pact, Colombia has experienced an increase in trade with its Andean partners. In keeping with the spirit of the Pact, Congress in 1975 "colombianized" foreign banks by requiring that within three years they offer ownership of 51 percent of their capital to Colombian nationals, although in some cases the foreign banks apparently partially circumvented the law by increasing their capital.[52] On the other hand, the Andean Pact has hardly revolutionized trade patterns or created a true common market. There has also been considerable difference among the members in their interpretations and applications of Decision 24, and its original stringent limitations on foreign investment have been eased somewhat, both in Colombia and elsewhere. While the Andean Pact is not moribund, by the mid-1980s it was clearly in a state of "transition" to something less than its original intent.

More recently Colombia has sought to expand its influence in the Caribbean. In 1974 it became a member of the Caribbean Development Bank, and it has taken various steps to expand its trade with Caribbean countries. Its diplomacy has also been more active in the region, partly as a means of strengthening its position vis-à-vis Venezuela and Nicaragua, with both of whom it has border disputes.

During the 1960s Colombia restored diplomatic relations with the Soviet Union—severed in the wake of the *bogotazo*, amid accusations of Soviet complicity in the rioting—and with other eastern European nations, and sought to intensify its minuscule trade with the Communist bloc. Diplomatic relations with Cuba, broken in 1962 in accordance with a vote of the Organization of American States (OAS), were resumed in 1975, only to be broken once more in 1981. President López Michelsen announced in 1975 that Colombia would henceforth do without U.S. economic assistance, on the grounds that "foreign aid breeds an unhealthy economic dependency and delays or undermines measures that should be taken for development."[53] López Michelsen also supported Panama in its renegotiation of the Canal Treaty with the United States, and the Turbay administration lent its voice to the deposition of the Somoza regime in Nicaragua and in opposition to a U.S. proposal for a peacekeeping force.

When President Betancur took office in 1982, he moved in the direction of a rapprochement with Cuba (although he did not renew diplomatic relations). He also announced that Colombia would join the group of nonaligned countries because "Colombia does not want to be a satellite of the United States."[54] Betancur was also instrumental in making Colombia one of the most active nations of the so-called Contadora Group (which included Mexico, Venezuela, and Panama) seeking to mediate the Central American conflict. This tended to place Colombia athwart U.S. policy, which, while nominally in support of the Contadora process, took a much harder line toward Nicaragua than did Colombia and other group members. President Betancur likewise proclaimed Colombia's solidarity with Argentina over the Falkland (Malvinas) Islands dispute with Great Britain after his predecessor (Turbay) had refused to join other Latin American countries in that position at the time of the 1982 war.[55] In the economic arena, the Betancur government played host (in Cartagena) to a conference of the Latin American debtor countries, somewhat to the displeasure of the international banking community, even as it took steps to ease a variety of restrictions on foreign investments.

Colombia's relationship with the United States, and its recent tentative attempts at greater autonomy, have been at the crux of its foreign policy, but certainly not its sole important dimension. In the early 1930s an attempt by Peruvian irregulars to occupy disputed territory on the Amazon River led to a brief (undeclared) conflict that ended with a settlement assuring Colombia access to the Amazon at Leticia. Currently two disputes over the delimitation of frontiers remain as legacies of independence more than a century and a half ago.

One is a dispute with Nicaragua over the islands of San Andres and Providencia and nearby uninhabited cays, lying not far off the Nicaraguan coast but governed by Colombia since the days of Gran Colombia. The new Sandinista government in Nicaragua reasserted that country's claims to the islands and the cays in 1979, leading Colombia to strengthen its military posture there and helping to distance Colombia from a revolution it had initially welcomed.

A dispute with Venezuela over the border in extreme northeastern Colombia, including the Gulf of Venezuela and nearby land areas, is of considerably greater moment. The area is thought to be rich in petroleum, and major coal deposits are nearby. Tensions periodically flare up—for example, when Venezuela acquired F-16 fighters from the United States—and then die down. The dispute has thus far been more of an irritant than something of crisis proportions. However, it is fed by negative stereotypes that each nation has of the other, and by the problems raised by the million or so Colombians who have illegally migrated to Venezuela.

Even so, what is surprising is the virtual absence of international conflict in Colombia's long history. With the exception of the brief conflict with Peru, Colombia has fought no wars with its neighbors. Those conflicts with which it has been associated, such as World War II and the Korean War (the latter under U.N. auspices) have been as a peripheral contributor to alliances headed by the United States, and fought and decided well beyond the confines of the hemisphere. Moreover, Colombia has from its earliest days been a pillar of the inter-American system and a proponent of international law and comity. Panama (then part of Gran Colombia) was the site of the first inter-American Congress in 1826, and the Organization of American States was founded at Bogotá in 1948. Colombia also played one of the more prominent Third World roles in the founding of the United Nations in 1945, arguing strongly against the great-power veto.

As of the mid-1980s, Colombia had hardly repudiated its close links to the United States. In some areas, as in combating the drug trade, those ties were perhaps closer than ever. Yet, compared with two decades earlier, Colombia's foreign policy was clearly less in lockstep with that of the United States: it was on the whole more autonomous, more oriented to its Caribbean and Andean neighbors and even to the Third World at large, and, at least temporarily, more assertive in commensuration with its relative size and importance. The nature of Colombia's relationship with the outside world could naturally be expected to vary according to particular presidents and situations. In any conflict with Nicaragua or Venezuela, Colombia could be expected to seek U.S. support or mediation, as well as the protection of international law. In fact, for a time during the Turbay administration there were indications that ties to the United States might be growing stronger than ever, notably with the break in relations with Cuba and Colombia's role as a kind of proxy in a U.S.-led campaign in 1979–80 to oppose Cuban membership on the U.N. Security Council. Nonetheless, a modestly greater degree of independence from the United States and enhanced involvement in Caribbean, regional, and Third World affairs seemed to be the long-term trend, albeit manifestly within the U.S. sphere of influence and still more securely linked to the United States than most of the other major Latin American countries.

CONCLUSION

Colombia's economic and political elites tend to predominate in the policy-making process, at least when they perceive their vital interests to be engaged, and the outcomes of the policy process clearly tend to favor them. This is true even in foreign policy, where alignment with the United States and the downplaying of nationalism serve in the broad view to preserve the basic structures of Colombia's society, economy, and polity. Thus it is, too, that policies promoting economic growth have been pursued more persistently, and have been more successful, than policies tending to foster a redistribution of resources, whether they be land, housing, or education.

Colombia's expenditures on health, education, and social welfare have over the years constituted a smaller share of central government expenditures than in most countries having comparable per capita income levels. Indeed, the government's share of the GNP is smaller than in most other countries having a similar income range.[56] It is nonetheless important to note that the overall impact of both taxation and government expenditures is at least mildly redistributive: "a strong case can be made that the separate and combined distributional impact of the two sides of the Colombian budget is progressive. It might lower the Gini coefficient by something on the order of 3 to 5 points."[57] Moreover, certain policies designed to promote growth—notably the expansion and improvement of education in recent years—have significant potential implications for broadening access to economic and political resources. It could well be said that Colombia's elites rather artfully blend the conservative and progressive approaches to modernization, stressing growth while recognizing that certain changes of a mildly redistributive stripe are on occasion necessary both to promote that growth and to prevent serious challenge to the system.

NOTES

1. Maurico Solaún, Fernando Cepeda, and Bruce Bagley, "Urban Reform in Colombia: The Impact of the 'Politics of Games' on Public Policy," in Francine Rabinowitz and Felicity M. Trueblood, eds., *Latin American Urban Research*, vol. 3 (Beverly Hills, Calif.: Sage, 1973), p. 117 and passim.

2. Harvey F. Kline, "The Coal of 'El Cerrejón': An Historical Analysis of Major Colombian Policy Decisions and MNC Activities," *Inter-American Economic Affairs* 35, no. 3 (Winter 1981): 69–90. President Turbay expressly noted (p. 84) that technical advisers did not make the decision.

3. Particularly good discussions of the Commission's recommendations and their fate in the legislative process are in Albert O. Hirschman, *Journeys Toward Progress* (New York: Twentieth Century Fund, 1963), chap. 3; and Bruce B. Bagley, "Political Power, Public Policy and the State in Colombia: Case Studies of the Urban and Agrarian Reforms During the National Front, 1958–1974" (Ph.D. diss., University of California, Los Angeles, 1979), chap. 3. A similar commission was appointed in 1967 by President Carlos Lleras Restrepo, but its recommendations were not so fully incorporated into the government's legislative proposals; see Bagley, "Political Power, Public Policy and the State," p. 201.

4. Cf. Jonathan Hartlyn, "Consociational Politics in Colombia: Confrontation and Accommodation in Comparative Perspective" (Ph.D. diss., Yale University, 1981), p. 169.

5. Cf. Miguel Urrutia, "Diversidad Ideológica e Integración Andino," *Coyuntura Económica* (Bogotá) 10, no. 2 (July 1980): 197.

6. Two "superministers," the minister of Hacienda (i.e., finance) and the minister of defense, have in recent years come to be considered more important

than others in the ministerial hierarchy; cf. Harvey F. Kline, *Energy Policy and the Colombian Elite: A Synthesis and Interpretation* (Washington, D.C.: American Enterprise Institute for Public Policy Research, 1982), p. 18.

7. Ibid., p. 7.

8. Kline, " The Coal of 'El Cerrejón,'" p. 86.

9. Cf. Hartlyn, "Consociational Politics in Colombia," p. 187.

10. Bagley, "Political Power, Public Policy and the State," chaps. 3-6; also see Pierre Gilhodes, *La Question Agraire en Colombie, 1958-1971* (Paris: Armand Colin, 1974), p. 147.

11. This seems to have been the case with regard to President López Michelsen's decreed tax reform, for example; cf. Hartlyn, "Consociational Politics," pp. 195-96.

12. They may also lack the technical expertise and "sophistication" on such matters as macroeconomic policy. Miguel Urrutia notes that labor failed to mobilize behind President López Michelsen's 1974 tax reform even though it favored workers; *Gremios, Política Económica y Democracia* (Bogotá: Fundo Cultural Cafetero, 1983), p. 194.

13. For instance, see Richard R. Nelson, T. Paul Schultz, and Robert L. Slighton, *Structural Change in a Developing Economy* (Princeton: Princeton University Press, 1971), chap. 7; see also Fernando Cepeda Ulloa, "La Influencia de las Agencias Internacionales en el Proceso de Desarrollo de Colombia, 1950-1974," *Estudios Internacionales* (Santiago) 11, no. 43 (July–September 1978): 57-75; and Edgar Revéiz, *Poder e Información* (Bogotá: Universidad de los Andes, Centro de Estudios Sobre Desarrollo Económico, 1977).

14. See William P. McGreevey, "Population Policy Under the National Front," in R. Albert Berry, Ronald G. Hellman, and Maurice Solaún, eds., *Politics of Compromise* (New Brunswick, N.J.: Transaction Books, 1980), chap. 14.

15. For an excellent analysis of the impact of international agencies during the National Front years, see Fernando Cepeda Ulloa and Christopher Mitchell, "The Trend Towards Technocracy: The World Bank and the International Labor Organization in Colombian Politics," in Berry et al., *Politics of Compromise*, chap. 8.

16. Cf. on this point ibid., p. 243; Nelson et al., *Structural Change*, pp. 238-39; Revéiz, *Poder e Información*, pp. 235-36; and Richard E. Hartwig, *Roads to Reason* (Pittsburgh: University of Pittsburgh Press, 1983).

17. Cf. Hartlyn, "Consociational Politics," pp. 121.

18. Solaún et al., "Urban Reform in Colombia," p. 121.

19. Richard Maullin, *The Colombia-IMF Disagreement of November–December 1966: An Interpretation of Its Place in Colombian Politics* (Santa Monica, Calif.: RAND Corp., 1967), p. 3.

20. This is the judgment of R. Albert Berry in "The National Front and Colombia's Economic Development," in Berry et al., *Politics of Compromise*, p. 314.

21. See International Bank for Reconstruction and Development, *The Basis of a Development Program for Colombia* (Baltimore: Johns Hopkins University Press, 1950). Currie was born in Canada and subsequently worked for the administration of Franklin D. Roosevelt. After his report on Colombia, he became a

Colombian citizen, and a leading spokesman and adviser on economic affairs. He headed the National Planning Department during the early 1970s.

22. República de Colombia, Consejo Nacional de Política Económica y Planeación, Departamento Administrativo de Planeación y Servicios Téchnicos, *Colombia, Plan General de Desarrollo Económico y Social*, 2 vols. (Bogotá: Imprenta Nacional 1961–62). In point of fact, this was a revised version of a four-year plan drawn up in 1960, prior to the launching of the Alliance.

23. Robert H. Dix, *Colombia: The Political Dimensions of Change* (New Haven: Yale University Press, 1967), p. 149.

24. See Jan Peter Wogart, *Industrialization in Colombia: Policies, Patterns, Perspectives* (Tübingen: J. C. B. Mohr, 1978).

25. See Harvey F. Kline, *Colombia: Portrait of Unity and Diversity* (Boulder, Colo.: Westview Press, 1983), chap. 5, for a useful, succinct portrayal of Colombian energy policy; see also Kline, *Energy Policy and the Colombian Elite*. The following discussion owes much to both.

26. The principal exception was the Colombian Petroleum Enterprise (ECOPETROL), formed in 1951 when the original concession granted to Tropical Oil (then a subsidiary of Standard Oil of New Jersey, now Exxon) expired.

27. For the controversy over Law 200, see Hirschman, *Journeys Toward Progress*, pp. 96, 108–13; and Orlando Fals Borda, *El Hombre y la Tierra en Boyacá* (Bogotá: Editorial Antares, 1957), pp. 103–05.

28. Official data cited in Everett Eggington and J. Mark Ruhl, "The Influence of Agrarian Reform Participation on Peasant Attitudes: The Case of Colombia," *Inter-American Economic Affairs* 28, no. 3 (Winter 1974): 30.

29. For an analysis of the inception, content, and passage of Law 135, see Hirschman, *Journeys Toward Progress*, pp. 141–58. For a thorough analysis of the problems of implementation of Law 135, see Roger W. Findley, "Problems Faced by Colombia's Agrarian Reform Institute in Acquiring and Distributing Land," in Robert E. Scott, ed., *Latin American Modernization Problems* (Urbana: University of Illinois Press, 1973), pp. 122–92; see also Ernest A. Duff, *Agrarian Reform in Colombia* (New York: Praeger, 1968).

30. Bruce M. Bagley, "The State and Peasantry in Contemporary Colombia" (paper prepared for delivery at the meeting of the Latin American Studies Association, Washington, D.C., March 1981), p. 26. The pattern of land concentration showed only minuscule change between the agricultural census of 1960 and that of 1970–71; see Albert Berry, "Rural Poverty in Twentieth-Century Colombia," *Journal of Interamerican Studies and World Affairs* 20, no. 4 (November 1978): 365. In addition, however, perhaps as many as 90,000 families had been given titles to land they already worked; see A. Eugene Havens, William L. Flinn, and Susanna Lastarria Cornhill, "Agrarian Reform and the National Front: A Class Analysis," in Berry et al., *Politics of Compromise*, p. 357.

31. For the passage of Law 1 of 1968 and its impact, see Bagley, "Political Power, Public Policy and the State," chaps. 4, 6; see also Bagley, "The State and the Peasantry," pp. 25–28.

32. Bagley, "The State and the Peasantry," p. 80.

33. For a discussion of these points with particular attention to the intendancy (territory) of Caquetá, see Robin Ruth Marsh, *Development Strategies*

in Rural Colombia: The Case of Caquetá (Los Angeles: University of California, Los Angeles, Latin American Center, 1983), esp. chap. 5.

34. See Eggington and Ruhl, "The Influence of Agrarian Reform Participation." Even among the campesino participants in the program, the lack of credit and technical assistance, and inadequate land distribution were major complaints; for a parallel assessment, see Marsh, *Development Strategies*, p. 127.

35. Michael Edwards, "The Political Economy of Low-Income Housing: New Evidence from Urban Colombia," *Bulletin of Latin American Research*, May 1982, pp. 48–49.

36. Solaún et al., "Urban Reform in Colombia," p. 103; for the following discussion, see this article and Bagley, "Political Power, Public Policy and the State," chaps. 7–9.

37. See John J. Bailey, "Bureaucratic Politics and Social Security Policy in Colombia," *Inter-American Economic Affairs* 29, no. 4 (Spring 1976): 3–19; and John W. Sloan, *Public Policy in Latin America* (Pittsburgh: University of Pittsburgh Press, 1984), pp. 124–25.

38. Charles L. Taylor and David A. Jodice, *World Handbook of Political and Social Indicators*, 3rd ed. (New Haven: Yale University Press, 1983), vol. 1, pp. 163–65, 28–30.

39. Berry, "Rural Poverty," pp. 359–60.

40. See Robert F. Arnove, "Education Policies of the National Front," in Berry et al., *Politics of Compromise*, p. 311, as well as for a general overview of Colombian educational policy up through the National Front period.

41. Ibid., p. 382.

42. World Bank, *World Development Report 1984* (New York: Oxford University Press, 1984), p. 267.

43. Ibid., pp. 149, 200–01. Only such Asian countries as China, Korea, and Singapore received an "A" rating.

44. For good, brief overviews of both the substance and the process of Colombian foreign policy, see Gerhard Drekonja-Kornat, "Colombia: Learning the Foreign Policy Process," *Journal of Interamerican Studies and World Affairs* 25, no. 2 (May 1983): 229–50; and Daniel Premo, "Colombia: Cool Friendship," in Robert Wesson, ed., *U.S. Influence in Latin America in the 1980s* (New York: Praeger, 1982), chap. 6.

45. Daniel L. Premo, "The Colombian Armed Forces in Search of a Mission," in Robert Wesson, ed., *New Military Politics in Latin America* (New York: Praeger, 1982), p. 166.

46. The death of Theodore Roosevelt, who opposed the treaty, and favorable treatment for Standard Oil of New Jersey seem to have made possible the long-delayed ratification of the treaty by the Senate; Kline, *Colombia*, p. 125.

47. Stephen J. Randall, *The Diplomacy of Modernization: Colombian-American Relations, 1920–1940* (Toronto: University of Toronto Press, 1977), p. 16.

48. U.S. Senate, Subcommittee on American Republic Affairs, Committee on Foreign Relations, 91st Congress, 1st Session, *Colombia—A Case History of U.S. Aid* (Washington, D.C.: U.S. Government Printing Office, 1969), pp. 4, 5.

49. David Bushnell, "Colombia," in Harold E. Davis and Larman C. Wilson, eds., *Latin American Foreign Policies: An Analysis* (Baltimore: Johns Hopkins University Press, 1975), p. 413.

50. Venezuela joined in 1973; Chile withdrew in 1975.

51. For further details on the Andean Pact, see Kline, *Colombia*, pp. 128–31. For a summary of the progress (or lack thereof) of the Andean Group and of ALALC—since 1980 reconstituted as the Latin American Integration Association (ALADI)—and Colombia's role in them, see *Quarterly Economic Review of Colombia, Ecuador* (London), annual supplement 1984, pp. 20–23.

52. "Decision 24" (1971) of the Andean Pact had in fact stipulated 80 percent domestic ownership of banks.

53. Quoted in Kline, *Colombia*, p. 126. Some economic and development assistance nonetheless did continue.

54. *Newsweek*, August 23, 1982. President Turbay had sent an observer to a meeting of the group in Havana in 1979, and in June of that year paid an official visit to Yugoslavia, one of the leaders of the nonaligned countries. 1983 brought official Colombian membership in the nonaligned bloc.

55. Colombia presumably had adopted its earlier position partly out of concern for sovereignty over its islands off the Nicaraguan coast. Its position also, of course, came close to the U.S. view.

56. See R. Albert Berry, "Some Implications of Elitist Rule for Economic Development in Colombia," in Gustav Ranis, ed., *Government and Economic Development* (New Haven: Yale University Press, 1971), p. 7, for the above evaluations and comparisons.

57. R. Albert Berry and Ronald Soligo, "The Distribution of Income in Colombia: An Overview," in R. Albert Berry and Ronald Soligo, eds., *Economic Policy and Income Distribution in Colombia* (Boulder, Colo.: Westview Press, 1980), p. 28.

9

CONCLUSION

Colombia's political system in the end appears to be a paradox: clearly democratic in form and in much of its practice, the resources of politics are nevertheless highly concentrated in a relatively few hands and rather frequent, albeit selective, use is made of repressive instruments and practices. Existing in a context of rapid social change even by Latin American standards, it has nonetheless retained a real degree of stability. Such traits make it difficult to classify according to the standard distinctions among political systems. Yet it is this very circumstance, as well as the polity's differences from its neighbors and the reasons for those differences, that make it well worth the attempt to summarize its major characteristics and to assess its future prospects.

THE POLITICAL SYSTEM CHARACTERIZED

How, then, do we categorize such a political system? What, in summary, is its nature? Is it a democracy or polyarchy?[1] Or an oligarchy? And is "dependent capitalism" an accurate way to characterize Colombia's relationship to the world outside its borders? Does the use of such a term clarify or obscure the realities of Colombian politics?

If political democracy (or its near approximation, polyarchy) is considered to have two dimensions—the free and fair competition for public office (public contestation) and the right of all citizens to participate effectively in that choice (inclusiveness)—historic Colombia has fallen considerably short on both counts and could at the very best be called a proto- or partial democracy.[2] Usually elections have been regularly held and civil liberties, including freedom of the press, respected. Yet in the long periods of party hegemony, competition was often limited to intraparty contests. Then, for 16 years after 1958, power was shared equally and only between the major parties by constitutional fiat, surely a limitation on full-blown competitive democracy whatever the other virtues of the National Front. As for inclusiveness, literacy and property qualifications limited the vote for much of Colombian history. Nor could the termination of such strictures in 1936 put an end to the manifestly unequal political resources that characterize Colombians, a situation that, if somewhat diminished by the growth of literacy and an urban electorate, very much continues today.

Is Colombia then an oligarchy, and democratic in form only? If a society is oligarchic when social status, education, wealth, and political influence tend to be united in the same hands, Colombia is—at least in comparison with most European and North American democracies—an oligarchy. The overlap among the holders of economic power, university degrees, social position, and political office is considerable, and the barriers to entry into such an elite tend to be high and difficult to cross. The proliferation of interest associations and financial-industrial conglomerates over the last several decades has had the effect more of institutionalizing the association among the several kinds of power and influence than of significantly diminishing it: producers' associations clearly far outweigh labor unions and peasant organizations in their access to the press, the parties, and governmental decision makers. The parties are very much characterized by patron-client relationships and the dominance of certain "natural chiefs," who tend to be men of high position and attainments in other spheres. Congressmen, presidents, and cabinet officers tend to come—to a strikingly disproportionate degree in comparison with their numbers in the population—from the ranks of the highly educated. The policy-making process demonstrates that powerful groups such as landowners or urban real estate interests are usually able to prevent the enactment of legislation inimical to their interests, or to block its effective implementation over the long run. Workers only seldom (and then often as the result of co-optative action by elites), and peasants almost never, get their way in the policy process.

Even the middle class is only weakly organized as an independent actor in Colombian politics.

Yet the term "oligarchy" masks other realities of Colombian society and politics. Individual upward mobility is, and always has been, possible, with President Betancur but the latest outstanding example. Moreover, Colombia's elites are hardly monolithic in their policy preferences, and are becoming more diverse in their social composition, and more varied in the available routes to power and influence. Some new sources of wealth (such as the drug trade) do not necessarily imply social position or education, while education (as in the case of the technocrats) does not always have its former close correlation with wealth or inherited social position. Finally, the state has a meaningful measure of autonomy vis-à-vis those who hold other forms of power in Colombian society. That is, the role of president, and often of cabinet minister and upper-level bureaucrat, carries its own measure of divorcement from social and economic power. The president and those with economic power frequently come into conflict over policy; moreover, at least some of those with little economic power, such as unions, are sometimes able to get their demands accommodated because of their electoral potential or threats to disrupt public order. Not least, elections and public opinion play something of a meaningful role in the system, placing constraints on both elite and state behavior.

In sum, there is little doubt that Colombian society is more nearly a system of cumulative than of dispersed inequalities. It might even be plausibly argued that a powerful, informal coalition of elites sustains the existing order—promoting capitalist growth, opposing threats to internal order and extant property arrangements, and favoring a pro-U.S. foreign policy—even while disagreeing from time to time on particular policies. Such a coalition would include the ex-presidents, the top leadership of the Liberal and Conservative parties, the hierarchy of the Church, the top ranks of the military, business leaders and large landowners and the management of the producers' associations, and even some elements of labor leadership. Yet given the diversity of such elites, the real possibilities for upward (and downward) individual social mobility, and the relative autonomy of the state, another term would seem better suited to accommodate Colombian political reality than the more constricting, if more colorful, designation *oligarquía*.[3]

This being the case, and given the real limitations on full-fledged democracy (or polyarchy) in Colombia, a qualified term such as "quasi democracy" or "near polyarchy" might be more accurate. Even more apposite might be a term such as "oligarchic democracy" or "elitist democracy," or "elitist pluralism,"[4] thus making more explicit the nature of Colombia's deviation from the democratic ideal—democratic in form and in some of its reality, but very largely controlled, in the interest of its self-preservation, by a self-perpetuating, though not entirely closed, elite.

What, then, of dependency? If "dependency" means that a country is relatively highly constrained by the international environment on most important issues most of the time, and if there is a substantial degree of penetration of a society by international actors, then Colombia—like most countries of Latin America and of the Third World, of whatever political hue—is clearly dependent. The disparities of power between it and the industrialized countries, and its vulnerability to outside economic, political, and even cultural forces largely beyond its control, are too great for it to be otherwise. But if "dependency" means that there is no meaningful measure of autonomy for the dependent country, or that Colombian politics can be explained largely on the basis of the country's relationship to external actors and forces, then the notion of dependency becomes overly simplistic. Rather than as a dichotomous concept—one either is or is not dependent—dependency is perhaps best thought of as a continuous, more-or-less, kind of variable. This has the further virtue of permitting comparisons with other countries concerning degrees of dependency, as well as the assessment of change over time. Indeed, the more interesting question may not be "Is Colombia dependent?" but "Has it become more or less dependent over time, and what is the prognosis for the future?"[5]

In addressing such a question in the case of Colombia, one finds that the country is highly vulnerable to the vagaries of international markets for its economic well-being, particularly in regard to the price of coffee. A sharp rise in coffee prices in the mid-1970s helped spur an economic boom, the rapid accumulation of foreign exchange reserves, and inflation. A subsequent decline in the world price of coffee (and of other primary products) helped to trigger a severe recession. Nonetheless, the diversification of exports beginning in the late 1960s has helped lessen the country's dependency on coffee to some degree. Not incidentially, between 1960 and 1975 Colombia substantially reduced its export reliance on a single trading partner (the United States).[6] Colombia's membership in the Andean Pact

TABLE 9.1. Latin American Dependency Indicators

	Relative Importance of the External Sector to National Economy (%) and Rank Order ( )[a]		Concentration Index of Export-Receiving Countries and Rank Order ( )			Concentration Index of Export Commodities and Rank Order ( )		
	1970	1980	1960	1975	Shift	ca. 1960	ca. 1975	Shift
Argentina	21(16)	51(12)	.105(17)	.066(18)	-.039	.113(16)	.174(9)	.061
Bolivia	43(6.5)	72(9)	.464(3)	.125(12)	-.339	.415(7)	.282(6)	-.133
Brazil	16(18)	30(18)	.065(18)	.102(15)	.037	.335(9)	.109(16)	-.226
Chile	39(9)	80(5)	.207(14)	.086(17)	-.121	.299(11)	.562(2)	.263
Colombia	**34(10)**	**47(13)**	**.454(4)**	**.186(8)**	**-.268**	**.555(1.5)**	**.265(7)**	**-.290**
Costa Rica	63(2)	90(4)	.374(7)	.245(7)	-.129	.403(8)	.193(8)	-.210
Dominican Rep.	43(6.5)	60(10)	.427(5)	.622(2)	.195	.304(10)	.423(4)	.119
Ecuador	33(11)	78(6)	.413(6)	.291(15)	-.122	.425(6)	.409(5)	-.016
El Salvador	42(8)	74(7)	.262(11)	.173(9)	-.089	.539(3)	.170(10)	-.369
Guatemala	29(13)	47(14)	.333(8)	.111(13)	-.222	.509(5)	.129(13)	-.380
Honduras	59(3)	96(3)	.277(9)	.379(4)	.102	.286(12)	.139(12)	-.147
Mexico	20(17)	44(16.5)	.557(2)	.706(1)	.149	.106(18)	.049(18)	-.057
Nicaragua	52(4)	74(8)	.257(12)	.151(11)	-.106	.231(13)	.115(15)	-.116
Panama	89(1)	196(1)	.933(1)	.441(3)	-.492	.555(1.5)	.493(3)	-.062
Paraguay	25(15)	44(16.5)	.265(10)	.159(10)	-.106	.169(14)	.072(17)	-.097
Peru	30(12)	46(15)	.184(15)	.109(14)	-.075	.108(17)	.145(11)	.037
Uruguay	27(14)	59(11)	.124(16)	.089(16)	-.035	.156(15)	.120(14)	-.036
Venezuela	45(5)	108(2)	.243(13)	.250(6)	.007	.526(4)	.877(1)	.351

	U.S. Aid per Capita, 1946–75 ($) and Rank Order ( )		Debt Service (1982) and Rank Order ( )		Composite Dependency Ranking (Mean Score) and Rank Order ( )[b]
	Economic	Military	As Percent of GNP	As Percent of Export Earnings	
Argentina	5.96(17)	1.98(14)	4.4(10)	24.5(6)	13.5(18)
Bolivia	148.97(2)	7.96(4)	4.0(11)	28.2(5)	6.6(3)
Brazil	no data	no data	3.5(12)	42.1(1)	13.4(17)
Chile	104.12(5)	10.00(2)	4.7(8)	18.8(7.5)	8.1(8.5)
Colombia	**78.05(8)**	**4.63(12)**	**2.2(15)**	**17.5(10)**	**8.9(10)**
Costa Rica	86.47(6)	1.18(16)	6.2(5)	12.5(14)	7.7(6)
Dominican Rep.	126.83(3)	7.32(6)	3.3(13)	18.7(9)	6.9(4)
Ecuador	61.90(12)	7.41(5)	9.7(3)	30.8(3)	6.2(2)
El Salvador	49.41(13)	2.65(13)	1.4(16.5)	4.6(17)	10.8(12)
Guatemala	64.49(11)	4.69(11)	1.0(18)	6.6(16)	12.2(14)
Honduras	80.83(7)	5.00(9.5)	5.7(6)	18.8(7.5)	7.3(5)
Mexico	6.13(16)	.04(17)	5.5(7)	29.5(4)	11.7(13)
Nicaragua	112.63(4)	8.95(3)	10.2(2)	N.A.	8.0(7)
Panama	357.86(1)	5.00(9.5)	15.4(1)	13.8(12)	3.4(1)
Paraguay	71.36(10)	6.36(8)	1.4(16.5)	10.3(15)	13.2(16)
Peru	77.52(9)	7.05(7)	7.4(4)	36.7(2)	10.6(11)
Uruguay	47.59(14)	16.21(1)	2.5(14)	13.4(13)	12.8(15)
Venezuela	43.40(15)	1.26(15)	4.6(9)	15.6(11)	8.1(8.5)

Note: Cuba is omitted because of lack of information in most categories.

aMeasured as the ratio between the combined value of exports and imports of goods and services, and the gross domestic product.

bAll columns are weighted equally.

Sources: Inter-American Development Bank, *Economic and Social Progress in Latin America. 1982 Report* (Washington, D.C.: the Bank, 1982), p. 24; Charles L. Taylor and David A. Jodice, *World Handbook of Political and Social Indicators*, 3rd ed. (New Haven: Yale University Press, 1983), vol. 1, pp. 230–35; David Scott Palmer, *Peru: The Authoritarian Tradition* (New York: Praeger, 1980), p. 86; and World Bank, *World Development Report 1984* (New York: Oxford University Press, 1984), pp. 248–49.

(Colombia was one of the leaders in its formation) has further helped to multilateralize the country's external economic relationships. Colombia has also joined with Brazil and others in a partially successful effort to stabilize coffee prices.

At the same time, foreign investment, now increasingly concentrated in mineral resources and in manufacturing sectors critical to the process of industrialization, has probably worked to increase dependency. However, even when, as in the case of several multinational automobile manufacturers, the provisions of contracts regarding production levels were not strictly fulfilled, this did not necessarily signify the government's weakness versus the multinationals. Rather, it appears that the companies' go-slow investment policies have coincided with government objectives, and with the interests of domestic financiers and industrialists as well.[7]

A new project designed to develop the El Cerrejón coalfields on Colombia's northeast coast in "association" with Exxon brings new foreign involvement in natural resource development. This agreement has been controversial, with some arguing that the country has surrendered too much control to a foreign enterprise. However, few seem to dispute the need for foreign capital in developing Colombia's coal resources, and the agreement with Exxon has sought to institute guarantees of a kind not generally characteristic of foreign resource investment in the past.[8]

Colombia's foreign debt increased substantially as the country's demands for imports grew to spur its industrialization and coffee prices fell. Although the government turned in a major way to a variety of external sources, particularly to multilateral lending agencies, to help fund its ambitious development plans in the early 1980s, Colombia's substantial debt burden has nevertheless not been in the category of most other major Latin American countries. And in a notable instance in the 1960s, President Carlos Lleras Restrepo faced down the International Monetary Fund (IMF), refusing to carry out the devaluation of the peso in the manner demanded by the IMF. For a time during the heyday of the Alliance for Progress, Colombia was a "showcase" of the Alliance and hundreds of millions of dollars in U.S. aid poured into the country, but in 1975 President López Michelsen formally pronounced an end to such aid.[9]

Foreign advisers, consultants, and technicians proliferated in Colombia during the National Front era, though their occasional presence dated from many years before. They included U.S. military advisers (and equipment) in the civic-military campaigns against the guerrillas in the early 1960s. The impact of those foreign techno-crats—and of Colombians educated abroad—was considerable, not only on policy but also on the shaping of institutions (such as, plan-ning and counterinsurgency forces). More recently, however, as the number and quality of Colombian technocrats (including the military) have noticeably increased, the weight of foreign influence has de-clined in comparison with the 1960s and 1970s, although it certainly continues to be important in the campaign against the drug traffic, for example.

Colombia has meanwhile shown an increased tendency to expand its foreign ties and influence in the Caribbean, among its neighbors, and in the Third World generally. President Betancur's initiatives in foreign policy, while hardly divorcing Colombia from its close ties to the United States, have created a sense of somewhat greater autonomy for Colombia in the international arena.

Colombia is therefore clearly vulnerable to the vagaries of inter-national markets and international politics, and its economic, social, and political systems are deeply penetrated by foreign actors and influences. Yet there are limits to those vulnerabilities and influences, ways in which Colombia is enabled to act that are at least semi-autonomous. On balance, the strengthening of the institutions and capacities of the Colombian state since the 1960s probably makes it less dependent today than a generation, or even a few years, ago.

CHANGE AND STABILITY

Whether polyarchy, oligarchy, or a system of elitist pluralism, whether dependent or not, Colombia has witnessed some striking changes in its society and economy compared with 1958, at the out-set of the National Front. The country is now more urban than rural, with some tendency toward increasing regional concentration. The transportation network links the country much more effectively than it did a generation ago. The population is now more literate than not, the reverse of 1958. Through the rapid commercialization of agricul-ture and the growth of financial-industrial conglomerates, Colombia's economy has become more "modern," and its land and wealth more concentrated. The drug trade has opened a vast new arena for the accumulation of wealth (and for its dissemination in the political arena), and industrialization has advanced apace. Economic diversification has brought less dependence on coffee as the source of foreign exchange. Population growth rates have begun to decline, and such indices of economic welfare as GNP per capita have started to climb.

Political changes have been significant as well. *La violencia*, with its combination of partisan warfare and revenge, economic extortion, and pure banditry, has come to an end in its old form, to be replaced by revolutionary guerrilla bands. In urban areas at least, there has been a decline in the ability of the parties to mobilize their traditional captive votes and some evidence that, in the wake of the National Front, at least some Colombians are now willing to vote for candidates with a party label other than their own. Could it be that a new version of populism, this time a successful one, is about to emerge in Colombia? There seems to be an increasing dichotomy between politics as practiced in the large urban centers and politics as practiced in smaller cities and towns, as well as, in parallel fashion, between the politics of presidential policy making and the politics of Congress and *el país político*. Party hegemonies—long periods of control of the presidency by one party, with the attendant "electoral bias" against the minority party—may well be a thing of the past; politics at the presidential level, at any rate, has become more genuinely competitive (and in that sense, at least, more genuinely democratic) than ever before.

The role of the parties has tended to decline in the wake of the growth of the state, and of the role of the executive branch and innumerable decentralized agencies in the making of economic and social policy. The increasing numbers and importance of *técnicos*, both national and international, have contributed to the same end, as have the proliferation and institutionalization of producers' associations and other interest groups. The relative role of Congress in the political process has, by the same token, tended to decline. Those groups with fewer resources, and with less effective access to the executive, Congress, and the bureaucracy—labor, peasants, students, for example—have become increasingly militant, increasingly willing to voice their demands by means of strikes, demonstrations, land invasions, and other forms of direct action. The role of the military in Colombia's internal political life has increased in tandem, making it at once a prime support of the existing order and a potential threat to the continuance of civil rule. On the other hand, the political role of the Church has probably diminished compared with the past. As important, its role has altered from that of political partisan to that of a buttress—but also sometime critic and conscience—of the post-National Front social and political order. Intellectuals seem markedly more critical of the system than they were in the early 1960s.[10]

Notwithstanding these changes, both socioeconomic and political, the bedrock of Colombian society and politics remains much the same. Coffee is still preeminent, striking diversities and disparities continue to prevail both among regions and between urban and rural areas, and the fundamental lines of social stratification and income distribution remain substantially intact. Government remains civilian and republican, and for the most part respectful of civil liberties and electoral freedoms, even though it continues to function much of the time under a state of siege, and even though in most elections a majority of Colombians stay away from the ballot box. The fundamental levers of political power remain only rather marginally altered, with no significant challenge, even of a reformist nature, to the prevailing order of things having made its appearance. This latter circumstance may be the greatest single contrast with the other major countries of Latin America.

How, then, is it possible to account for the underlying stability of the Colombian system and the lack of serious challenge to its continuance, despite the many other changes in Colombian society and politics? How is it possible to account for the maintenance of a quasi-democratic polity in the face of high levels of social mobilization, one of the more unequal patterns of income distribution in the hemisphere, and one of the most elitist political systems? Nor is such a political system merely a creation of the last few years. Historically Colombia has been more open politically, with fewer periods of dictatorship, than virtually any other nation in Latin America, while policy changes have been at most incremental, and antisystem parties uncommonly weak.

To start with, the stability and continuity of Colombia's civilian institutions doubtless is partly an illusion. The frequent use of violence for political ends—*la violencia*, the *bogotazo*, the coups of 1953 and 1957, the increasing use of direct-action tactics, and the sporadic acts of several revolutionary guerrilla bands, not to mention the threat of violence posed by the drug "mafia", among the more prominent instances in the post-World War II period—is not the mark of stable democratic government by most definitions. Much of the same might be said of the recurrent utilization of the state of siege and the accompanying use of force by the government and its armed forces.

Statistically high levels of social mobilization can be somewhat deceptive. The recent migrants to urban areas and the marginally employed have in Colombia, as elsewhere in Latin America, thus far tended to remain politically passive, at least at the level of national politics. They tend to be more concerned with daily survival, and the attainment of urban services for their barrios, than with structural changes. Rapid urbanization does not, therefore, automatically translate into political radicalization.

Still, much else remains to be explained. Among other things, those largely left out of the elite-dominated economic, social, and political systems have seldom sought radical changes in those systems. Labor has been too weak, and largely uninfluenced by European immigrants' ideas of labor militancy. Until recently, at least, peasants have been too isolated and traditional, and perhaps there have been too many smallholders among them, for them to seek change. Even students and intellectuals, in recent decades increasingly militant and articulate on behalf of social and political change, lagged well behind their counterparts in Venezuela and Peru, where as early as the 1920s university students took the lead in founding such movements as Acción Democrática (AD) and the American Popular Revolutionary Alliance (APRA), respectively. Nor was there any lasting challenge to the system from a new group of industrialists. Although for a time during the 1930s and 1940s something of a split did appear between a rising industrial bourgeoisie and traditional landed and commercial elites, it was largely healed by the late 1950s as they joined against a common set of perceived dangers and as, with the increasing commercialization of agriculture, their interests tended to fuse. The very fact that much of the capital for Colombian industry came from agricultural (coffee) income tended to mute any such conflict in the first place. The industrializers and the export sector were closely allied, and by and large each accepted the demands of the other. The classic populist alliance among workers, industrialists, and the middle class—together seeking to promote industrial development in the face of opposition from landowners and their allies—therefore never really formed in Colombia on any sustained basis.[11]

The diversion and division of counter-elite claimants go a long way toward explaining their ineffectiveness. The "hereditary hatreds" and the attendant loyalties of most Colombians both to the traditional parties and to the elites who led them have made it unusually difficult to mobilize a political movement along class lines. The nature of Colombia's regionalism, producing not only fragmentation but also dispersion among roughly equal regional centers, added to those difficulties. Today the migration of tens of thousands of Colombians to Venezuela (and elsewhere) in search of employment and higher wages, and the advent of the drug "industry," providing jobs, income, and a measure of upward mobility to many, perhaps help to divert Colombians from challenging the established order.

Similarly, economic and political co-optation by the incumbent elites has almost certainly played a major role in harnessing any potential challenge to the established order. Economically, this has meant that growth has been constant enough throughout most of the last several decades to provide the perception of an expanding pie—and for long periods genuinely improving real wages—for a significant portion of the urban work force. Politically, the traditional parties have been able to include under their broad, multiclass umbrellas most of the challengers to their leadership, and at critical junctures such as the 1930s to enact sufficiently reformist policies to defuse, at least for a time, any potential threat to themselves and to the system. In fact, to a large extent Colombia's elites have by their actions anticipated needs or demands for reforms, rather than responding to groups that were in most cases poorly organized and not very articulate. Reforms have "resulted from the political will of groups fully integrated with the nation's exclusivist social circles,"[12] rather than from the initiative or pressure of any counter-elite.

The pattern of patron-clientism that pervades the parties and society generally, and has the effect of distributing the public largesse particularistically to persons and localities, has worked to a similar end. It might well be argued that Colombia's traditional party system survives essentially because of its regionally distributive policy-making style—that is, its ability to allocate jobs, goods, and services to regional elites and their supporters in a reasonably equitable manner.[13] It is in this way that Colombia's *pais politico*, which in one sense has an inhibiting effect on the government's (and international agencies') goal of the efficient allocation of resources, in a different sense is fundamental to the success of the developmental process in Colombia, at least under auspices that are at least semidemocratic. For Colombia a measure of horizontal (regional) equity has substituted for the lack of it on the vertical (class) dimension in helping to stabilize the system and inhibit the emergence of radical discontent.[14]

Finally, would-be opponents of the status quo have generally lacked a catalyst that might unite them, as well as erstwhile supporters of the regime, into the kind of widespread movement necessary to overturn or significantly modify it. Anti-imperialism has seldom loomed large in Colombia. Nor has the country experienced the sort of prolonged, harsh dictatorship—like those of Fulgencio Batista in Cuba and the Somoza family in Nicaragua—that might lead to such a coalesence of opposition forces, whatever their otherwise divergent objectives or ideologies.[15]

Weakness and lack of revolutionary impetus among potential regime opponents; their division, diversion, and co-optation; and the lack of a unifying catalyst may together help to explain the absence of an effective challenge from the Left to Colombian social and political patterns.

Interestingly, neither has Colombia's elitist democracy been effectively challenged from the Right. So far, at least, it has not fallen victim to a bureaucratic-authoritarian (B/A) regime like those of the countries of South America's southern cone, involving military rule and the suppression of unions and other mass organizations. Given Colombia's persistent use of the state of siege, and periodic use of the military against strikers and other manifestations of popular discontent, it might be argued that Colombia already has a B/A regime in all but name. There is a measure of truth in such an assertion, yet the distinctions between civil rule and a relatively open political system in Colombia, and the regimes in Chile and pre-1983 Argentina, remain too substantial to sustain the argument; Colombian presidents bear little resemblance to Augusto Pinochet, the dictator-president of Chile.

A number of factors help to explain Colombia's failure to follow the political path of authoritarianism. Among them may be the nature and history of the Colombian military, and the country's relative success in recent decades in avoiding overwhelming economic crises. Two principal factors seem to be overriding, however: the strength and persistence of Colombia's civilian elites and their dependent institutions, such as the parties, and, perhaps most basically, the absence of a sustained populist or revolutionary challenge. The strength and militancy of Colombian labor do not compare with those of labor in Uruguay, Chile, and Argentina prior to the onset of their respective B/A regimes.[16] In fact, in Colombia labor has traditionally had close ties to the parties and to the Church. Neither Gaitán nor Rojas—let alone Camilo Torres, General Ruiz Novoa, or others—was able to mount a more than momentary (and partial) threat to elite rule. The only regime in Colombian history that might be termed populist, that of the *revolución en marcha*, was directed (and was soon contained) by members of the Colombian elite.[17]

Put succinctly, Colombia has avoided military rule because the elite's objectives of economic growth and the containment of mass mobilization have been accomplished without yielding to the uncertainties and inconveniences of harsh repression and what is for Colombians the alien phenomenon of military rule. Nonetheless, Colombia's political system has failed to become as fully democratic as, say, those of Venezuela and pre-1973 Chile, for the process of development never really had the effect of broadening the system to include new social classes in its effective membership.

> Such a system is characterized by "limited modernization" carried out by an elite that holds a virtual monopoly of resources within a political framework of representative government, a condition that leads to intra-elite political competition and factionalism. The wellsprings of reform are found mainly at the elite level itself. The limits to reformism are found in the desire of the elite to retain power.[18]

To this end, presidents and would-be presidents continue to engage in recurrent efforts at reform, even when they often seem incapable of rallying the requisite political support to enact it or to sustain its implementation, especially if the reform implies significant structural change. As one scholar has put it with regard to education: "The failure of many reforms cannot be attributed to the lack of adequate administrative bureaucratic structure to implement decisions or to the lack of highly trained personnel in the different national educational agencies. The reforms failed because a fundamental change would have challenged the dominance of the existing elites in Colombia and, therefore, was never intended."[19] In fact, "when 'rhetorical reformism' has been transformed in Colombia into real reform, as during the López [Pumarejo] and Lleras Restrepo administrations, the consequence has been division within the traditional political elite and temporary increases in the political strength of middle-class counter-elites. Thus from the point of view of the traditional elite, actual reformism has resulted in threatening situations."[20] Nevertheless, "rhetorical reformism," plus the occasional periods of "real" reform, combined with moderately successful economic performance—continued fairly steady growth and the avoidance of major crises—have thus far been sufficient to head off or defeat any challenges to elite rule.

PROSPECTS

In no country does the past equal the future, no matter how strongly it may condition it. Thus in Colombia social and economic change can be expected to continue at a rapid pace, and it may be increasingly translated into demands for political change, or at least to lead to a further erosion in the legitimacy of the system, particularly in the eyes of the growing urban population. The apparent decline in allegiance to the two traditional parties may be one such indication. System tensions can therefore be expected to increase. At any rate, an observer of Colombian politics must assume that distinct possibility, especially if the poor economic performance of the early 1980s fails to improve substantially. What, then, of the country's political prospects for the next decade or so?

The radicalization of society to the point of revolution, or at least a strong reformist thrust from below, would be one conceivable possibility. Some recent developments argue for the likelihood of such an alternative, particularly the increasing radicalization since the mid-1970s of peasants, blue-collar workers, students, and even such white-collar groups as teachers and other government employees, and their more frequent resort to direct-action tactics. Continuing guerrilla activities (despite the partially effective truce instituted in 1984) are further evidence of such a prospect. There is a recurrent antisystem (though essentially reformist) strain in Colombian politics, as reflected in Gaitanismo during the 1940s and Rojismo more than two decades later. Presumably there are some outward limits to the co-optative capacities of even Colombia's elites and their multiclass parties, now put to an increasing test by the bevy of claimant groups only recently become articulate. Co-optation is much easier, after all, if a group is weakly organized and only minimally self-conscious. Yet the abject failure to date of the Colombian Left either to unite or to make any noteworthy electoral showing argues against this alternative future, as does the weight of Colombia's political past.

In quite another vein, what has not been true of Colombia thus far, in contrast with other South American nations, could become true of its future. Certainly in terms of their size, their organizational capacities, and their attitudinal predispositions the Colombian armed forces have greater potential for self-initiated political intervention than at almost any other time in the country's history. The strength, capacities, and relative unity of the country's civilian elites would seem for the present to preclude such an option, however, for the military would find few civilian allies for such a move.

The country's most recent experience with military government, though fading from memory, proved overwhelmingly negative for the private sector. From the perspective of producer groups, for example, there would be many unknowns if a military regime should come to power. It would be difficult to predict whether its economic orientation would be one of liberal orthodoxy, or more statist and nationalist in nature, and civilian access to the policy-making process would probably diminish.[21] Yet given the emergence of a full-blown threat to public order, or to the essentials of the established system, this could well change. It seems fair to say that under the right conditions, and in spite of the vaunted dedication to civilian politics, important segments of Colombia's elites might well collaborate in changing the terms of the current tacit alliance between civilian elites and the military, in which the former are dominant, into one in which the latter prevails. More plausible—in fact, arguably already in place—is a situation in which the armed forces and the national police slip the effective bonds of civilian control in their effort to combat the guerrillas. Even members of the government have criticized them for acts of violence, torture, and "disappearances" that go beyond legitimate bounds and threaten a kind of "Argentinisation" of the country.

There is at the same time little sign that Colombia is about to take a marked turn toward the genuine democratization of its political system. For there is little evidence that the country's elites are about to surrender their control over the major institutions, or that the more equitable distribution of skills and resources that might make that possible, or even mandatory, has made significant progress since the early 1960s. Though other alternatives, particularly the military one, are certainly not out of the question, the continuation of Colombia's elitist democracy therefore seems the more likely course for the present, a kind of muddling through of a political system that seems often on the verge of complete immobility in the face of unattended social and economic problems, a persistent undercurrent of violence and public disorder, both criminal and political,[22] and even some of it "official," and an uncomfortable sense that the tentacles of the drug trade extend through unknown reaches of the society, with untold political, social, and economic ramifications. It is also a system whose legitimacy seems persistently in doubt. The recurrent states of siege have thus seemed at the same time necessary for the survival of the system and an indication of its underlying weakness.

Since no major issues separate the parties, and the era of *la violencia* now seems long past, the time may not be too far distant when Article 120 of the constitution, mandating a sharing of power on a proportionate basis, is brought to an end, and with it the last formal remnants of the National Front that served the country, or at least its elites, so well for so long. The end of Article 120 (and the direct election of mayors) could have the further effect of opening access to power to third parties, long a demand of the Left. Any real changes, either in the structure of the party system or in the policy alternatives offered the country, would most likely not be the result of competition between the parties as such, but of a fracturing of one (or both) along factional lines, perhaps accompanied by the rise of a new Gaitán or a new Rojas, or the emergence of another Alfonso López Pumarejo from the ranks of the elite.

However, no such figure is immediately apparent. Today's most critical dissident faction, Nuevo Liberalismo, is still too confined to the middle class of the largest cities, and especially to Bogotá, to constitute such a movement; and its principal champion, Luis Carlos Galán, appears to be neither a new Gaitán nor a new Rojas Pinilla. By all the evidence the Liberal Party remains the "natural" majority party, as indicated by the outcome of the 1986 elections. The populism of Belisario Betancur was proved to be of a distinctly ephemeral nature, with no enduring organizational base and no personal successor.[23]

In fine, there is little to indicate that Colombia's politics will, in the short run, be much different from that of the recent past. In the longer view, it seems probable that eventually, by some means, Colombia's immobilist politics will be brought into closer harmony with its rapidly changing society and economy, and the increasing political consciousness of its people, to produce some form of "democratic opening."[24]

NOTES

1. Robert A. Dahl, in *Polyarchy* (New Haven: Yale University Press, 1971), uses "polyarchy" essentially as a surrogate for "constitutional democracy," but without the connotations of relative economic and social equality, or direct popular rule, sometimes attaching to "democracy."

2. Such terms are used, for example, by Mauricio Solaún in his "Colombian Politics: Historical Characteristics and Problems," in R. Albert Berry, Ronald G. Hellman, and Mauricio Solaún, eds., *Politics of Compromise* (New Brunswick, N.J.: Transaction Books, 1980), pp. 1–57.

3. For a critique of the use of "oligarchy" to depict Colombian reality, see James L. Payne, "The Oligarchy Muddle," *World Politics* 20 (April 1968): 439–53.

4. The term "elitist pluralism" is employed by John J. Bailey in his "Pluralist and Corporatist Dimensions of Interest Representation in Colombia," in James M. Malloy, ed., *Authoritarianism and Corporatism in Latin America* (Pittsburgh: University of Pittsburgh Press, 1977), pp. 259–302. The term "controlled democracy," applied particularly to the National Front by Miles W. Williams, "El Frente Nacional: Colombia's Experiment in Controlled Democracy" (Ph.D. diss., Vanderbilt University, 1972), is arguably still pertinent. Another descriptive term for the Colombian political system is "interwoven factionalisms" (*faccionalismos trenzados*), employed by Enrique Ogliastri Urribe, "Liberales Conservadores Versus Conservadores Liberales: Faccionalismos Trenzados en la Estructura de Poder en Colombia" (paper presented to the annual meeting of the Latin American Studies Association, Mexico City, October 1983). Yet another term is "inclusive authoritarianism," employed by Bruce M. Bagley, "Colombia: National Front and Economic Development," in Robert Wesson, ed., *Politics, Policies, and Economic Development in Latin America* (Stanford, Calif.: Hoover Institution Press, 1984), pp. 124–60.

5. For an attempt to assess Brazilian dependency along such lines, see Robert A. Packenham, "Trends in Brazilian National Dependency Since 1964," in Riordan Roett, ed., *Brazil in the Seventies* (Washington, D.C.: American Enterprise Institute, 1976), pp. 89–115.

6. Charles L. Taylor and David A. Jodice, *World Handbook of Political and Social Indicators* (New Haven: Yale University Press, 1983), vol. 1, pp. 231, 234, 261. At the same time, as in every other country in Latin America, the relative importance of the external sector grew between 1970 and 1980 (see Table 9.1). Colombia continued to rank at the lower end of the scale among Latin American countries in this respect, however (tie for 13th out of 18), and the increase was less than that for any other Latin American country during the decade.

7. Cf. Michael Fleet, "The Politics of Automobile Industry Development in Colombia," *Journal of Interamerican Studies and World Affairs* 24, no. 2 (May 1982): 211–39.

8. For the controversy over El Cerrejón, see Harvey F. Kline, "The Coal of 'El Cerrejón': An Historical Analysis of Major Colombian Policy Decisions and MNC Activities," *Inter-American Economic Affairs* 35, no. 3 (Winter, 1981): 69–90.

9. A U.S. diplomat lamented that the end of a role for the Agency for International Development (AID) in Colombia would put an end to the embassy's "leverage"; Harvey F. Kline, *Colombia: Portrait of Unity and Diversity* (Boulder, Colo.: Westview Press, 1983), p. 128.

10. The best-known of these is the internationally acclaimed novelist Gabriel García Márquez, who can fairly be called an independent leftist. In recent years he has lived mainly abroad (mainly in Mexico), out of fear he would be arrested for allegedly consorting with guerrilla groups and their supporters.

11. For an elaboration on some of these and related points, see Jonathan Hartlyn, "The Impact of Patterns of Industrialization and of Popular Sector Incorporation on Political Regime Type: A Case Study of Colombia," *Studies in Comparative International Development* 19, no. 1 (Spring 1984): 29–60; see also J. Mark Ruhl, "An Alternative to the Bureaucratic-Authoritarian Regime: The Case of Colombian Modernization," *Inter-American Economic Affairs* 35, no. 2 (Autumn 1981): 43–69.

12. Solaún, "Colombian Politics," p. 8.

13. This is the argument made in John W. Sloan, "Regionalism, Political Parties and Public Policy in Colombia," *Inter-American Economic Affairs* 33, no. 3 (Winter 1979): 38–39.

14. Equity among Colombia's diverse regions should not be exaggerated; the disparity in the levels of development among the Colombian departments is quite great (see chap. 4). Nevertheless, as pointed out in chaps. 7 and 8, the Colombian political process operates to distribute the goods and services of government fairly widely. A term such as "balanced inequities" might be more appropriate for Colombia, in that "development" is dispersed among several regions, even while some areas of the country remain quite poor.

15. See Robert H. Dix, "Why Revolutions Succeed and Fail," *Polity* 16, no. 3 (Spring 1984): 423–46.

16. For the relevant data, see Jonathan Hartlyn, "Consociational Politics in Colombia: Confrontation and Accommodation in Comparative Perspective" (Ph.D. diss., Yale University, 1981), pp. 359–61.

17. The Rojas dictatorship (1953–57) also had populist overtones, but it was halfhearted and largely ineffective in its efforts at mass mobilization.

18. Mauricio Solaún, Fernando Cepeda, and Bruce Bagley, "Urban Reform in Colombia: The Impact of the 'Politics of Games' on Public Policy," in Francine F. Rabinowitz and Felicity Trueblood, eds., *Latin American Urban Research*, vol. 3 (Beverly Hills, Calif.: Sage, 1973), p. 98.

19. Robert F. Arnove, "Education Policies of the National Front," in Berry et al., *Politics of Compromise*, p. 404.

20. Solaún et al., "Urban Reform in Colombia," p. 124.

21. See Jonathan Hartlyn, "Producer Associations, the Political Regime and Political Processes in Contemporary Colombia" (MS, Vanderbilt University, 1984), pp. 27–28.

22. Mario Latorre Rueda refers to Colombia as *"una sociedad bloqueada,"* in which the effective blocking of legal channels for genuine opposition to the system helps to produce the violent protests of contemporary Colombia; see his *Política y Elecciones* (Bogotá: Universidad de los Andes, Facultad de Artes y Ciencias, 1980), esp. p. 282.

23. The 1986 Conservative candidate, Alvaro Gómez Hurtado, one of the party's long-standing "natural chiefs," was unable to transcend the appeals of sectarian politics. The winning Liberal candidate, Virgilio Barco, was a venerable politician who is a close associate of former president Turbay.

24. For a discussion of the prospects and dimensions of such an "opening," see Ricardo Santamaría S. and Gabriel Silva Lujan, *Proceso Político en Colombia: Del Frente Nacional a la Apertura Democrática* (Bogotá: Fondo Editorial CEREC, 1984).

BIBLIOGRAPHY

The following is a selected bibliography of items dealing primarily or substantially with Colombia that were consulted during the writing of this book. Only items published after 1966 have been included; for earlier bibliography, see Robert H. Dix, *Colombia: The Political Dimensions of Change* (New Haven: Yale University Press, 1967).

Abstención, La. Bogotá: ANIF, 1980.

Americas Watch. *The "MAS Case" in Colombia: Taking on the Death Squads.* New York: Americas Watch, 1983.

——. *Human Rights in the Two Colombias: Functioning Democracy, Militarized Society.* New York: Americas Watch, 1982.

Arrubla, Mario, ed. *Colombia Hoy.* Bogotá: Siglo XXI, 1978.

Bagley, Bruce M. "Colombia: National Front and Economic Development." In Robert Wesson, ed., *Politics, Policies, and Economic Development in Latin America*, pp. 124–60. Stanford, Calif.: Hoover Institution Press, 1984.

——. "The State and the Peasantry in Contemporary Colombia." Paper prepared for the meeting of the Latin American Studies Association, Washington, D.C., March 1982.

——. "Political Power, Public Policy and the State in Colombia: Case Studies of the Urban and Agrarian Reforms During the National Front, 1958–1974." Ph.D. dissertation, University of California, Los Angeles, 1979.

Bailey, John J. "Pluralist and Corporatist Dimensions of Interest Representation in Colombia." In James M. Malloy, ed., *Authoritarianism and Corporatism in Latin America*, chap. 9. Pittsburgh: University of Pittsburgh Press, 1977.

——. "Bureaucratic Politics and Social Security Policy in Colombia." *Inter-American Economic Affairs* 29, no. 4 (Spring 1976): 3–19.

Bakke, E. Wight, and Mary S. Bakke. *Campus Challenge: Student Activism in Perspective.* Hamden, Conn.: Archon Books, 1971.

Berquist, Charles W. *Coffee and Conflict in Colombia, 1886–1910.* Durham, N.C.: Duke University Press, 1978.

——. "The Political Economy of the Colombian Presidential Election of 1897." *Hispanic American Historical Review* 56, no. 1 (February 1976): 1-30.

Berry, R. Albert. "Rural Poverty in Twentieth-Century Colombia." *Journal of Interamerican Studies and World Affairs* 20, no. 4 (November 1978): 355-76.

——. "Some Implications of Elitist Rule for Economic Development in Colombia." In Gustav Ranis, ed., *Government and Economic Development*, pp. 3-29. New Haven: Yale University Press, 1971.

Berry, R. Albert, Ronald G. Hellman, and Mauricio Solaún, eds. *Politics of Compromise*. New Brunswick, N.J.: Transaction Books, 1980.

Berry, R. Albert, and Ronald Soligo, eds. *Economic Policy and Income Distribution in Colombia*. Boulder, Colo.: Westview Press, 1980.

Berry, R. Albert, and Miguel Urrutia. *Income Distribution in Colombia*. New Haven: Yale University Press, 1976.

Blutstein, Howard I., et al. *Area Handbook for Colombia*. Washington, D.C.: U.S. Government Printing Office, 1977.

Booth, John A. "Rural Violence in Colombia: 1948-1963." *Western Political Quarterly* 27, no. 4 (December 1974): 657-79.

Broderick, Walter J. *Camilo Torres*. New York: Doubleday, 1975.

Bushnell, David. "Colombia." In Harold Eugene Davis and Larman C. Wilson, eds., *Latin American Foreign Policies: An Analysis*, pp. 401-18. Baltimore: Johns Hopkins University Press, 1975.

Campos, Judith Talbot, and John F. McCamant. *Cleavage Shift in Colombia: Analysis of the 1970 Election*. Beverly Hills, Calif.: Sage, 1972.

Cepeda Ulloa, Fernando. "Que Pasó en las Mitacas?" *Boletín de Sociedad Económica de Amigos del País*, April 1984, pp. 1-4.

——. "Los expresidentes." *Estrategia Económica y Financiera* (Bogotá), August 1980, pp. 44-48.

——. "La Influencia de las Agencias Internacionales en el Proceso de Desarrollo de Colombia, 1950-1974." *Estudios Internacionales* (Santiago) 11, no. 43 (July-September 1978): 57-75.

——. "La Desigualdad de la Representación en el Congreso y en la Constituyente." *Separata de la Revista de la Cámara de Comercio.* Bogotá: Cámara de Comercio, n.d.

Cepeda Ulloa, Fernando, and Claudia González de Lecaros. *Comportamiento del Voto Urbano en Colombia: Una Aproximación.* Bogotá: Universidad de los Andes, Departmento de Ciencia Política, 1976.

Corr, Edwin R. *The Political Process in Colombia.* Denver: University of Denver, 1972.

Craig, Richard B. "Colombian Narcotics and United States-Colombian Relations." *Journal of Interamerican Studies and World Affairs* 23, no. 3 (August 1981): 243-70.

Deas, Malcolm. "Algunas Notas Sobre la Historia del Caciquisimo en Colombia." *Revista de Occidente* (Madrid) 43, no. 127 (October 1973): 118-40.

Departamento Administrativo Nacional de Estadística (DANE). *Colombia Política.* Bogotá: DANE, 1972.

Dix, Robert H. "Consociational Democracy: The Case of Colombia." *Comparative Politics* 12 (April 1980): 303-21.

——. "The Varieties of Populism: The Case of Colombia." *Western Political Quarterly* 31, no. 3 (September 1978): 334-51.

——. "The Colombian Presidency: Continuities and Changes." In Thomas V. DiBacco, ed., *Presidential Power in Latin American Politics*, pp. 72-95. New York: Praeger, 1977.

——. *Colombia: The Political Dimensions of Change.* New Haven: Yale University Press, 1967.

Drekonja-Kornat, Gerhard. "Colombia: Learning the Foreign Policy Process." *Journal of Interamerican Studies and World Affairs* 25, no. 2 (May 1983): 229-50.

Duff, Ernest A. "The Role of Congress in the Colombian Political System." In Weston Agor, ed., *Latin American Legislatures: Their Role and Influence*, pp. 369-402. New York: Praeger, 1971.

——. *Agrarian Reform in Colombia.* New York: Praeger, 1968.

Edwards, Michael. "The Political Economy of Low-Income Housing: New Evidence from Urban Colombia." *Bulletin of Latin American Research*, May 1982, pp. 45–61.

Eggington, Everett, and J. Mark Ruhl. "The Influence of Agrarian Reform Participation on Peasant Attitudes: The Case of Colombia." *Inter-American Economic Affairs* 28, no. 3 (Winter 1974): 27–43.

Fajardo, Luis H. *Social Structure and Personality: The Protestant Ethic of the Antioqueños.* Cali.: Ediciones Departamento del Valle, n.d.

Fals Borda, Orlando. *Subversion and Social Change in Colombia*, trans. Jacqueline D. Skiles. New York: Columbia University Press, 1969.

Fernández, Raúl A. "Imperialist Capitalism in the Third World: Theory and Evidence from Colombia." *Latin American Perspectives* 6, no. 1 (Winter 1979): 38–64.

Findley, Roger W. "Presidential Intervention in the Economy and the Rule of Law in Colombia." *American Journal of Comparative Law* 28 (Summer 1980): 423–73.

———. "Problems Faced by Colombia's Agrarian Reform Institute in Acquiring and Distributing Land." In Robert E. Scott, ed., *Latin American Modernization Problems*, pp. 122–92. Urbana: University of Illinois Press, 1973.

Fleet, Michael. "The Politics of Automobile Industry Development in Colombia." *Journal of Interamerican Studies and World Affairs* 24, no. 2 (May 1982): 211–39.

Gallón Giraldo, Gustavo. *Quince Años de Estado de Sitio en Colombia: 1958–1978.* Bogotá: Editorial América Latina, 1979.

Gilhodes, Pierre. *La Question Agraire en Colombie, 1958–1971.* Paris: Armand Colin, 1974.

———. "Agrarian Struggles in Colombia." In Rodolfo Stavenhagen, ed., *Agrarian Problems and Peasant Movements in Latin America*. Garden City, N.Y.: Doubleday, 1970.

Gómez, Fabio Hernán. *Concentración del Poder Económico en Colombia.* Bogotá: Centro de Investigación y Acción Social, 1974.

Gott, Richard. *Guerrilla Movements in Latin America*. Garden City, N.Y.: Doubleday, 1971.

Harkness, Shirley, and Patricia Pinzón de Levin. "Women, the Vote, and the Party in the Politics of the Colombian National Front." *Journal of Interamerican Studies and World Affairs* 17, no. 4 (November 1975): 439-64.

Hartlyn, Jonathan. "The Impact of Patterns of Industrialization and of Popular Sector Incorporation on Political Regime Type: A Case Study of Colombia." *Studies in Comparative International Development* 19, no. 1 (Spring 1984): 29-60.

——. "Military Governments and the Transition to Civilian Rule: The Colombian Experience of 1957-58." *Journal of Interamerican Studies and World Affairs* 26, no. 2 (May 1984): 245-81.

——. "Producer Associations, the Political Regime and Political Process in Contemporary Colombia." MS, Vanderbilt University, 1984.

——. "Colombia: Old Problems and New Opportunities." *Current History* 82, no. 481 (February 1983): 62-65, 83-84.

——. "Consociational Politics in Colombia: Confrontation and Accommodation in Comparative Perspective." Ph.D. dissertation, Yale University, 1981.

Hartwig, Richard. *Roads to Reason: Transportation, Administration, and Rationality in Colombia*. Pittsburgh: University of Pittsburgh Press, 1983.

——. "Cabinet Instability and the Colombian Political System." MS, Vanderbilt University, 1971.

Havens, A. Eugene, and William L. Flinn, eds. *Internal Colonialism and Structural Change in Colombia*. New York: Praeger, 1970.

Henao, Jesús María, and Gerardo Arrubla. *Historia de Colombia*, 8th ed. Bogotá: Talleres Editoriales de la Librería Voluntad, 1967.

Herrán, María Teresa. *El Sindicalismo por Dentro y por Fuera*. Bogotá: Editorial La Oveja Negra, 1981.

Hoskin, Gary. "The Colombian Political Party System: The 1982 Reaffirmation and Reorientation." Paper prepared for the annual meeting of the Latin American Studies Association, Mexico City, 1983.

——. "Belief Systems of Colombian Political Party Activists." *Journal of Inter-american Studies and World Affairs* 21, no. 4 (November 1979): 481–504.

——. "Post-National Front Trends in the Colombian Political Party System: More of the Same?" Paper prepared for the annual meeting of the Latin American Studies Association, Pittsburgh, 1979.

——. "Dimensions of Representation in the Colombian National Legislature." In Weston Agor, ed., *Latin American Legislatures: Their Role and Influence*, pp. 403–59. New York: Praeger, 1971.

Hoskin, Gary, et al. *Estudio del Comportamiento Legislativo en Colombia*, vol. 2. Bogotá: Universidad de los Andes/Cámara de Comercio, 1975.

Kalmanovitz, Salamón. *Desarrollo de la Agricultura en Colombia*. Bogotá: Editorial la Carreta, 1978.

Kline, Harvey F. "New Directions in Colombia." *Current History* 84, no. 499 (February 1985): 65–68.

——. *Colombia: Portrait of Unity and Diversity*. Boulder, Colo.: Westview Press, 1983.

——. "The Colombian Debates About Coal, Exxon, and Themselves." *Inter-American Economic Affairs* 36, no. 4 (Spring 1983): 3–28.

——. *Energy Policy and the Colombian Elite: A Synthesis and Interpretation*. Washington, D.C.: American Enterprise Institute, 1982.

——. "The Coal of 'El Cerrejón': An Historical Analysis of Major Colombian Policy Decisions and MNC Activities." *Inter-American Economic Affairs* 35, no. 3 (Winter 1981): 69–90.

——. "Committee Membership Turnover in the Colombian National Congress, 1958–1974." *Legislative Studies Quarterly* 2, no. 1 (February 1977): 29–43.

——. "Interest Groups in the Colombian Congress." *Journal of Interamerican Studies and World Affairs* 16, no. 3 (August 1974): 274–99.

——. "Las Ideologías en la Política Colombiana." *Razón y Fábula* (Bogotá) no. 31 (January–March 1973): 45–58.

Latin America Regional Reports. Andean Group Report (London).

Latin America Weekly Report (London).

Latorre Rueda, Mario. *Política y Elecciones.* Bogotá: Universidad de los Andes, Facultad de Artes y Ciencias, 1980.

——. *Elecciones y Partidos Políticos en Colombia.* Bogotá: Universidad de los Andes, Departamento de Ciencia Política, 1974.

Leal Buitrago, Francisco. "La Frustración Política de una Generación. La Universidad Colombiana y la Formación de un Movimiento Estudiantil 1958–1967." *Desarrollo y Sociedad* no. 6 (July 1981): 299–325.

——. *Análisis Histórico del Desarrollo Político Nacional, 1930–1970.* Bogotá: Ediciones Tercer Mundo, 1973.

Levine, Daniel. *Religion and Politics in Latin America.* Princeton: Princeton University Press, 1981.

——. "Church Elites in Venezuela and Colombia: Context, Background and Beliefs." *Latin American Research Review* 14, no. 1 (1979): 51–79.

Levine, Daniel, and Alexander W. Wilde. "The Catholic Church, Politics, and Violence: The Colombian Case." *Review of Politics* 39, no. 2 (April 1977): 220–49.

Losada, Rodrigo. *Pérfil Socio-Político del Congresista Colombiano.* Bogotá: Universidad de los Andes, 1972.

Lupsha, Peter A. "Drug Trafficking: Mexico and Colombia in Comparative Perspective." *Journal of International Affairs* 35, no. 1 (Spring–Summer 1981): 95–115.

Maingot, Anthony P. "Colombia." In Lyle N. McAlister et al., *The Military in Latin American Sociopolitical Evolution: Four Case Studies.* Washington, D.C.: Center for Research in Social Systems, 1970.

Marsh, Robin Ruth. *Development Strategies in Rural Colombia: The Case of Caquetá.* Los Angeles: University of California, Los Angeles, Latin American Center, 1983.

Maullin, Richard L. *The Colombia-IMF Disagreement of November–December 1966: An Interpretation of Its Place in Colombian Politics.* Santa Monica, Calif.: RAND Corp., 1967.

McGreevey, William Paul. *An Economic History of Colombia, 1845–1930.* Cambridge: Cambridge University Press, 1971.

Medhurst, Kenneth N. *The Church and Labour in Colombia.* Manchester: University of Manchester, 1984.

Murillo Castaño, Gabriel. *Migrant Workers in the Americas*, trans. Sandra del Castillo. La Jolla, Calif.: University of California, San Diego, Center for U.S.-Mexican Studies, 1984.

Murillo Castaño, Gabriel, and Israel Rivera Ortiz. *Actividades y Estructura de Poder en los Partidos Políticos Colombianos.* Bogotá: Universidad de los Andes, Departamento de Ciencia Política, 1973.

Nelson, Richard R., T. Paul Schultz, and Robert L. Slighton. *Structural Change in a Developing Economy.* Princeton: Princeton University Press, 1971.

Ogliastri Uribe, Enrique. "Liberales Conservadores Versus Conservadores Liberales: Faccionalismos Trenzados en la Estructura de Poder en Colombia." Paper presented to the annual meeting of the Latin American Studies Association, Mexico City, October 1983.

Ogliastri Uribe, Enrique, and Carlos Dávila L. de Guevara. "Estructura de Poder y Desarrollo en Once Ciudades Intermedias en Colombia." *Desarrollo y Sociedad* (Bogotá) no. 12 (September 1983): 149-88.

Oquist, Paul. *Violence, Conflict and Politics in Colombia.* New York: Academic Press, 1980.

Palacios, Marco. *Coffee in Colombia, 1850–1970.* Cambridge: Cambridge University Press, 1980.

Parra Sandoval, Rodrigo, ed. *Dependencia Externa y Desarrollo Político en Colombia.* Bogotá: Imprenta Nacional, 1970.

Payne, James L. "The Oligarchy Muddle." *World Politics* 20 (April 1968): 439-53.

——. *Patterns of Conflict in Colombia.* New Haven: Yale University Press, 1968.

Pecaut, Daniel. *Política y Sindicalismo en Colombia.* Bogotá: La Carreta, 1973.

Peeler, John. "Colombian Parties and Political Development." *Journal of Interamerican Studies and World Affairs* 18, no. 2 (May 1976): 203-24.

Phelan, John Leddy. *The People and the King.* Madison: University of Wisconsin Press, 1978.

Pollock, John. "The Political Attitudes and Social Backgrounds of Colombia's Urban Housing Bureaucrats." In Francine Rabinowitz and Felicity True-blood, eds., *Latin American Urban Research*, vol. 3, pp. 133-52. Beverly Hills, Calif.: Sage, 1973.

Posada F., Antonio J., and Jeanne de Posada. *The CVC: Challenge to Underdevelopment and Traditionalism.* Bogotá: Ediciones Tercer Mundo, 1966.

Premo, Daniel. "Colombia: Cool Friendship." In Robert Wesson, ed., *U.S. Influence in Latin America in the 1980s*, chap. 6. New York: Praeger, 1982.

——. "The Colombian Armed Forces in Search of a Mission." In Robert Wesson, ed., *New Military Politics in Latin America.* New York: Praeger, 1982.

——. "Alianza Nacional Popular: Populism and the Politics of Social Class in Colombia, 1961-70." Ph.D. dissertation, University of Texas at Austin, 1972.

Ramsey, Russell. "Critical Bibliography on La Violencia in Colombia." *Latin American Research Review* 8, no. 1 (Spring 1973): 3-44.

Randall, Stephen J. *The Diplomacy of Modernization: Colombian-American Relations, 1920-1940.* Toronto: University of Toronto Press, 1977.

Reading, Reid. "Political Socialization in Colombia and the United States: An Exploratory Study." *Midwest Journal of Political Science* 12 (1968): 352-81.

Registraduría Nacional del Estado Civil. *Estadísticas Electorales.* Bogotá: Registraduría various years.

República de Colombia, Superintendencia de Sociedades. *Conglomeradas de Sociedades en Colombia.* Bogotá: Editorial Presencia, 1978.

Revéiz, Edgar, et al. *Poder e Información.* Bogotá: Universidad de los Andes, Centro de Estudios Sobre Desarrollo Económico, 1977.

Ruhl, J. Mark. "An Alternative to the Bureaucratic-Authoritarian Regime: The Case of Colombian Modernization." *Inter-American Economic Affairs* 35, no. 2 (Autumn 1981): 43-69.

——. "Civil-Military Relations in Colombia: A Societal Explanation." *Journal of Interamerican Studies and World Affairs* 23, no. 2 (May 1981): 123-46.

——. *Colombia: Armed Forces and Society.* Syracuse, N.Y.: Syracuse University, Maxwell School of Citizenship and Public Affairs, 1980.

——. "Party System in Crisis? An Analysis of Colombia's 1978 Elections." *Inter-American Economic Affairs* 32, no. 3 (Winter 1978): 29-45.

Safford, Frank. *The Ideal of the Practical: Colombia's Struggle to Form a Technical Elite.* Austin: University of Texas Press, 1976.

——. "Social Aspects of Politics in Nineteenth-Century Spanish America: New Granada, 1825-1850." *Journal of Social History* 5, no. 3 (Spring 1972): 344-70.

Santamaría S., Ricardo, and Gabriel Silva Lujan. *Proceso Político en Colombia: Del Frente Nacional a la Apertura Democrática.* Bogotá: Fonda Editorial CEREC, 1984.

Schmidt, Steffen W. "Patrons, Brokers, and Clients: Party Linkages in the Colombian System." In Kay Lawson, ed., *Political Parties and Linkages*, chap. 12. New Haven: Yale University Press, 1980.

——. "Bureaucrats as Modernizing Brokers? Clientelism in Colombia." *Comparative Politics* 6, no. 3 (April 1974): 425-50.

Schoultz, Lars. "Urbanization and Changing Voting Patterns: Colombia, 1946-1970." *Political Science Quarterly* 87, no. 1 (March 1972): 22-45.

Sepúlveda Niño, Saturnino. *Elites Colombianos en Crisis.* Bogotá, 1970.

Sharpless, Richard E. *Gaitán of Colombia, a Political Biography.* Pittsburgh: University of Pittsburgh Press, 1978.

Silva Colmenares, Julio. *Los Verdaderos Dueños del País.* Bogotá: Fondo Editorial Suramérica, 1977.

Sloan, John W. "Regionalism, Political Parties and Public Policy in Colombia." *Inter-American Economic Affairs* 33, no. 3 (Winter 1979): 25-46.

Solaún, Mauricio, Fernando Cepeda, and Bruce Bagley. "Urban Reform in Colombia: The Impact of the 'Politics of Games' on Public Policy." In Francine

F. Rabinowitz and Felicity Trueblood, eds., *Latin American Urban Research*, vol. 3, chap. 4. Beverly Hills, Calif.: Sage, 1973.

Solaún, Mauricio, and Sidney Kronus. *Discrimination Without Violence*. New York: John Wiley and Sons, 1973.

Tiempo (El) (Bogotá).

Twinam, Ann. *Miners, Merchants and Farmers in Colonial Colombia*. Austin: University of Texas Press, 1982.

Ungar, Elizabeth Bleier. "La Organización Popular y los Servicios Públicos: Política de Concertación o Política de Confrontación? El Caso de Acción Comunal." *Carta Financiera* (Bogotá) no. 49 (April-June 1981): 217-31.

Ungar, Elizabeth Bleier and Angela Gómez de Martínez. *Aspectos de la Campaña Presidencial de 1974: Estrategias y Resultados*. Bogotá: Ediciones Tercer Mundo, 1977.

Urrutia, Miguel. *Gremios, Política Económica y Democracia*. Bogotá: Fondo Cultural Cafetero, 1983.

——. *The Development of the Colombian Labor Movement*. New Haven: Yale University, 1969.

U.S. Senate, Subcommittee on American Republic Affairs, Commitee on Foreign Relations, 91st Congress, 1st Session. *Colombia—A Case History of U.S. Aid*. Washington, D.C.: U.S. Government Printing Office, 1969.

Vásquez Carrizosa, Alfredo. *El Poder Presidencial en Colombia*. Bogotá: Sociedad Ediciones Internacionales, 1979.

Vidal Perdomo, Jaime. "The 1968 Administrative Reforms in Colombia." *International Review of Administrative Sciences* no. 1 (1982): 77-84.

——. *Historia de la Reforma Constitucional y Sus Alcances Jurídicos*. Bogotá: Universidad Externado de Colombia, 1970.

Visión. (Mexico City).

Weinert, Richard S. "Violence in Pre-Modern Societies: Rural Colombia." *American Political Science Review* 60, no. 2 (June 1966): 340-47.

Whiteford, Michael. *The Forgotten Ones*. Gainesville: University of Florida Press, 1976.

Wilde, Alexander. "Conversations Among Gentlemen: Oligarchical Democracy in Colombia." In Juan J. Linz and Alfred Stepan, eds., *The Breakdown of Democratic Regimes*, vol. 3, *Latin America*, pp. 28-81. Baltimore: Johns Hopkins University Press, 1978.

———. "A Traditional Church and Politics: Colombia." Ph.D. dissertation, Columbia University, 1972.

Williams, Miles W. "El Frente Nacional: Colombia's Experiment in Controlled Democracy." Ph.D. dissertation, Vanderbilt University, 1972.

Wogart, Jan Peter. *Industrialization in Colombia: Policies, Patterns, Perspectives*. Tübingen: J. C. B. Mohr, 1978.

INDEX

ABOUT THE AUTHOR

ROBERT H. DIX is professor of political science at Rice University, and a former chairman of the department. He previously taught at Yale University, and from 1957 to 1960 served in the U.S. Foreign Service in Bogotá, Colombia. He received his B.A., M.A., and Ph.D. degrees from Harvard in 1951, 1953, and 1962, respectively.

Professor Dix's publications include *Colombia: The Political Dimensions of Change*, and articles and book chapters on such subjects as Colombian politics, populism, political oppositions, and revolutions.

POLITICS IN LATIN AMERICA
A HOOVER INSTITUTION SERIES
Robert Wesson, Series Editor

POLITICS IN CENTRAL AMERICA: Guatemala, El Salvador, Honduras, Costa Rica
Thomas P. Anderson

SOCIALISM, LIBERALISM, AND DICTATORSHIP IN PARAGUAY
Paul H. Lewis

PANAMANIAN POLITICS: From Guarded Nation to National Guard
Steve C. Ropp

BOLIVIA: Past, Present, and Future of Its Politics
Robert J. Alexander

U.S. INFLUENCE IN LATIN AMERICA IN THE 1980s
Robert Wesson

DEMOCRACY IN LATIN AMERICA: Promise and Problems
Robert Wesson

MEXICAN POLITICS: The Containment of Conflict
Martin C. Needler

DEMOCRACY IN COSTA RICA
Charles D. Ameringer

NEW MILITARY POLITICS IN LATIN AMERICA
Robert Wesson

BRAZIL IN TRANSITION
Robert Wesson and David V. Fleischer

VENEZUELA: Politics in a Petroleum Republic
David E. Blank

HAITI: Political Failures, Cultural Successes
Brian Weinstein and Aaron Segal

GEOPOLITICS OF THE CARIBBEAN: Ministates in a Wider World
Thomas D. Anderson

PUERTO RICO: Equality and Freedom at Issue
Juan M. Garcia-Passalacqua

LATIN AMERICA AND WESTERN EUROPE: Reevaluating the
Atlantic Triangle
Wolf Grabendorff and Riordan Roett

GEOPOLITICS AND CONFLICT IN SOUTH AMERICA: Quarrels
Among Neighbors
Jack Child

LATIN AMERICAN VIEWS OF U.S. POLICY
Robert Wesson

CLASS, STATE, AND DEMOCRACY IN JAMAICA
Carl Stone